The Politics of European Citizenship

The Politics of European Citizenship

Deepening Contradictions in Social Rights and Migration Policy

Peo Hansen and Sandy Brian Hager

Berghahn Books
New York • Oxford

First published in 2010 by
Berghahn Books

www.berghahnbooks.com

©2010, 2012 Peo Hansen and Sandy Brian Hager
First paperback edition published in 2012.

All rights reserved. Except for the quotation of short passages
for the purposes of criticism and review, no part of this book
may be reproduced in any form or by any means, electronic or
mechanical, including photocopying, recording, or any information
storage and retrieval system now known or to be invented,
without written permission of the publisher.

Library of Congress Cataloging-in-Publication Data

Hansen, Peo.
　The Politics of European Citizenship : Deepening Contradictions in Social Rights and Migration Policy / Peo Hansen and Sandy Brian Hager.
　p. cm.
　Includes bibliographical references and index.
　ISBN 978-1-84545-733-4 (hbk.) – ISNB 978-0-85745-621-2 (pbk.)
　1. Citizenship–European Union countries. 2. Civil rights—Europe. 3. European Union countries—Emigration and immigration. 4. European Union. I. Hager, Sandy Brian. II. Title.
　JN40.H36 2010
　323.6094–dc22

2010013458

British Library Cataloguing in Publication Data

A catalogue record for this book is available from the British Library

Printed in the United States on acid-free paper.

ISBN: 978-0-85745-621-2 (paperback)　ISBN: 978-0-85745-622-9 (ebook)

For historical and structural reasons, *a European "constitution of citizenship"* can only emerge on the condition of being *more democratic* than the traditional constitutions of the "national states"—or it will be deprived of any legitimacy, any capacity to "represent" the populations and solve (or mediate) their social conflicts (be they conflicts of economic interests or cultural-religious loyalties).

—Étienne Balibar
(*We, the People of Europe?*, 2004)

Contents

Preface	viii
Abbreviations	xi
Introduction. European Integration and the Problem of Citizenship	1

I. Theory and History of EU Citizenship

Chapter 1. Theorizing Citizenship in the EU: Towards a Critical History	21
Chapter 2. The Origins of EU Citizenship (1950–1980)	38
Chapter 3. A Citizens' Europe for Whom? Social Citizenship, Migration, and the Neoliberal Relaunch of European Integration (1980–1995)	58

II. The Current Trajectories of Citizenship Politics in the EU

Chapter 4. "No Rights Without Responsibilities": Adapting Citizens for the New European Economy	93
Chapter 5. A New EU Politics of Migration, a New Politics of EU Citizenship? Analyzing the Amsterdam Treaty and Tampere Program	127
Chapter 6. "At the Heart of Citizens' Interests": EU Migration Policy in the Hague Program	162
Conclusion. The Politics of European Citizenship: Power Asymmetries, Contradictions, and Trajectories	197
Afterword to the Paperback Edition	207
References	219
Index	245

Preface

This book traces the politics of European citizenship as it has unfolded since the beginning of the European integration project in the 1950s to the present day. Our main focus, though, lies with the more contemporary developments, stretching from the mid-1980s—or the commencement of the EU's Single Market project—until the present. The idea of writing this book took shape in the aftermath of the French and Dutch No votes in the referenda on the EU's Constitutional Treaty in 2005. Ironically enough, as we were about to finish writing the book, in the summer of 2009, we found ourselves in the still uncertain aftermath of yet another "shocking" EU referendum: the Irish No to the Lisbon Treaty. (At the time of going to press, the Lisbon treaty had been ratified, in November 2009, via a second Irish referendum, held in October 2009.)

Given the serious challenges that the French and Dutch referenda were to pose to the direction of the European project, we felt an urge to craft an analysis that could provide both a broad and thorough understanding of the social purpose and historical trajectory of EU citizenship. We thus aimed to move beyond the existing approaches to the study of EU citizenship, which are largely dominated by rather narrow foci on normative prescriptions and visions, on the one side, and legal-institutional descriptions and policy recommendations, on the other. Through our broad focus on the interrelated matters of political economy, social rights, and migration—all of which were central elements in the heated referenda debates—we instead wanted to highlight the enormous stakes, deep-seated contradictions, and widening power asymmetries that shape the content, purpose, and struggle of EU citizenship. In essence, our intention was to speak to the urgency involved in the current politics of European citizenship: to a European Union plagued by increasing social exclusion and labour insecurity, rampant exploitation of rightless undocumented migrant workers, growing anti-immigration and anti-Muslim sentiments, rising support for the racist extreme right, and blatant disregard for refugee and human rights, as seen in the almost daily tragedies resulting from the EU's militarized 'fight against illegal immigration' in the Mediterranean and elsewhere.

As we write this, with Europe experiencing the worst economic crisis since the 1930s, none of these grave predicaments have been mitigated; on the contrary, they have just grown more severe. In addition the voter turnout for the European Parliament elections held in June 2009 reached another historic low (at around 43 percent), with the extreme right making significant gains. Yet again, we have thus heard Brussels and EU capitals resort to the well-rehearsed rhetoric calling for vigorous action to regain the confidence of Europeans and move Europe closer to its citizens.

Although we regard the EU project's growing legitimacy crisis as momentous, we are also careful to emphasize the historical continuities that underpin these recent developments—and that is our whole motivation for writing a "critical history" of EU citizenship politics. Indeed, to cast the most recent referenda rejections as a structural break with the past would be to erroneously gloss over the longstanding crisis of legitimacy that has plagued the EU since the Maastricht reforms of the early 1990s. While most EU scholars are quick to lament this legitimacy crisis, we are hesitant to level such a hasty judgement. After all, any un-, pre-, or post-democratic formation with a significant and growing influence over people's lives that does *not* suffer from a permanent crisis of popular legitimacy is to be feared even more.

This book has benefited from the help, support and encouragement of numerous people. We are particularly grateful to Joseph Baines, Erik Berggren, Gurminder Bhambra, Andreas Bieler, Arne Bjärgvide, Anna Bredström, George Comninel, Julian Germann, Jeremy Green, Ragnar Haake, Stefan Jonsson, Paula Mulinari, Anders Neergaard, Henrik Nordvall, Dermot O'Connor, Magnus Ryner, Carl-Ulrik Schierup, Bastiaan van Apeldoorn, and Charles Wolfson, all of whom provided constructive feedback on the whole or parts of the book in draft. We are equally grateful to the two anonymous peer-reviewers, whose valuable comments helped to improve the manuscript. We also wish to thank the colleagues in the weekly seminar at the Institute for Research on Migration, Ethnicity and Society (REMESO), at Linköping University, where earlier drafts of two chapters have been presented. Responsibility for errors and shortcomings that remain in the text is of course ours alone. The initial work for this book got off to a good start thanks in part to a generous Senior Fellowship awarded to one of us (P.H.) by the Remarque Institute at New York University in 2006; special thanks to Remarque's directors, Tony Judt and Katherine Fleming. Warm thanks too to Marion Berghahn, Ann Przyzycki,

Melissa Spinelli, and Michael Shally-Jensen of Berghahn Books for their generous encouragement and assistance. The research for this book was made possible in part by a departmental research grant to the Institute for Research on Migration, Ethnicity and Society (REMESO) provided by the Swedish Council for Working Life and Social Research (FAS).

Last but by no means least, thanks to Anna, Carin, and Hakeem, for love, encouragement, and patience.

Norrköping and Toronto
July, 2009

Abbreviations

ACP	African, Caribbean, and Pacific countries
AU	African Union
BEPG	Broad Economic Policy Guidelines
CEC	Commission of the European Communities
CEAS	Common European Asylum System
CEE	Central and Eastern Europe
Council EU	Council of the European Union
ECB	European Central Bank
EC	European Community
ECRE	European Council on Refugees and Exiles
ECSC	European Coal and Steel Community
EEC	European Economic Community
EES	European Employment Strategy
EMU	Economic and Monetary Union
ERF	European Refugee Fund
ERT	European Roundtable of Industrialists
ESF	European Social Fund
ESM	European Social Model
ETUC	European Trade Union Congress
EU-RPP	EU Regional Protection Programs
FRONTEX	European External Borders Agency
ICMPD	International Center for Migration Policy Development
ICT	Internet Communications Technology
JHA	Justice and Home Affairs
KBE	Knowledge-Based Economy

KWNS	Keynesian Welfare National State
LCEC	Lisbon Council for European Competitiveness
MLG	multilevel governance
OECD	Organization for European Cooperation and Development
OMC	Open Method of Coordination
PNC	post-national cosmopolitanism
QMV	Qualified Majority Voting
RPAs	regional protection areas
SEA	Single European Act
SPA	Social Policy Agenda
TCNs	third-country nationals
UNHCR	United Nations High Commissioner for Refugees

INTRODUCTION

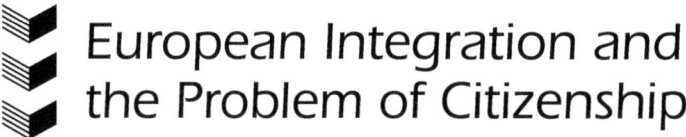
European Integration and
the Problem of Citizenship

On People, Parrots, and the Politics of EU Citizenship

Popular appreciation and European integration are two phenomena that rarely seem to coincide these days. Two decades of heartbreaking referenda have clearly taken their toll; so much that parts of the EU establishment at times convey the impression of having lost confidence in the EU citizenry. As the chasm has widened, so has the stream of invectives being hurled against the unappreciative public. In the summer of 2008, after the Irish had cast their No vote to the EU's Lisbon Treaty, it was time for this lack of confidence to resurface yet again. In fact, many EU leaders' and pundits' reactions to the No vote brought to mind the lines in Bertolt Brecht's 1953 poem "The Solution" ("Die Lösung"): "Would it / not be easier / In that case for the government / To dissolve the people / And elect another?". Indeed, "The Irish will have to vote again," was President Sarkozy's immediate reaction. His foreign minister, Bernard Kouchner, did not mince matters either, lambasting the Irish as "ungrateful," adding: "It would be very, very awkward if we couldn't count on the Irish, who themselves have counted a great deal on Europe's money" (quoted in Barber 2008). For his part, the Irish prime minister, Brian Cowen, derided the naysayers as epitomizing the egoistic "me generation." "We have an obligation," his reprimand went on, "to those who have gone before us and sacrificed so much for our national progress to conduct ourselves as citizens not just as consumers" (quoted in Murray Brown 2008). (It had become high time, in other words, to replace the entrepreneurial cubs of the "Celtic Tiger" with the God-fearing sheep of Europe.) Apart from accusations of ungratefulness and selfishness, No voters were also branded as anti-immigration and intolerant, even racist, these having become standard epithets used to morally disparage those who allegedly hold negative views of Europe.

But in addition to the poetic (in)justice, there was also an element of humor to the story. In its swift answer to the question whether the parrot really was dead, a Monty Pythonesque European Commission delivered a resounding No, its president, Jose Manuel Barroso, simply stating that "the treaty is alive" and that "the European Commission believes that the remaining ratifications should continue to take their course" (quoted in Vucheva 2008). In so doing, President Barroso, not the Irish No voters, was actually contravening both the letter and spirit of one of the EU's most basic principles, namely, that all new treaties have to be taken unanimously by all member states. Faced with an Irish electorate of selfish and intolerant ungratefuls, however, such contravention seemed like a price worth paying; or, more likely, there was not even a conception of such a price in the first place. Today, rather, the stakes in the European project seem too high to make room for much level-headed reflection and dialogue on the part of the EU leadership, let alone any serious explication of what those stakes are that seemingly cannot afford the least bit of popular hesitation as to the EU's allegedly benign influence on people's livelihoods and future prospects. After all, and as expressed with utter clarity for many years now, the EU claims as its first priority the service of the European citizens. Yet if the EU truly wants a relationship with citizens, and not merely with subjects, few would argue that such a relationship could rest solely on the latter's *obligations* to the former—since that would be in radical breach of everything smacking of a modern conception of citizenship. Instead, such a relationship would necessarily also have to be built on a conception of citizens as possessors of *rights* whereby they could gain a stake in the EU project. In the Irish referendum, as on so many other occasions when the EU project stands at the direct mercy of popular scrutiny, the majority of voters were not approached as citizens of the European Union. In other words, they were not seen as worthy of a stake.

Outlining the Historical Background

This book aims to describe and analyse the current nexus of citizenship and the EU project, recognizing, however, that such an analysis could not go very far unless it proceeds from a historical perspective. Before we spell out our more specific aims, and before we delve any further into the current problematic, let us therefore take a moment here to preview some of the historical antecedents of the contemporary predicament.

To begin with, it is important to remember that although the project of European integration was launched already in the 1950s, it would wait until the 1970s before the matters of popular legitimacy and participation were to enter the integration equation in any noticeable fashion. Cast in the still prevalent social democratic mold at the time, these matters, as we discuss in Chapter 2, were to form part of various initiatives pushing for greater European Community authority and involvement in the 1970s economic crisis management. For such Community involvement to be legitimate and effective, it was argued, it had to proceed in tandem with the launch of a "European citizenship" scheme, establishing a direct link of substantial social rights and policy influence between member-state citizens and the Community level. However, falling prey to the so-called Eurosclerosis (or Euro-pessimism) hitting the Community in the mid-1970s, which stalled much of the progress on European integration up until the early 1980s, these initiatives would basically all come to naught. Yet, what had been shown with some force was that many Community policy makers had become convinced that if European integration was to go forward it had to be able to enthuse the general public and so find a mobilizing argument outside the realm purely concerned with market integration.

After the initiatives in the 1970s it would take until the mid- and late 1980s before the time proved ripe again for the question of "European citizenship" to gain a foothold on the Community agenda. Unlike in the 1970s, however, this time the efforts to boost the Community's popular legitimacy were neither of a primarily social democratic bent, nor were they principally initiated in order to pave the way for integration steps not yet taken. Rather, they were launched so as to bestow retroactive popular legitimacy onto giant integration steps that had already been taken, without prior consultation with the member-state citizens. These giant steps of European integration of course refer to the Single Market project, launched in 1985, and to the new treaty that underwrote it: the Single European Act (SEA, ratified in 1987), which made up the first sizeable revision of the Community's founding treaties. As we shall discuss at some length in Chapter 3, the neoliberal-inspired Single Market—with its attempts to subject ever greater areas of social life to the commodifying logic of the market and the principle of free movement—was to induce significant social and political transformations in the member states. Igniting a development whereby more and more policy areas and future challenges to the member states started to take on a "European dimension"—in everything from social welfare and macroeconomy to third-country migration and asylum policy—these transformations continue to cast their shadow on today's developments. Suffice it to say, too, that the vexed question of the EU's "democratic deficit" derives its origin from the changes brought about by the Single Market and the SEA. To be sure, the architects of the Single Market and the SEA were well aware of the consequential impact of their creations. In addition, many of these same architects, the most important among them being the president of the European Commission himself, Jacques Delors, were also aware of these creations' potentially adverse effects, particularly for the Community's laborers.

It is therefore no coincidence that the Single Market transformations were to walk hand in hand with a concerted effort to rally member-state citizens around the reborn European integration. This effort can be broken down into roughly four subsets of initiatives. First, there was the launch of the extensive campaign to foster a popular sense of "European identity," broadcast under such headings as "People's Europe" and "Citizens' Europe," urging member nationals to embrace and unite around their common European cultural values and civilizational heritage. As part of this, Brussels worked hard to both introduce new and revive old Community symbols, as seen in the promotion of an EU anthem, a flag, a Europe Day and a new EU passport design. Second, citizens were to be made aware of the new opportunities presented by the Single Market's open internal borders (free movement) and deregulated markets, highlighting the benefits to be reaped by European entrepreneurs, professionals, students, consumers, and tourists. In addition, and third, Europeans were promised the creation of a "social Europe," working so as to counterbalance any socially unfavorable effects that might result from the new "market making" Europe. Fourth, and finally, popular legitimacy for the Single Market transformations was also sought via Brussels and member-state governments' firm assurance that the new Europe of open internal borders by no means was to imply an increase in immigration from non-member countries, or that international crime was to be allowed to take advantage of the abolition of internal border controls. In this sense, the budding European citizenship fashioned itself as a security bulwark protecting citizens against a number of perceived new threats, among which "illegal" immigration and "bogus" asylum seeking increasingly were being placed on the same footing as international crime and drug trafficking, even terrorism.[1] This also meant that from now on the EU's politics of citizenship was to be indissolubly bound up with the EU's politics of third-country migration.

As the EU entered the 1990s and the period for the launching of the next treaty revisions in Maastricht—paving the way for the Union's subsequent great step toward monetary union (the EMU)—the question of popular legitimacy was similarly to be taken to the next level. It was not long after the Maastricht Treaty had been signed (in the winter of 1992), then, before it became evident that the EU's legitimacy efforts and citizenship policy so far had fallen short of their goals. When member-state populations began in the 1990s to feel the socioeconomic impact of the Single Market more directly, it seemed as if they had also started to develop feelings about European integration. And although popular involvement with the integration project had for years been sought by EU institutions and governments, once such involvement started to germinate in the 1990s much of it turned out to be an unpleasant surprise. It was thus telling that the very same treaty, i.e. the Maastricht Treaty, which endowed member-state nationals with a formal "European citizenship"—or "Citizenship of the Union"/EU citizenship[2]—should also set off a referenda induced ratification crisis that soon put a damper on the Single Market's "Euro-optimism."

Regardless of the eventual ratification of the new treaty in 1993, thanks to a Danish referendum revote overriding its initial No to the treaty, Maastricht was to become emblematic of an emerging rift between the "new Europe" and large strata of the EU citizenry. For the EU leadership this constituted a development of great concern, a fact that was to be emphatically confirmed in countless public statements and initiatives throughout the 1990s. Hence, the European Commission took great pains to stress that the Union "depends for its very legitimacy on its citizens" (Commission of the European Communities 1993a: 15; henceforward abbreviated as CEC); and that the "penalty for failure" to gain the citizens' confidence "is that citizenship of the Union may appear to be a distant concept for citizens engendering confusion as to its means and objectives even fuelling anti-EU feelings" (CEC 1997a: 1). Maastricht, as Wallace and Smith (1995: 150–151) argue, thus meant that not only had "the democratic credentials of European integration" come under public scrutiny; it had also "forced European elites to accept that public support for further integration could not be taken for granted" (see also Beetham and Lord 1998: 15).

A Harrowing Option

There can be no gainsaying that the experiences from the early 1990s made clear that popular consent to further integration had to be earned, rather than simply assumed. What was made much less clear, though, was the extent to which "European elites" would be ready to "accept" popular discontent and thus bow to the fact that their subsequent plans for "further integration" might fail to earn sufficient popular consent. Today, some fifteen years after the Maastricht ratification crisis, this latter question still lingers unanswered; and we take it to be no wild guess that the failure to provide an unambiguous answer goes some way to explain why successive EU referenda, on the whole, have turned out to be such distressing, even harrowing events. By not answering the question in favor of the verdict of the popular vote, European elites have instead retained the (pre-democratic) option to nullify the vote at will, by for instance forcing revotes, as in the Irish case in 2008–9, or, as in the case of the Franco-Dutch No to the EU's Constitutional Treaty in 2005, by simply applying cosmetic changes. This option, it seems, has not only proven harrowing for voters. That is, once decision makers start to eye the option—always in breach of pre-election promises to the contrary—they are also forced to reframe the referenda in terms of a moral choice, rather than a political one. (In reality, all the referenda on the EU so far have undoubtedly been formulated as political choices, formally speaking, some add "technical" choices, but never have they been formally designed as moral choices.) As borne out by practically all the post-referenda debates up until now, the reason for overturning a popular judgment is thus primarily motivated with a more or less implicit reference to a moral imperative. The popular verdict gets disqualified not because it is deemed politically unfeasible, but because it is deemed morally reprehensible. Hence, voters throwing wrenches into the EU works are branded as ungrateful, selfish, racist, nationalist, intolerant, ignorant, lazy, irresponsible, and so on and so forth. This is where it gets harrowing also for "European elites," since we must assume that most of them know full well that this type of obvious manipulation always tends to backfire. As *The Economist* (2008) noted, commenting on the debate following upon the Irish referendum: "Why would Irish mainstream politicians want to scapegoat immigration, and paint their own voters as intolerant? Perhaps because they know that they ran a wretched yes campaign." For students of European integration, this is also where we can get a sense of the enormous stakes involved in the European integration of today, of the enormous public credibility gaps that the EU's political leadferships are prepared to open up in order to have their will.

EU Referenda and the Politics of EU Citizenship

Since these stakes were nowhere more evident than in the debates surrounding the French and Dutch referenda on the EU's Constitutional Treaty in 2005—where a high turnout of voters overwhelmingly said No to the political proposal put before them—we also need to take a moment to reflect on what took place here. While this book is not about EU referenda per se, we take the referendum's character, as a rare medium whereby citizens are put in direct political contact with the EU project, to be offering exceptionally pertinent clues as to the meaning and content of EU citizenship. That is to say, the referenda and the reactions they engender provide exceptionally good starting points for reflection on the various and often contradictory and situation-specific registers of EU citizenship—specifying the traits distinguishing an "ideal," or "model," EU citizen—that EU institutions, political leaders and other influential actors decide to make use of, or not make use of, in different contexts.

In line with our account above, the approach adopted by Brussels, governments, and most other elite voices to the French and Dutch referenda was very much articulated in *moral* terms, thus seeing little merit in discussing the outcome as an expression of a conscious *political* choice, based on what voters took the Constitutional Treaty to stand for in a political sense. The refusal to take the No vote for a political answer was underscored too by the fact that the results had barely been made public before the news media was brimming with voices asking what it was that people *actually* had voted No to. While the answers provided were many and varied the great majority of them agreed on a basic message that held the No vote in more or less moral contempt. As would be the case in the subsequent debate on the Irish referendum, voters were depicted as ignorant, uninformed, anti-immigration, intolerant, nationalist, and as inimical to globalization, "open economies," and "employment-friendly" labor markets.

In contrast to the Irish case, though, the commentary on the French and Dutch referenda, both prior to and after the elections, was much more prone to depict the No side as anti-immigration, anti-Muslim and racist. In particular, No voters were made out to be hostile to labor migrants from the new Eastern and Central European member states, epitomized by "the Polish plumber," as well as to a Turkish EU membership. True, such sentiments did exist among those voting No—as they did exist among those voting Yes (see e.g. Hainsworth 2006). But the allegation that virulent xenophobia, racism, and the like had a significant impact on the solid majority of the No voters—made up of leftists and greens in both France and the Netherlands—was at best the cry of a sore loser.[3] Above all, what these accusations in effect served to achieve was to relocate the referenda beyond the pale of liberal democracy. Like in previous and subsequent ones, the referenda were rather cast as inverted votes of moral confidence; instead of respecting citizens' free political choice to decide whether or not they had confidence in the proposal put before them, it was governments, Brussels, and scores of pundits, intellectuals, and corporate voices who, in the end, decided to declare the great majority of voters morally incapacitated. Accordingly, you were either with the enlightened (some would say cosmopolitan) Europeans, or you were with the bigoted nationalists.

In essence, such was also the message from Jürgen Habermas—European post-nationalism's most renowned interpreter—who, together with a group of other intellectuals, called on voters to do the right thing and vote Yes: "We owe it to the millions and millions of victims of our senseless wars and criminal dictatorships" (quoted in Watkins 2005: 7). "If we look at Auschwitz," said the Dutch prime minister, Jan Peter Balkenende, "we know why we must accept the European Constitution" (quoted in European Citizen Action Service 2006: 14). First vice president of the European Commission, Margot Wallström, issued a similar admonition when advocating a Yes in a speech in the former Jewish ghetto of Terezin. As if this was not enough, the Dutch minister for justice went on to warn that naysayers were paving the way for "Balkanization" and war in Europe (Watkins 2005).

Such were the elite reactions to allegedly anti-European votes that, as borne out by numerous polls, after all just bore the stamp of an old arch-European tradition that refuses to call it quits; in reality, that is, they were reactions to votes largely anchored in class politics and mundane socioeconomic issues. Besides low-income constituencies and allies of the political left, however, also the young and women voted strongly against the treaty. Apparently, a treaty giving no indications of trying to dilute the long-standing EU formula of neoliberal "market making" for the benefit of welfare and social rights protection proved the wrong recipe for the types of socioeconomic problems that large cohorts within the No camp were addressing. And we should like to note that there were a few voices from within the moderate Yes camp that eventually came around to concede this banal point. Although reproaching No voters for "nationalist" and "isolationist thinking," even a couple of hardliners could be heard echoing the self-evident; said Ulrich Beck and Anthony Giddens (2005): "We know that the 'no' votes in France and the Netherlands were motivated substantially by social and economic anxieties."

In no uncertain terms, then, the referenda evince that when people fail to comply with the political-economic register of European citizenship, as laid down in the EU's Lisbon Agenda/Lisbon Strategy (adopted in 2000 and distinct from the 2009 Lisbon treaty), they are promptly vilified as intolerant nationalists, anti-immigration, ignorant, selfish, and so on. To have qualms about the political economic orientation of European integration, and thus being in favour of setting the EU onto a different political economic course, more attuned to social welfare objectives, are consequently positions that are relegated from serious consideration on the EU agenda. As we shall discuss in some detail ahead, however, such has not always been the case. Well into the 1990s, calls to dilute neoliberal orthodoxy could be heard from the highest levels of the EU. Also today, as we shall examine at length as well, the EU's pledge to respect the "European Social Model" (ESM) testifies to the fact that the social question by no means has fallen silent on the EU agenda. By the same token, neither has social issues ceased to make up a register of EU citizenship. Yet, what is important to keep in mind is that during the past decade, or since the launch of the Lisbon Agenda in 2000, the key watchword, and thus also the key to such a register, has not been the European Social Model as such, but rather the "reforms" to which this model by necessity must submit. It seems reasonable to argue, then, that recent referenda signal that such "reforms"—e.g., greater labor market flexibility, privatization, and overall cutbacks in social entitlements—have failed to draw sufficient popular support, thereby also preventing people from conforming to the prescribed social register of EU citizenship.

But the EU referenda in question are equally interesting to explore for what they make less explicit with regards to the question of citizenship. Anyone just vaguely acquainted with EU politics will know of the enormous attention it has come to pay to the question of migration in recent years. To the "problems" of "illegal immigration" and asylum seekers, to the need for more labor migrants from third countries in order to ensure economic growth and to alleviate the Union's demographic deficit and to the migrant integration challenges faced by EU societies, particularly as concerns the growing Muslim minority. As already noted above, moreover, the question of third-country migration has also come to occupy central stage in EU citizenship policy in recent years. And here things get really convoluted. Because if we juxtapose the registers of EU citizenship that came to the fore in the elite reactions to the No votes in the Dutch, French, and Irish referenda with those registers of EU citizenship conveyed by EU migration policy, we encounter a number of startling contradictions. What we encounter, then, is an inversion of citizenship registers of sorts. That is to say, many of those deplorable attitudes, particularly with regards to migration, that are said to be typical of No voters in EU referenda are to no insignificant extent recast as legitimate attitudes when it comes to EU migration policy.

In fact, it is by adopting a migration policy commensurate with such negative attitudes toward migration that the EU, since the late 1980s, is hoping to convert its migration policy into a concrete and indeed popularly legitimate manifestation of citizenship policy. As the EU's chief decision-making body, the Council of Ministers (or formally the Council of the European Union) puts it: "In order to meet the expectations of its citizens the European Union must respond to the security threats of terrorism and organised crime, and to the challenge of managing migration flows" (Council of the European Union 2005: 1; henceforward abbreviated as Council EU). Similarly, the EU's executive body, the European Commission, holds that an "effective common management of the external borders of the Member States of the Union will boost security and the citizen's sense of belonging to a shared area and destiny. It also serves to secure continuity in the action undertaken to combat terrorism, illegal immigration and trafficking in human beings" (CEC 2002a: 2). Furthermore, as our subsequent analysis will show, the EU citizen whom the European Commission has tasked itself to serve is also a citizen said to be greatly in favor of more stringent asylum rules combined with an increase of forced deportations of rejected asylum seekers. We could also add that the Commission has promised EU citizens to pursue a tougher approach to migrant integration, in general, and toward Muslims, in particular. As the EU's Commissioner in charge of migration and citizenship matters (also Vice-President of the European Commission) brusquely remarked in 2006: "We are not governed by sharia, after all" (quoted in Kubosova 2006a).

However, and to introduce yet another layer of contradictions, we should also emphasize that the European Commission on other occasions, particularly within the framework of the EU's anti-discrimination policy, is very eager to promote intercultural understanding and tolerance towards migrants and Muslims. To some extent the same applies whenever the issue of the Union's professedly enormous economic and demographic need for labor migrants is on the agenda. In this context, often prefaced with references to the Lisbon Agenda's grave warnings concerning the detrimental impact on economic growth should the Union fail to meet this need, the Commission urges EU citizens to adopt a positive attitude to new labor migration in exchange for Brussels' promise to adopt an even more relentless attitude towards "illegal immigration."

To broaden the contradictory picture a bit further, let's also bring in some illustrations from the national level. Take, for instance, the whole fuss about the "Polish plumber" and the allegations that No voters were motivated by negative attitudes toward labor migration from the new eastern members. Now, if the political establishment really believed that to have been the case, we must also ask why governments across the old EU did not take the opportunity to rejoice instead, crediting themselves for having succeeded in persuading public opinion as to the merits of restrictions on labor migration from the new member states. After all, these restrictions, or "transition rules," which barred the new members' citizens from enjoyment of the EU citizenship's most esteemed right—i.e., "free movement" of labor—that practically all of the fifteen old members had imposed just the year before the Franco-Dutch referenda, were to no minor extent justified under the pretext of protecting citizens from being swamped by wage dumpers and welfare scroungers from the new member states. In other words, the transition rules were imposed for the alleged reason of protecting citizens from the same Polish plumber whom EU governments a year later were to soak in crocodile tears.

An equally paradoxical picture unfolds when we turn, finally, to the sweeping charges of intolerance and murky nationalism made against No voters in EU referenda. It is interesting to note that the same Dutch government who scolded No voters for having forgotten about Auschwitz and for fueling a dangerous "Balkanization" of Europe, at the same time had its hands full with developing compulsory so-called integration tests for the purpose of inculcating certain migrant groups, particularly Muslims, with allegedly superior Dutch national values. Here, the ruling Christian Democrats promised voters that migrants, among other things, were to be forced to learn the national anthem by heart (*BBC News*, 16 May 2002). Dutch and French governments branding No voters as nationalist and xenophobic were thus, in effect, contradicting their own long-standing xenophobic and anti-Muslim agendas. "Like it or not," said President Chirac in 2003, "wearing a veil is a kind of aggression" (quoted in Scott 2007: 84). Right before the Irish referenda, moreover, similar statements about Muslims could be heard from the Yes camp there, the Labour Party's education spokesman declaring: "Nobody is formally asking them [the Muslims] to come here. In the interest of integration and assimilation, they should embrace our culture" (quoted in McDonagh 2008). As part of a new brand of migrant and minority integration policy at both national and EU levels—something we scrutinize in detail further on—messages such as these have become increasingly common in recent years, giving rise to ever more exclusive and ethno-culturally articulated notions of national and European citizenships.

Grasping the Politics of EU Citizenship: Aims and Approach

Above we have pointed to the centrality of the interrelated matters of political economy, social rights, and migration for our grasp of the content, registers, and purpose of EU citizenship. Not least have our illustrations from the messy world of EU referenda sought to give a glimpse of how these matters impinge upon the huge stakes and hefty contradictions that are involved in the struggles over EU citizenship. But if this somewhat impressionistic picture that we have painted so far tries to speak to the urgency involved in the current politics of European citizenship, it has also tried to show that in order to grasp this politics we need to situate it in a historical context. Before we turn our attention to these tasks in the chapters ahead, however, we need to specify our aims, approach, and research questions in more precise terms.

The overall purpose of this book is to critically conceptualize and analyze the historical development of EU citizenship as it has developed alongside the deepening cleavage between the power of EU institutions on the one hand and popular legitimacy among its citizenry on the other; charting its long-range movements vis-à-vis the broader transformations of the EU integration project. We stress that although formal legal EU citizenship was only introduced in 1993 with the Maastricht Treaty, what we term a "de facto transnational citizenship regime" has existed at least since the establishment of the European Economic Community (1957), and can even be traced to the establishment of the European Coal and Steel Community (1951), and its legal provisions for intra-EU labor mobility (see Maas 2005).

Grounded in the tradition of critical political economy (see van Apeldoorn, Drahokoupil and Horn 2008), the approach developed here identifies and illuminates the historically contingent political struggles that shape citizenship politics in the EU. More specifically, our approach sets out to uncover the relations of power underpinning the EU as a historically specific *capitalist* social formation, to determine how these relations shape the trajectories of the integration project and its concomitant citizenship model (see Chapter 1; van Apeldoorn, Overbeek and Ryner 2003). The central premise guiding this approach is that in order to understand and explain the limits of EU citizenship in securing legitimacy, we need to examine its "social purpose," attempting not only to normatively assess or to describe the institutional form of EU citizenship, but also to uncover its socioeconomic content by explaining who benefits from it and what kind of citizenship model it seeks to promote (Holman 2004; van Apeldoorn 2002; Hager 2008). Uncovering this social purpose, we argue, requires an empirically thick, historical account that is careful not to isolate EU citizenship from the historical dynamics of the broader integration project from which it stems. As we seek to motivate throughout the book, such an account—which anchors the study of EU citizenship in an empirically sustained critical-historical framework—is glaringly absent from the extensive current literature on the subject.

The three central and interrelated research questions guiding the development of our conceptual framework, and employed in our subsequent empirical analysis can be briefly summarized as follows:

1.) How have the politics or "social purpose" of EU citizenship transformed over time? How do we explain this historical transformation?

2.) What are the particular configurations of social and political forces that shape the form and content of EU citizenship in any given historical period?
3.) What are the specific structural barriers or limitations within citizenship practices that help account for the EU's deepening crisis of legitimacy?

In outlining these specific aims, we should also be careful to explicitly delimit our analysis; to outline from the beginning what our book is *not* trying to cover. Firstly, this is not a book replete with citizenship and migration policy recommendations. As we will describe more fully in our theoretical framework developed in Chapter 1, our critical approach attempts to stand back from the existing literature's fixation with policy prescription and endorsement, to uncover historically the social power relations underpinning citizenship politics in the EU. This does not mean that we accept a separation of theory and practice, but rather that the political practice we envision is not limited to given formal institutional structures. As is implied in critical analysis, the radical nature of the knowledge offered in this book is more likely to inform the political practices that go beyond mere policy recommendations to EU institutions. Second, this is not a book that engages systematically with quantitative data on migration. We do undoubtedly make reference to this data to back up our arguments in empirical analysis, yet this is by no means our focal point. This data is readily available in the EU documents we cite and also in some of our existing works (see Schierup, Hansen and Castles 2006). In all, we feel strongly that this book is venturing into the relatively uncharted territory of critical political economy analysis in the realm of EU citizenship studies. As an exploratory exercise, we hope that our analysis will pave the way for more specific engagement with various facets of citizenship politics, including critical analysis of the relationship between EU and the various national citizenship regimes.

The Outline of the Book

In terms of expositional structure, the book is divided into two parts. We begin in Part I by both theoretically anchoring and historically contextualizing our analysis of citizenship politics in the EU. Chapter 1 systematically outlines our alternative theoretical approach to EU citizenship—a "critical history"—which in shorthand refers to our application of insights from critical political economy to the analysis of EU citizenship from a long-term historical perspective. Here we set out to qualify further our point of departure in the social purpose of EU citizenship: firstly by critiquing existing approaches to EU citizenship for their narrow foci on normative prescription or institutional problem solving; and secondly by developing a conceptual apparatus that examines how the historically contingent asymmetrical power relations engendered by capitalist market structures shape and transform citizenship politics in both its form and content.

The remainder of Part I traces the historical development of EU citizenship over the second half of the twentieth century. The historical background provided in these chapters establishes a foundation for understanding the current state of affairs in EU citizenship policy, first and foremost by dispelling a prevailing misconception that a specifically *supranational* citizenship politics have only existed since the Maastricht Treaty's introduction of a formal EU citizenship category in 1993.

In Chapter 2 we analyze the struggles to implement substantive pan-European citizenship rights, including social rights, to facilitate intra-EU labor migration and thus labor mobility in line with imperatives of economic growth during the postwar embedded liberal period (see Ruggie 1982). The de facto transnational citizenship regime that emerged through these dynamics, we argue, highlights the fact that migration policy has been central to EU citizenship policy from the very outset of the integration project, while the regime's rigid exclusion of third-country nationals (TCNs) from citizenship provisions marked the creation of a *dualized* citizenship order that remains at the heart of EU citizenship politics to this day.

Chapter 3 focuses on the transformations in EU citizenship policy during the Single Market induced "relaunch" of the integration project from the mid-1980s to the mid-1990s. We argue that the introduction of the EU's own formal citizenship model in the Maastricht Treaty was bound up with the ideological re-orientation of the EU toward "embedded neo-liberalism" (see van Apeldoorn 2002) and the domination of the Single Market project's "market making" negative integration; a contradictory combination attempting to embed market forces within a limited social-institutional framework (e.g., welfare policy, research and development, education and skills training) (van Apeldoorn 2003a). This was the case insofar as EU citizenship was itself based on neoliberal precepts of the individualized "market citizen." Crucially, however, we show that the "socially thin" market citizenship model was also underpinned by an exclusivist "ethno-cultural" dimension emphasizing the (Judeo-Christian) civilizational, cultural, and religious facets of a European identity that Brussels took great pains to promote as part of its new European citizenship policy. In consequence of the Single Market, external migration also emerged as a common European "problem," calling for common action and solutions that increasingly were to couch migration in terms of control, security and crime. The securitization and criminalization of the migration problématique during the relaunch—motivated as part of a greater concern to "protect" EU citizens against new external as well as internal threats—can be regarded as another component in the EU's attempt to compensate for the absence of supranational social rights; a move that furthermore served to bolster the dualized order of EU citizenship policy discussed in Chapter 2.

Part II of the book focuses on the citizenship politics in the contemporary context of the Lisbon Strategy, the ambitious strategic blueprint launched in 2000 seeking to transform the EU into the most competitive knowledge-based economy (KBE) in the world by 2010. As our account moves into the contemporary scene, the analysis becomes empirically richer and more detailed, compelling us to make an empirical division between EU migration policy, on the one hand, and the EU's more explicitly articulated, or "formal," citizenship policy, on the other. This should be read as a practical, or pragmatic division, rather than one implying that these two main sides of citizenship politics have become analytically separated from each other. As the reader will no doubt notice, the analysis in Part II also gives more weight to migration policy. This was a conscious decision on our part rather than a case of haphazard lopsidedness: as we will seek to motivate throughout Part II, this emphasis on migration policy is necessary precisely because migration has become articulated by the EU as a key issue within its contemporary citizenship politics. Here we should emphasize that "EU migration policy" in our account refers to a complex conceptualization that bridges the commonly invoked analytical and empirical separation between the *external* and *internal* dimensions of EU migration policy. As such, we scrutinize both the external dimension of EU migration policy—as in labor migration from non-EU countries, asylum policy, and policy to prevent "illegal" or irregular immigration—on the one side, *and* the internal dimension—as in migrant integration policy, anti-discrimination policy, and labor migration, or "free movement" within the EU area—on the other. Moreover, by conceiving of these dimensions as analytically inseparable, this, what we may term, *integrated approach* provides for a discussion of causes as well as consequences of EU migration policy that accounts for the dynamic of oftentimes contradictory political and economic driving forces that are at work in the formation and execution of migration policies. Such a wide-ranging approach provides a comprehensive picture of a complex development. What is more, this approach is becoming all the time more important. Thus, as the external and internal dimensions of EU migration policy have become thoroughly interdependent, the analytical separation between the external and internal dimensions is turning out to be increasingly untenable.

The opening chapter of Part II, Chapter 4, takes on the task of uncovering how EU citizenship—particularly in terms of social citizenship—has developed since the launching of the Lisbon Strategy (2000–2010). Considered by many to have ushered in a new era for the integration project, the Lisbon Strategy is analyzed in detail in order to determine to which extent it actually deviates from the "embedded neoliberal" hegemonic order and socially thin market citizenship model of the relaunch era. We argue that contrary to some enthusiastic academic and political assessments, the Lisbon Strategy does not mark a "positive" turning point for EU-level social citizenship, but instead remains firmly grounded within the framework of embedded neoliberalism. Yet the novelty of the Lisbon Strategy as it relates to social citizenship is that it focuses almost solely on citizen responsibilities or duties to make themselves employable in light of the inevitable restructuring involved in the transition to a globally competitive KBE. We go on to explain how this has been further intensified since the shift in early 2005 to a streamlined "growth and jobs" agenda under the Commission headed by José Manuel Barroso.

In Chapters 5 and 6 we return to EU migration policy as it unfolds in the areas of migrant integration and anti-discrimination policy, extra-EU labor migration policy, asylum policy, and EU policy to fight so-called illegal immigration; current EU estimates put the number of "illegal" (or irregular) migrants in the EU-25 at about 8 million.[4] Chapter 5 concerns itself with the developments in migration policy under the auspices of the EU's Tampere Program (1999–2004), while Chapter 6 deals with Tampere's multi-annual successor agenda, the Hague Program (2005–10). Both of these chapters examine the contradictory interplay between internally and externally directed supranational initiatives within the broad field of EU migration policy. Here, we put stress on what we identify as growing tensions between the EU's agenda to crack down on "illegal" immigration and "bogus" asylum seeking, and to toughen measures aimed at migrant "integration," on the one hand, and on the other hand the EU's simultaneous promises to base EU asylum policy on humanitarian values, to combat migrants' social exclusion and to institute vigorous measures to fight racism and discrimination. As part of this we discuss the implications of the EU's developing migration policy for the issue of EU citizenship, in general, and for the prospects of migrants' access to social rights in the EU, in particular.

Finally, the Conclusion offers a synthesized treatment of the book's empirical analysis by summarizing the various power relations that have underpinned citizenship politics over the more than half century old history of the EU project. We then return to a discussion of the post-referenda dynamics of EU integration that we started in this introductory chapter, reflecting on the implications that the EU's current crisis of legitimacy have for the current configuration of power asymmetries that underpin citizenship politics. We conclude the book with a brief discussion of what constitutes the "model" or "ideal" EU citizen in the eyes of social and political forces at the heart of the integration project.

Notes

1. For detailed accounts of the efforts to secure popular support and legitimacy for European integration following in the wake of the Single Market transformations, see e.g. Hansen (2000); Shore (2000); Scott-Smith (2003); Martiniello (1995).
2. As was stipulated in the Maastricht Treaty (EC Treaty, Part Two, Article 8(1)), "Every person holding the nationality of a Member State shall be a citizen of the Union". The rights provided by the "Citizenship of the Union" include, inter alia, "the right to move and reside within the territory of the Member States"; "the right to vote and to stand as a candidate" at municipal and European Parliament elections for residents in a member state other than the one where they are nationals; expanded diplomatic and consular protection; and "the right to petition the European Parliament" and to "apply to the Ombudsman" (Council of the European Communities, CEC 1992).
3. For a substantiation of this point, as well as a comprehensive analysis of the referenda, see Watkins (2005).
4. See CEC (2008a: 6). For more comprehensive EU migration statistics, covering both irregular and regular migration, see CEC (2008a: Annex 4). See also e.g. Eurostat (http://epp.eurostat.ec.europa.eu/portal/page/portal/population/introduction); OECD (http://www.oecd.org/topic/0,3373,en_2649_37415_1_1_1_1_37415,00.html); and International Organization for Migration (IOM) (http://www.iom.int/jahia/jsp/index.jsp).

PART I

Theory and History of EU Citizenship

CHAPTER 1

Theorizing Citizenship in the EU
Towards a Critical History

Introduction

The growing importance of citizenship within the EU political arena has been paralleled by a surge of academic interest in its subject matter (see e.g. Rosas and Antola 1995; Wiener 1998; Bellamy and Warleigh 2001; Bellamy, Castiglione and Shaw 2006; Maas 2007). What stands out within this wide-ranging, and ever-growing, body of literature has been the diverse range of social scientific fields, from philosophy and sociology to industrial relations and gender studies, that have grappled with the extension of EU supranational (or as some would have it "post-national") competencies in the realm of citizenship, and the implications this has for contemporary European societies. Yet for all this diversity in disciplinary terms, the study of EU citizenship is still dominated heavily by a narrow set of theoretical frameworks which take the current political parameters of EU citizenship as given, either endorsing it as a progressive model or seeking to correct what are regarded to be more or less surmountable institutional deficiencies in citizenship practice. Drawing inspiration from van Apeldoorn, Overbeek and Ryner's (2003) critique of mainstream integration theories, we argue here that although these approaches are not necessarily uninterested in issues of power and legitimacy, their very conceptual designs render them inherently unable to explain the contradictions between citizenship practice and principles of legitimacy which are at the heart of the EU's currently unfolding legitimacy crisis (see Introduction).

Accessing these dynamics, we suggest, therefore requires that analyses of EU citizenship go beyond narrow concerns with normative prescription and institutional problem solving, and instead take up the central problématique that unites a varied set of approaches within the theoretical tradition of critical political economy: "to understand the nature of

21

power in the EU, including its organization and distribution, and to access the implications of a given set of power relations for legitimacy" (van Apeldoorn, Overbeek and Ryner 2003: 17). In attempting to historically uncover the "social purpose" of EU integration, *who benefits* from it, and *what kind* of polity it seeks to promote, critical political economy has the potential to contribute unique insights describing not only how EU citizenship has been limited in securing legitimacy, but also to *explain why* this has been the case (Holman 2004; van Apeldoorn 2002). Essential to this explanatory critical-historical framework is the examination of capitalist market structures in engendering asymmetrical power relations, which crucially shape the content of citizenship politics.

To this point, however, save for a few book chapters and conference papers, there has been no systematic attempt to develop a critical political economy approach to EU citizenship. In this chapter we aim to begin filling this void in the literature by outlining the ways in which critical political economy contributes to our understandings of citizenship politics in the EU. In developing what we prefer to call a "critical history"—shorthand for this book's application of critical political economy insights to the long-term history of citizenship in the EU since the early 1950s—the central purpose here is to intervene in the existing literature by rendering explicit the social purpose of EU citizenship within the EU as a hybrid, but nevertheless capitalist, form of statehood (Jessop 2002). Before proceeding to outline this alternative approach in detail, we begin by first fleshing out our conceptual critique of what we broadly identify as the predominant theoretical approaches to EU citizenship. Considering the enormous body of work already existing in this area, any attempt to review and critique this literature in its entirety within the space allocated here would tend toward caricature. We choose here to focus on the debates and issues surrounding two theoretical perspectives that we argue to be most significant in regards to EU citizenship: namely, the moral philosophical approach known as "post-national cosmopolitanism," and the legalist-institutionalist approach with affinities to the "multilevel governance" approach to EU integration.

"Post-National Cosmopolitanism" and EU Citizenship

Is it desirable, or even possible, for legitimate and democratic citizenship to function outside the confines of the nation-state? Should EU citizenship be endorsed as the basis for a progressive post-national European identity? These are the main questions that have concerned approaches to EU citizenship falling within the moral philosophical tradition, which involves competing interpretations of the European "demos," its possibilities, ethical implications, and consequences for traditional political concepts associated with the nation-state. By far the most influential theoretical perspective on EU citizenship within moral philosophy has been "postnational cosmopolitanism" (hereafter PNC), also referred to as "cosmopolitan democracy".[1] As a normative theoretical perspective located within the tradition of "Kantian-Habermasian critical theory" (Patomäki 2006: 116), PNC seeks to advance an academic and political project of an "international system based on the rule of law and democracy" and respect for universallyrecognized human rights (Archibugi and Koenig-Archibugi 2003: 273). PNC holds that in an era of "globalization," defined as the "transcontinental or interregional flows and networks of activity, interaction and power" (Held, interviewed by Guibernau 2001: 427), new constraints have been placed on the nation-state, which increasingly serve as barriers to, rather than as facilitators of, effective political cooperation and democratic participation.[2]

As a result, PNC prescribes the establishment of new democratic institutions at the local, regional and global levels, to accommodate and politically harness the diffusion of power across the different levels at which it is exercised. Crucially, the formation of a multilayered democratic world order would require the establishment of a universal form of political membership based upon "global citizenship" (Falk 2000; Carter 2001), with the rights and obligations of global civil society and global institutions being based on civil, political, economic, social, and reproductive rights (Held 1991; see also Held 2006). PNC scholarship has been engaged in efforts to assess existing regional and global institutions to serve as prospective "models" for the establishment of an alternative world order.

According to the criteria set by PNC, the EU represents "the last politically effective utopia" (Beck and Grande 2007: 2), and the "the only normatively satisfactory alternative ... an alternative that points to a cosmopolitan order sensitive to both difference and social inequality" (Habermas 2001a: xix, cited in Manners 2007: 81). In this way the institutional setup of the EU serves as a nascent cosmopolitan polity, and a blueprint for further development:

> The first international organization which begins to resemble the cosmopolitan model is the European Union. Its members are in fact sovereign states which have voluntarily transferred increasingly broad tasks (from coal and steel policy to human rights) to the Union.... The centripetal force of the European Union is even greater than that of the United States, which has extended geographically without absorbing culturally heterogeneous communities. From the constitutional point of view, it is extremely significant that intergovernmental insti-

tutions such as the Council of Ministers are now backed by technical institutions such as the Commission, and even by a body directly elected by citizens, such as the European Parliament. The principle of subsidiarity has allowed European institutions to intervene in selected policy areas of member countries. Seen from a global perspective, the European Union is an experiment of great importance. We can only hope that it will be imitated by other regional organizations, be it the Union of African Unity or the Organization of American States. At the same time, the European Union offers interesting cues for a possible reform of the United Nations and the setting up of new institutions (Archibugi 1998: 219–220).

EU citizenship, which serves as the legal embodiment of a European identity based on "the secularization of the egalitarian and individualist universalism that informs our normative self-understanding" (Habermas 2001b: 20; see also Delanty 2005), serves an essential function within PNC's conception of the EU. The potential of EU citizenship to act as an avenue toward the establishment of a cosmopolitan democracy of global citizens lies in the fact that it represents the only concrete example of a legally established citizenship model not based upon the boundaries of the nation-state. In their penchant for normative prescription, PNC theorists argue that EU citizenship should continue to evolve along the lines of "constitutional patriotism" (as coined by Habermas), under which loyalties and allegiances are derived not from national or ethnic origin but instead from an identification with a truly inclusive "post-national" and multicultural EU polity, where rights and obligations are accessible to all, including migrant third-country nationals (TCNs) residing within EU member states (Soysal 1994; for an overview, see Prentoulis 2001).

In order to secure the support of citizens, and to foster their self-consciousness as members of the EU polity based on "common values" (Habermas and Derrida 2003), PNC advocates an expansion of EU-level citizenship, beyond the socially thin and market facilitating citizenship currently on offer, to include the whole constellation of rights previously guaranteed by the nation-state during the "thirty glory years" of the postwar period (Habermas 2001b). From the perspective of PNC, EU citizenship therefore has the potential to combat two main obstacles to the realization of a progressive cosmopolitan order: namely, the destructive effects of twentieth-century European nationalism and the "hollowing out" of national citizenship rights as a result of neoliberal globalization. Despite the academic and political influence of PNC, and indeed the merits of many of its goals and visions, we hold that its conception of EU citizenship faces severe limitations.

To begin, we take issue with PNC's conceptualization of the interrelations between globalization, the nation-state, and EU integration. While we agree with claims that globalization represents a diffusion of power across multiple scales of governance and that state functions have been *adjusted,* if not necessarily *diminished,* as a result, we find problematic the fact that there is no systematic attempt within PNC scholarship to explain why it has come into being, and who (in terms of concrete social and political actors) is pushing it forward in the first place. Instead globalization is treated as an independent variable, an exogenous, almost inevitable, and most crucially, agent-less process bearing down on the political capabilities of nation-states. In focusing on globalization as a process, this "logic of no alternative" (Hay and Rosamond 2002: 158; see Chapter Four) within PNC ignores the fact that globalization is just as much a project reflecting the interests and power of identifiable social and political actors (Overbeek 2004), with many of its key facets authored by nation-states habitually portrayed by PNC as globalization's victims (Görg and Hirsch 1998; Panitch 1996; Murray 1971). Thus if globalization is, as PNC is willing to concede, primarily about the acceleration of global capitalism, then the role of "critical" theory, from which PNC finds its lineage, should accordingly be to scrutinize the role of capital as a class actor, explaining the role of its structural power in disciplining and ultimately subordinating the interests of other competing class forces (Morton 2006).

This critique of PNC's conception of globalization and its relation to the nation-state has direct implications for the perspective's approach to EU integration and citizenship. While PNC is primarily interested in endorsing the EU as a "buffer" against the apparent negative effects of globalization on the nation-state, it is not equipped with the conceptual and analytical tools to inquire into the historical and material dimensions of the EU project: explaining its origins and limitations, in addition to identifying the power relations that underpin it. Much like in its assessment of globalization, PNC is willing to concede that EU integration has, to this point, been primarily about market-making integration (Habermas 2001b), and subsequently argues in favor of market-correcting mechanisms to counter market integration along the lines of an EU project envisioned by former Commission President Jacques Delors. Yet at no point does it take into consideration the structural barriers in place that have historically constrained the realization of EU-level market-correcting mechanisms (Deppe 2004: 311), explaining for instance why Delors' social democratic vision for the EU was eventually cast aside (see further Chapter 3). Processes linked to EU integration, therefore, much like the PNC account of globalization, are taken as given instead of serving as phenomena to be explained in their own right. Thus the PNC's endorsement of the EU project serves as a "totalizing blueprint" that is "not grounded in realist analysis of the relevant context, concrete embodied actors, social relations and mechanisms, and transformative possibilities" (Patomäki 2003: 347).

Similar shortcomings also plague PNC's views on citizenship, which involve declaring support for the EU project and its citizenship policy on the basis of their supposed promotion of progressive, cosmopolitan values without inquiring into the historical and material context through which EU citizenship has developed. To cosmopolitan reasoning, however, there is little room for such hesitation. For many within this school of thought, one of the chief intellectual tasks is rather to venerate the EU's past achievements and outline hopeful visions for the EU's future. "The historical success of the European Union," writes Jürgen Habermas (2006: 48, italics in original), "has confirmed Europeans in the conviction that the *domestication of the state's use of violence* also calls for a *reciprocal* restriction of the scope of sovereignty at the global level." Given, moreover, that this enterprise is founded on a passionate conviction that the EU project eventually will yield a progressive cosmopolitan return—working, for instance, to the advantage of migrants' rights and inclusion—it can neither afford any agnosticism as regards the EU project's allegedly benign founding intentions, nor as regards its allegedly benign teleology (for examples of this passionate conviction, see Beck 2006: 168; Beck and Grande 2007: 2; Giddens 1998: 142–7). This, in much the same way, then, as yesterday's nationalist intellectuals could not afford such questioning of the national project. To declare support for, and invest hope in, this form of cosmopolitan subject making while neglecting the power relations through which subjects "forge themselves" (Davies 2005: 135) is tantamount, as André Drainville (2004: 31) has argued in his critique of PNC, to treating citizens as "ghosts."

A more nuanced power perspective, anchored in the critical-theoretical procedures of negative dialectics, which assess conceptual frameworks and analytic models "in terms of how they are not serving" humanity's material needs and "self- and mutual recognition of human subjectivities and their aspirations" (Ryner 2005: 145), would place two burdens of proof on the PNC endorsement of EU citizenship. First, the extent to which EU citizenship actually entails a more effective and democratic guarantor of rights vis-à-vis national citizenship; and second, the reasons why EU citizenship serves as a more inclusive basis for identity and rights formation and not merely as a regional mode of exclusiveness based on a new *European platform* of anti-immigrant nationalism and ethno-cultural chauvinism (Hansen 2000, 2009; Kveinen 2002). Today's cosmopolitans may assert that Islamophobia only can be tackled above the nation, since, as Beck (2006: 166–7) claims, it is "utterly un-European" to be anti-Muslim—a fact that Beck links directly to the condition that, in sharp contrast to the nation-state, "[r]adical openness is a defining feature of the European project and is the real secret of its success". Yet, when searching for the empirical corroboration of this and other assertions holding forth the EU project's inherently benign and anti-racist spirit, one looks in vain for any systematic account demonstrating how such "radical openness" actually manifests in more concrete terms and how it serves to mitigate the current plight of Muslims (see further Chapters 5–6). When a disjuncture exists between the exercise of power and legitimacy (whether defined in terms of social rights, inclusiveness or non-discrimination), as is the case in the contemporary EU project, the task of critical theory must therefore be to scrutinize the contextual environment in which this disjuncture has emerged, to grasps the limits that EU citizenship faces in its task of popular legitimation. PNC, in endorsing EU citizenship on the basis of an abstract model, clearly falls short of this task.

"Nested Membership": EU Citizenship in a Multilevel Governance Polity

The second body of literature, grounded primarily in the disciplinary traditions of legal studies and political science, goes beyond the narrow focus of PNC to analyze the legal interactions between citizenship models at the EU and national levels. With direct affinities to multilevel governance (hereafter MLG) integration theory, this approach is interested in uncovering potential areas of conflict and congruence that characterize the overlapping competencies of the EU and national governments with specific reference to their formal institutional arrangements for citizenship. The MLG approach relates citizenship to processes of integration and seeks to highlight the ways in which EU citizenship is shaped by actors within the "fragmented, complex, and multi-sited" EU polity (Bellamy and Warleigh 1998: 466). Ultimately the MLG approach to EU citizenship, though characterized by a diverse range of theoretical positions and empirical applications, is captured succinctly by Thomas Faist (2001: 37), who observes that "European citizenship is nested in various sites: regional, state and supranational forms of citizenship function in complementary ways—while the associated norms, rules and institutions are subject to constant revision and further development on all governance levels." Discussions of social citizenship and rights, on the one hand, and the status of migrants, ethnic minorities and third-country nationals, on the other, have figured prominently in the MLG citizenship literature, and it is to these two themes that we now turn.

There is a general consensus between scholars working within the MLG approach to EU citizenship that, to this point, there has been an absence of EU-level social rights. Disagreement exists however, over the implications of "de-socialized" EU citizenship, and whether or not EU-level social rights are obtainable or even a necessary component of a legitimate EU polity. Pessimists argue that the lack of EU social rights is a main factor contributing to the EU's legitimacy crisis, and that the current institutional configuration of the EU imposes severe limits on the realization of a "social Europe" underpinned by social citizenship provisions (Closa 1996; Downes 2001).

Though not dealing explicitly with the issue of EU citizenship, the work of Fritz Scharpf serves as one of the most sophisticated, and we think justifiably respected, frameworks effectively capturing the MLG line of thinking of European social rights. For Scharpf, the lack of EU social rights can be attributed to the fact that the relationship between positive market-correcting integration and negative market-making integration has become increasingly asymmetrical: while economic policies have been progressively Europeanized, social-protection policies have remained at the national level (see further Chapter 3). "As a consequence," Scharpf (2002: 666) argues, "national welfare states are constitutionally constrained by the 'supremacy' of all European rules of economic integration, liberalization and competition law."

Intensifying economic interdependence in the EU has proceeded rapidly. This has imposed restrictions on national governments' abilities to provide social goods. At the same time, according to Scharpf, a "joint decision trap" has prevented governments in the Council of Ministers from agreeing on integration in areas of social policy. The EU therefore suffers from a multilevel and dual-faceted legitimacy crisis of both input-legitimacy (government-by-the-people) and output-legitimacy (government-for-the-people) (Scharpf 1999). Scharpf's solution to this dual crisis of legitimacy runs counter to the proposals of PNC based on strengthening collective European identity and the input-based model of constitutional patriotism. Instead Scharpf (1999: Ch. 1) argues that the diversity of the EU's member states prevents the formation of a collective European identity and that this diversity, in turn, renders input-based models of legitimacy based on majoritarian democracy unsuitable in the EU context (Thomassen and Schmitt 2004). The EU should therefore concentrate on strengthening output-based legitimacy, an important component of which would be to strengthen the social dimension of EU governance. Although the nature of the EU polity places daunting obstacles to

EU-level social rights, Scharpf (2001: 19) suggests that a more effective route, against both supranational and intergovernmental decision making, may lie in the "open method of coordination" (OMC) and the hopes that EU-level "monitoring, benchmarking and peer review could increase the effectiveness of national employment and social policies" (see Chapter 4).

The second theme that has preoccupied much of the MLG literature involves the status of non-citizen migrants or resident third country nationals (hereafter TCNs). MLG scholars working on this issue have come to a simple yet significant observation: since the claim to EU citizenship is tied to national citizenship in a member state, it excludes the more than 18 million TCNs[3] resident in the EU from its provisions. Whereas barriers to free movement and residence are increasingly removed for Union citizens, possession of member state nationality remains a qualifying criterion for eligibility to the benefits afforded by Community rules in the post–Amsterdam Treaty Europe. Union citizenship remains conditioned on possession or acquisition of state nationality. This has resulted in the relegation of long-term resident nationals of third countries to the periphery of the emerging European civil society, despite the fact that they are an integral part of the EU and contribute to the development and flourishing of European societies (Kostakopoulou 2002: 444).

The exclusionary and limited nature of EU citizenship as relates to TCNs, as MLG scholars are keen to point out, runs contrary to the assertions made by cosmopolitans that it forms the basis for a more progressive post-national identity detached from the nation-state (Kostakopoulou 2005: 240). MLG scholars also point to the fact that the position of TCNs challenges the notion that EU citizenship serves as a route to popular legitimacy for the EU project, as a large base of the EU population, directly subject to supranational policy making, are denied the democratic right to participate in the political process (Geddes 2000a; Day and Shaw 2002). This also raises concerns about the abilities of the EU to promote the social integration of TCNs, given the increased institutional capacities of the EU in areas of migration and asylum policy since the Amsterdam Treaty (ratified in 1999) (Kostakopoulou 2005). In terms of possible solutions, the MLG approach advocates a number of institutional reforms that could remedy the precarious position of TCNs and expand upon EU citizenship beyond its current exclusionary nature. This would entail either modifying EU citizenship, basing it on residence rather than nationality ("denizenship," as coined by Hammar [1990]) (Hansen, R. and Weil 2001; Hansen, R. 1998), or building upon existing EU initiatives that seek to give TCNs rights and obligations that are comparable to those of EU citizens (Kostakopoulou 2002: 449; see also Chapters 5–6).

The MLG approach to citizenship thus has several advantages over PNC: most importantly, it situates EU citizenship within the concrete historical context of EU integration, recognizing how the politics of citizenship in the EU is influenced by several actors and institutions at multiple levels of governance. It also, especially in the work of Scharpf, offers a more nuanced approach to the scalar dimensions of EU citizenship, challenging the portrayal of globalization and EU integration as necessarily negative exogenous pressures on national citizenship models. At the same time, however, the MLG approach to citizenship suffers from the same pitfalls that characterize MLG integration theory. In narrowly focusing on the institutional form of EU citizenship, the MLG approach to EU citizenship fails to address its socioeconomic content, explaining why it has emerged, who benefits from it, and what kind of citizenship model it seeks to promote (Holman 2004). Although MLG recognizes that certain elements of society have indeed lost out when it comes to EU citizenship (social rights beneficiaries, TCNs), it does not make any systematic attempt to explain why this has been the case. Thus the institutional reforms that MLG proposes tend toward pluralism—failing to take into account the power relations that limit the efficacy of such measures (van Apeldoorn et al 2003). As a descriptive theory concerned mostly with the "problem solving" (see Cox 1986) dimensions of EU citizenship, MLG cannot account for the origins and trajectories of structural power that underpin the provision of rights and responsibilities in the multilevel governance polity. Much like PNC, the explanatory dimensions of EU citizenship, especially as they relate to issues of power and legitimacy, are largely out of reach.

Towards a Critical History

Despite their obvious differences, the two broadly categorized streams of thought outlined above are likely to accept as a starting point a basic definition of citizenship as the concept or category defining the rights and responsibilities of civil society to the polity/state and vice versa (Hay 1996; Tilly 1995). As our critique suggests, PNC tends to focus its energies completely on a nascent European civil society, the coming together of diverse European peoples who have supposedly begun to shed their outdated, regressive allegiances to the nation-state. It cannot, however, due largely to crude conceptualizations of globalization and the concomitant process of EU integration, provide any compelling reasons as to why a European polity as a political organization would differ fundamentally from the nation-state. The MLG approach to EU citizenship on the other hand concentrates narrowly on the institutional dynamics between the EU and national levels or polities, thus largely ignoring the role of civil society in shaping and influencing the content of supranational and national laws and institutions. Most crucially furthermore, both of these approaches tend toward pluralism in failing to systematically explain the ways in which different social and political actors are differentially impacted by citizenship politics in the EU. In the absence of any such treatment of the power relations underpinning EU citizenship, PNC is limited in its abilities to account for the structural barriers preventing the realization of its progressive vision of the EU; whereas MLG, though it recognizes asymmetries between national and European social citizenship regimes and between EU citizens and TCNs, faces troubles in trying to explain why or how these asymmetries came into being, and how they can be transformed.

Citizenship and Capitalist Power Relations

Our alternative critical history starts out from the same basic definition of citizenship, but radically departs from the dominant approaches by analyzing the historical *power relations* underpinning the relationship between civil society and the polity. As such, we emphasize that the politics of citizenship is never isolated from broader processes of social transformation; and while the phenomena of societal change have certain transformative effects on the rights and responsibilities of citizenship, at the same time rights and responsibilities entrenched in prior social struggles can have an impact on, and even limit the degree of such change (Purcell 2002). By explicitly situating our analysis within the broader historical context of EU integration, we start our analysis from the obvious but nevertheless crucial argument that since the EU is a capitalist social formation, our explanatory approach must place primary emphasis on the role of capitalist social relations as a key mode of power shaping the content of citizenship politics in the EU. Of course the state, civil society, and indeed citizenship have all historically preceded the emergence of capitalist social relations, and so our first task will be to explicate historically the social purpose of citizenship within a capitalist context. This, we argue, will help to address the charges of "economic reductionism" that inevitably arise to challenge these observations regarding the centrality of capitalist social relations.

In order to think historically about the relationship between citizenship and capitalism, we feel that it is useful to draw insights from the literature tracing the gradual rise of industrial capitalism in eighteenth-century England. This is by no means the place to revisit the controversial and protracted debates over the precise origins of capitalism (for an instructive overview, see Wood 2002); instead, we single out the work of Ellen

Wood (1995) as particularly helpful in elucidating the historical specificity of citizenship in capitalist societies. For Wood (1995), the transition from feudalism to capitalism in England brought with it a new form of state embodied by the principles of the Glorious Revolution of 1688 (see also van der Pijl 1998). Whereas feudal communities were characterized by (1) peasant possession of the "means of labour and subsistence," (2) "extra-economic" modes of surplus extraction by feudal lords in the form of rent and taxation, and (3) formal inequality excluding peasants from political participation in the state, emergent capitalist communities were predicated on a combination of relative political and civil equality in the form of representative liberal democracy, and socioeconomic inequality whereby the institution of private property ensured that "purely economic advantage [took] the place of juridical privilege and political monopoly" (Wood 1995: 211).[4]

This explication of the specific rise of capitalist citizenship in England gives us clues as to what the primary function or social purpose of citizenship within the capitalist state is in general; namely, to *legitimate* the unequal power relations in the realm of capital accumulation through a discourse of purportedly equal political subjects. Echoing Dannreuther and Petit's (2006: 184) regulationist approach, we see that the state's role in conferring (or denying) citizenship status can be conceptualized as a mode of social regulation over processes of capital accumulation:

> One of the clearest ways that the state has contributed to the maintenance of capital accumulation has been in its exclusive ability to grant rights to its subjects. In their constitutional form, rights provide cultural as well as formal references for acceptable behaviour through statements of ideals and beliefs that inform legislative behaviour. More practically, rights establish the primary legislation from which secondary legislation is enacted to, for example, empower voters, secure property, and enable trade.

Dannreuther and Petit (2006: 185) go on to explain convincingly how the historical development of rights and responsibilities—which spell out the need for citizens "to not steal, to accept the primacy of market forces, to vote and to work when well"—have played a crucial role in maintaining the compliance of subjects by regulating social behavior in a manner that not only sustains, but also legitimately reproduces particular regimes of accumulation. In other words, the composition of citizenship and especially social rights, as the "constituent element of citizenship" and the "cement of social cohesion" (Aglietta 1998: 64), act as a bridge between accumulation and regulation.

At the same time it is crucial to emphasize that the *politics* of citizenship cannot be reduced to an instrumentalist reading whereby citizen rights and responsibilities serve merely as a "top-down" instrumentalist tool of legitimation for the ruling class. As an institutionalized outcome of (politically contingent) class struggles (Mann 1987), the content of citizenship reflects the balance of social power relations that vary considerably over time and space. For example, explaining the emergence of, but also the considerable variations in, social citizenship regimes in advanced capitalist states during the post–World War II period must take into account not only ruling class strategies, but also situate these in relation to working class strategies for social protection (see Chapter 2).

We therefore prefer to anchor our conceptual framework within what Bob Jessop (1990) terms "hegemonic projects," a concept denoting the competing strategies through which competing class forces vie for "moral and intellectual leadership" over the state. Crucially, the actual historical formation of hegemonic projects in terms of strategies, interests and allegiances (in short, politics and ideology) cannot merely be reduced to their structural positions in the original process of accumulation, and must instead be identified in terms of class *agency*, whereby open-ended political struggles play a defining role. In moving from narrow "economic" objectives toward uniting together the "divergent views, identities and interests" (van Apeldoorn 2002) into a "general interest" incorporating subordinate groups, most successful hegemonic projects all rely on notions of equality, fairness and the "common good." In capitalist societies these find their fullest expression in particular constellations of civil, political, and social citizenship rights and responsibilities. This view of citizenship has obvious affinities with the framework of T. H. Marshall, whose classic work *Citizenship and Social Class* (1950) made plain the contradictory nature of citizenship under capitalism. While citizenship, as Marshall argued, had been at war with the class system for centuries, citizenship simultaneously harbored the potential to serve as a "legitimate architect of social inequality" that characterizes capitalist social relations.

The Politics of Citizenship: Being and Becoming a Citizen

Marshall's analysis of the historical evolution of Anglo-Saxon citizenship from civil rights in the eighteenth century, political rights in the nineteenth century, culminating in the institutionalization of social rights in the twentieth century (Mann 1987), never addressed the issue of migration, which as our introduction suggest, is central to a broader understanding of the underlying politics of citizenship in the EU. It is important in this regard to take into account the historical context in which Marshall wrote, where, at least in terms of social rights, migrants in the advanced capitalist countries were included, or at least about to become included, in the "nationally oriented settlements of the Keynesian Welfare [National] State" (Ryner 2000: 51; Schierup, Hansen and Castles 2006). Nevertheless, in the contemporary context of the increasing political salience of migration and the decline of the Keynesian Welfare National State (KWNS) (Jessop 2002) it has become imperative, both for positive (empirical) and normative reasons, to render explicit the inextricable linkages between citizenship and migration. We feel it is useful to draw on Castles and Davidson's (2000: 84) distinction between "being a citizen," implied in our basic definition of citizenship offered above, and "becoming a citizen":

> Becoming a citizen is clearly of crucial importance to an immigrant, but gaining formal access to citizenship—symbolized by getting the passport of the country of residence—is only one aspect of this. Equally important is the extent to which people belonging to distinct groups of the population actually achieve substantial citizenship, that is, equal chances of participation in various areas of society, such as politics, work, welfare systems and cultural relations.

As these authors go on to point out, the distinction between "being" and "becoming" a citizen is always a blurred one "because of the discontinuities and fluidity of different aspects of citizenship" (Castles and Davidson 2000: 103). The blurring of reality that occurs when migration is added to the citizenship equation has direct implications for Marshall's evolutionary depiction of the line from civil to political to social rights. As discussions of the migrant integration, or incorporation, experiences in Western Europe during the postwar "golden age" attest to, the Marshallian formula was actually reversed for migrants and ethnic minorities, who most often were drawn into social welfare schemes before being given the political right to vote (Guiraudon 2000; Schierup, Hansen and Castles 2006). In the case of EU citizenship, however, these matters are further complicated as it appears as though this model has been reversed back to its original Marshallian formulation, with the EU recently introducing a "civic citizenship" model for TCNs—"but with no guarantees of an evolutionary follow-up in the future in terms of a *social* citizenship of the Union" (Schierup, Hansen and Castles 2006: 63, italics in original; see further Chapter 5–6).

We therefore suggest that it makes sense to speak of *differential degrees of inclusion* into particular citizenship regimes and their accompanying rights and responsibilities. Schematically, these may be divided into separate regimes, for instance, for "formal" citizens, legally, "illegally" or irregularly resident TCNs, asylum seekers, and those on the borderlands trying to enter a specific territory—all of which are further complicated by the differential power relations that divide societies along class, gender, sexual, ethnic, racial, and religious lines. In this way, the centrality of hegemonic projects to our critical-historical framework enables us to identify the structural division between capital and labor in the accumulation process, but is also sensitive to the fact that this must give way to an overtly political discussion of the divisions and fractures within classes themselves (e.g. organized labor lobbying alongside employer associations for stricter migration controls for employment and social protection reasons). Overall, it is crucial to the critical aspect of our framework to be able to highlight such disjunctions between the structural and political, not the least in order so that knowledge can be used to formulate alternative projects that identify the barriers and offer tangible strategies toward the mobilization of subordinate social forces in ways that cut across these political divides.

Conclusion: Citizenship and the EU Polity

Thus far our conceptual framework has been concerned with the historical interrelations between citizenship and the state. In what ways does it need to be modified in order to take into account the interrelations between the EU, a different form of political organization from the nation-state, and EU citizenship, a category which is at the same time distinct from, yet still necessarily linked to the national citizenship models of EU member states? In general terms, we accept the premises of both PNC and MLG that the EU has taken on several policy-making and governance powers that were once the exclusive domain of the nation-state. We also accept the argument that the rescaling of power to the EU level has altered the functions and powers of EU member states in certain respects. Finally, we agree that the rescaling of policy making and governance to the EU level has been heavily biased toward market-making negative integration, and also that EU citizenship has, as a result, been limited especially in terms of social rights.

According to our alternative approach, the EU can be conceived of not as a nation-state in the traditional sense but, as James Caporaso (1996: 46) makes clear, as an "ongoing structure of political authority and governance." It is a hybrid and evolving form of polity, one that contains its own modes of regulation that govern and coordinate the pan-European regime of accumulation (reflected in the Single Market). This in turn means that the EU takes on several important functions of statehood, mediating competing hegemonic projects that operate within simultaneous and interrelated levels and arenas of governance (van Apeldoorn and Horn 2007). Thus far however, this account does not give us much indication as to how our alternative approach differs from the predominant PNC and MLG conceptions of the EU polity. We depart from these conceptions by suggesting that although the institutional setup of the EU is distinct from the state in many ways, it still fulfils the same role as a site of accumulation and competing class interests, contained within a hybrid EU state/civil society complex. As in the case of state citizenship outlined above, EU citizenship also acts as a mode of social regulation, this time within the EU polity, creating "new and compatible social identities to match the European social body" (Scott-Smith 2003: 261) while attempting to legitimate configurations of power relations that underpin EU policy making and governance.

Taken as a whole, we argue that this alternative critical history equips us with the conceptual tools for explaining the historical emergence and movement of the politics of citizenship in the EU, with the overall aim of elucidating its underlying social purpose. As a result, we do not seek to merely describe the current state of EU citizenship and endorse it as a route to a more progressive world order (in the case of PNC) nor to propose narrow problem-solving solutions that portend to modify EU citizenship in ways that make it into a mechanism for the legitimation of EU policy making and governance (as in MLG). Given the current crisis of EU legitimacy, we feel there is a dire need for social scientific research that instead directs its energies toward uncovering the limits and contradictions of EU citizenship from a historical perspective. Ultimately, the overall efficacy of the alternative problématique and underlying theoretical assumptions sketched here to sustain it can only be assessed based on how well the empirically thick historical account they buttress can capture the dynamics of citizenship politics as they have developed in the EU through more than half a century. It is to this task that we now turn.

Notes

1. For a key critique of PNC from within the moral philosophical tradition—one that we draw theoretical inspiration from and attempt to give empirical grounding to—see Balibar (2004).
2. We consider this conception of the nation-state within PNC to be the most common, "moderate" position, espoused by figures such as Daniele Archibugi and David Held. There is, however, a considerable divergence of thinking on the nation-state within PNC, so that it makes sense to plot differing views on a continuum ranging from moderates of a more realist bent to those with more doctrinaire outlooks, such as the one espoused by Ulrich Beck (2006: 170), who likens

the nation-state to an "experimental chamber of horrors," the one responsible for "the two world wars, the Holocaust, the atomic bombs dropped on Hiroshima and Nagasaki, the Stalinist death camps and genocides." For a thorough delineation and critical scrutiny of the various cosmopolitan and post-national perspectives and positions, see Calhoun (2007).
3. According to Eurostat figures for 2006, there were approximately 18.5 million third-country nationals residing in the EU-25 (CEC 2007f: 3).
4. Wood's argument thus relies on the notion that early forms of capitalist social relations relied upon market compulsion ("economic" versus "extra-economic" power) as the central mechanism through which workers are drawn into wage labor and capitalists are drawn to "maximize" profits. The dichotomy between "economic" and "extra-economic," we argue, is blurred in the initial transition to capitalism through its reliance on violent forms of "primitive accumulation" (Marx 1976), and also with the rise of oligopolistic corporations in the late nineteenth and early twentieth centuries (Josephson 1934).

CHAPTER 2

The Origins of EU Citizenship (1950–1980)

Introduction

Although it would take until the early 1970s before any real explicit discussion concerning a European Community citizenship was to emerge (Wiener 1998: 10–11), a very tangible, what we could term, supranational citizenship regime had been set to develop from the onset of European integration in the 1950s (see Meehan 1993). Certainly, this supra- and transnational citizenship regime was rarely perceived as such at the time. That is to say, in sharp contrast to the EU citizenship's current image and formal status, the historical citizenship regime did not constitute a freestanding policy area but was inextricably bound up with migration policy. Hence, the emerging catalogue of transnational rights in the Community was almost exclusively conferred on one single target group, namely intra-Community labor migrants, and so derived from the EU's migration policy regime (Koslowski 1998) that the Rome Treaty instituted in order to stimulate labor migration between the Community's six member states. Elements of citizenship policy and migration policy were thus directly bound up with the political economic scheme devised by the Rome Treaty and the Community's *four freedoms:* the free movement of goods, persons, services, and capital. From the very beginning, then, migration policy at the EU level also implied a transnational citizenship policy at the EU level. In this chapter we shall remove the dust from this important historical relationship, one that often gets lost in today's debate and scholarship on EU citizenship.

The common neglect of the historical symbiosis between supranational migration and citizenship policy owes much to the fact that contemporary scholarship tends to perceive of migration as a latecomer on the EU agenda. In *Encyclopedia of the European Union* (Dinan 2000: 269), for instance, where a number of scholars account for the EU's historical trajectory, it is established that "[i]mmigration emerged as an explicit

38

European level policy area only in the [Maastricht] Treaty on European Union," which was ratified in 1993.¹ According to this prevalent view, such tardiness is mainly attributable to the alleged fact that member states until the 1990s considered the area of migration to be wholly off-limits to any supranational competence and meddling. Migration, the story goes, was, and still is, simply too delicate of a matter for national governments to compromise, too intimately bound up with matters of borders, security, citizenship, national identity, and a host of other purportedly "sensitive" issues which are said to define the very essence of the sovereign nation-state. And although it is acknowledged that the Amsterdam Treaty (ratified in 1999) did, in fact, bring about a certain transfer of migration policy competence from the national to the supranational level, the (what we could call) *sensitivity thesis* stays in control and can readily claim corroboration with reference to the, after all, quite limited relocation of competence to the supranational level that has taken place in recent years. Hence, member-state governments can still be said to be to "jealously guarding" their sovereignty over migration policy vis-à-vis the EU level.

There is certainly an element of truth in this account; but it is also an account that significantly overstates and (inadvertently) misrepresents its case. Upon closer scrutiny it soon becomes obvious that the story largely earns its coherence from an erasure of the longstanding supranational migration policy of "free movement" within the EU for member state citizens. These days, free movement is thus rarely conceptualized in terms of migration and so is exempted from discussions of the larger migration policy complex in the European Union, past and present (see further Hansen 2008: Ch. 1).

This way of defining away the positively charged phenomenon of *free movement*—connoting, as it does, open borders and labor markets, European unity, modern economy, and, last but not least, European citizenship—from the context of *migration,* which in today's political vocabulary mostly spells "problems," is, needless to say, an even more firmly established, albeit much more premeditated, practice within the sphere of European politics and policy making. As such, it walks hand in hand with an established and steadily growing discrepancy in the way people who move across national borders are treated and represented in and by the European Union. Although referring specifically to this discrepancy's manifestation in the Spanish case, Gunther Dietz and Belén Agrela's (2004: 431) delineation loses none of its accuracy when applied to the situation in the EU as a whole:

> The large segment of intra-European Union migrants is made statistically and politically invisible by virtue of its being excluded from of-

ficial immigration data, from the discourse on migration, and from governmental integration measures.... Thus immigration is officially— and artificially—perceived and treated as a south-north phenomenon. The formal and legal classifications of migrants—refugees or asylum seekers, settled or temporary immigrant workers, undocumented immigrants, and so on—are combined with ethnocultural and symbolic labels that reflect an implicit ethno-religious hierarchy of "others."

Notwithstanding the reality of national borders within the EU having been open to labor migration for member-state citizens ever since the start of European integration, and regardless of the fact that member states handed over the responsibility for such migration policy to the supranational level, today's literature, save for a few notable exceptions (e.g. Miles 1993; Geddes 2003), persists in designating migration policy as a latecomer on the EU agenda. As Sassen (1999: 129) put in 1999: "there is still no EC immigration policy as such, nor a EC citizenship policy." In this literature, migration policy in the EU is thus almost exclusively made to refer either to member states' individual immigration, asylum, and migrant integration policies with regard to people from outside the Union and the OECD sphere, or to the intergovernmental cooperation on migration in the EU (e.g. Schengen). This provided, it is only when this latter and more comprehensive dimension of migration policy formally enters the supranational policy picture in the 1990s that scholars in any general sense start to perceive of a relationship between *migration policy* and *citizenship policy* at the EU level. Prior to the 1990s, current scholarship rarely detects such a relationship; it only catches one between *free movement* and *EU citizenship*.

Interestingly enough, this approach has not always been predominant. As will be evinced below, up until the late 1970s, even into the 1980s, the literature quite commonly referred to free movement as a form of migration policy and those who utilized free movement as migrants or "immigrants" (see e.g. Collins 1975). Even more so this held true for the terminology employed by EU institutions. Such historical changes of definitions and categorizations (as well as the disappearance of categorizations and inventions of new ones) of people who migrate function as telling indicators of the impact European integration has had on institutionalized and public perceptions of identity, belonging, and spatial frames of reference. In parallel with the politically driven process and project of European integration, the definitions and categories employed to describe this process are also transformed. In turn, this parallel change of signification often entails that the consequences of European integration are endorsed and made imperceptible at one fell swoop. Not too long ago, people in Sweden with Italian origin were routinely described as "immigrants." Nowadays, this connection is rarely made in the public debate and official policy. The designation of people with Spanish origin in France, Portuguese in Belgium, or Irish in Britain point to similar cases of changing categorizations (see Miles 1993: 206–7).

Against this background, we now go on to survey and analyze the EU-level's approach to migration, citizenship, and transnational rights during the first decades of European integration (ca. 1950–1980). As we have already demonstrated, such an account cannot confine itself to the nexus of migration and citizenship as it played out in the context of free movement. Instead, the chapter explains why the supranational influence was limited to the migration policy of free movement, whereas the member states effectively kept control over all other areas of migration policy. As part of this, member-state governments made sure to exclude third-country nationals (TCNs)—the great majority of whom had been recruited as labor migrants or "guest workers"—from free movement and the rights belonging to it. This provided, it becomes important to account for the consequences of this division, or *dualization,* of migration policy in the EU, not least since this dualized order still exists today, manifesting in an unequal treatment between migrants with citizenship in a member state and TCNs. This means that the chapter seeks to weave together the question of EU citizenship historically not only with the migration policy of free movement; rather, the complex historical trajectory of EU citizenship compels us to also locate it in the context of migration policy writ large. That there is ample reason for such a pursuit will, not least, become evident as we account for the European Commission's attempts in the 1970s to utilize Community citizenship and social rights as an articulatory platform to confer rights on external migrants and TCNs and thus remedy their lot in the Community as a whole. Such calls to expand a transnational regime of rights, or citizenship, also formed an integral part of the larger struggle over the political economic orientation of the European Community in the 1970s. Citizenship was thus to surface as a watchword in the debate over European integration's role in the looming economic crisis in Western Europe during the 1970s. Conversely, the provision of substantial supranational rights of citizenship was also seen as a means to amend the legitimacy crisis hitting the project of European integration itself at this historical juncture.

Regimes of EU Citizenship and Intra-EU Migration

In the Treaty of Rome, labor migration was assigned an important function. This partly grew out of the assessments made in *The Brussels Report on the General Common Market* from 1956—or the Spaak Report, named after the Belgian foreign minister Paul-Henri Spaak, who was its author and principal instigator. The report, which made up the chief preparatory work for the Rome Treaty and the design of the European Economic Community (EEC), made it clear that labor migration formed part of the EEC's elementary logic, a necessary precondition for an association built on "free competition" (Maas 2005: 1019). A large market and competitive production, it was argued, did not only require facilitated mobility for the interchange of goods, capital, and services; it also required access to a mobile labor force. Imbalances on the Community's labor market such as when one member state was unable to supply its growth industries with enough labor, or labor with sufficient skills, would in this way be resolved by having the member state in need gain access to labor from the other members. In theory, the allocation gains reaped from enhanced labor mobility also implied that unemployment in one region of the Community and labor shortage in another were to balance each other out in a way beneficial to both regions. The mobility of the factors of production (in this case labor) in the six member states was no longer to be constrained by national borders; instead, it was to be extended in order to benefit the entire transnational common market and enlarged production base that the integration project intended to create. Important to keep in mind, though, is that this by no means entailed a transfer of national labor market and migration policies to the supranational level. However, since migration policy as regarded the intra-EEC movement of workers was subjected to such a transfer, this change did, indirectly, involve a certain supranational influence on labor market policy. But this was as far as the member states were ready to go at this point (Romero 1993).

The Rome Treaty's labor mobility provisions originated in the Treaty of Paris (1951) and its institution of the European Coal and Steel Community (ECSC) (Maas 2005). Through persistent pressure from the Italian government, the ECSC opened up for the free movement of qualified coal and steelworkers. Italy saw itself suffering from an acute problem of overpopulation and was, therefore, very anxious to secure means for emigration in order to, as the expression often goes, export its surplus population, and, with it, its unemployment problem. This also constituted one of the main reasons behind the Italian support for and participation in postwar European integration (Willis 1971).

Italian unemployment problems also influenced the Rome Treaty's institution of free movement for labor. This time, however, the other five signatories were also in favor of more open intra-EEC labor migration. But for them, and in contrast to Italy, it was labor shortage, rather than unemployment, that prompted their approval. The five other members, and West Germany in particular—now the emerging economic motor of Western Europe—had difficulties in meeting the 1950's great labor demand on their own, and thus saw free movement of labor as a means to amend the problem (Collins 1975: 13). The motives are clearly mirrored in the migration statistics for the years immediately following the ratification of the Treaty of Rome, where Italian workers made up over half of all labor migrants admitted in the Community countries, while less than two fifths came from countries outside of the EEC. In the beginning of the 1960s, almost half of West Germany's labor migrants came from Italy (Ascoli 1985: 186–7).

Free movement of labor within the EEC was not introduced over night at the ratification of the Treaty of Rome in 1958, but would be gradually implemented during the 1960s. More precisely, free movement meant that citizens in the member states were given the same rights and opportunities to seek and acquire work in the Community as a whole. Citizens in one member state were entitled to travel to another member state to accept an employment offer; and they were entitled to stay on in that country after the employment had been concluded. Exceptions were made for employment in the civil service, e.g., the police, military, taxation authorities, government, and the court system. Over and above that, member states were also permitted to restrict the free movement in cases where it was judged to compromise law and order, public safety, and health (see Weiss and Wooldridge 2002).

The work to implement the free movement was carried out in different stages during the 1960s and was completed (tentatively) through legislative decision by the Council of Ministers in 1968 (Council EC 1968a, 1968b). This took place at the same time as the Customs Union was completed, which also had been gradually implemented. 1968 thus marks an important date in EU history; two of the Treaty of Rome's most important transitional goals were now completed. The work to develop, expand, and improve the rights tied to free movement did not stop in 1968, however, but was to continue during the 1970s, and has done so ever since. Hence, even today free movement is not fully accomplished. In fact, the introduction of the so-called transition rules that all old member states (except for Sweden[2]) imposed on the ten new members in 2004 and the two new ones in 2007, and which substantially limit the right of free labor movement for the new EU citizens, inflicted a major blow to free movement, both as a principle and practice. But also citizens of the old member states are still met by certain obstacles when they move, work and settle across borders within the EU (see Baldoni 2003). Even if one disregards the transition arrangements, then, free movement—in the sense of denoting the total equality of rights (and thus the total absence of discrimination based on nationality) between the intra-EU migrants and the citizens of the member state to which they migrate—is still not fully implemented, but even now subjected to some restrictions. The phasing out of such lingering restrictions, as we will discuss further in the next chapter, has been one of the primary aims of the EU's formal citizenship regime ever since its inception in the early 1990s.

Returning to the historical development, it is important to remember that the implementation and development of the free movement provisions implied so much more than a catalogue of *formal rights* and prohibitions against one member state's labor market discriminating against another member's citizens on grounds of nationality. In order to stimulate transnational labor mobility and create incentives for labor to work across borders in the Community, it also became necessary to ensure that such migration entailed a set of *substantial rights*. As we shall see below, the labor migration occurring within the regime of free movement was therefore also to become equipped with an accentuated social welfare dimension.

Migration Policy as Transnational Social Citizenship

When we speak of the EU's social and welfare policy it must be kept in mind that, from the very outset, such EU policy has differed markedly from its national counterparts in the member states. EU competence within social policy was, and still is, very limited and has for the most part consisted of general policy statements lacking binding legal force (see Hix 1999: 226–30). The Treaty of Rome, for instance, emphasized the importance to work for improved living standards and working conditions, increased employment, and reduced social disparities in the Community. The treaty also assigned the Commission the task of establishing member-state cooperation on social policy. As the generality and vagueness of these objectives indicate, EU social policy was never intended to replace its national counterpart; neither can it easily be described as a complement to national social policy, even if this constituted one of its stated purposes. Instead, it was foremost put in place to complement the EU's own economic, or "market making," policy. And since the Community's supranational bearing on economic policy centred on measures to enhance factor mobility, this meant that Community social policy came to be primarily directed toward stimulating labor migration between the member states (see Flanagan 1993: 168–9). EU social policy, as the European Parliament (2000) has described it, was thus fashioned "as an adjunct to economic policy and remained broadly speaking an accompanying policy. The only practical achievements recorded between 1958 and 1974 were the implementation of freedom of movement for migrant workers and the associated social security arrangements and the establishment of the European Social Fund." The intimate connection between the Community's social policy and the free movement's migration policy was also made apparent by the fact that the Rome Treaty's binding and most important social policy provisions were incorporated into the section on the free movement of labor, capital, and service—and not in the treaty's section on social policy (see Majone 1993).

This provided, from the late 1950s to the beginning of the 1970s Community initiatives within the social policy area were almost exclusively geared toward free movement and the issue of intra-Community labor migration (Dinan 1999: 421; Williams 1994: 182). In large part, therefore, it was the implementation and development of social rights for internal labor migrants that came to define supranational social policy during the Community's first decades.

This should not lead one to interpret the role of Community social policy solely in mechanistic terms, as if social policy only functioned as a crass handmaiden to economic imperatives calling for greater cross-national labor mobility. While this certainly was an important part of the story, the European Commission also aspired to provide Community social policy with a stronger and more wide-ranging mandate, one that would also encompass redistributory instruments and thus go beyond the confines of compensatory measures targeted at internal migrant workers and their families. In the 1960s, for instance, the Commission endeavored to set in train a gradual harmonization of national social policy, arguing for an elevation of social policy standards and living and working conditions across the Community. For this purpose the Commission established a close collaboration with national trade unions, a move that greatly incensed both governments and employers' associations. This, not the least, since unions soon tried to make use of the platform afforded to them by the Commission for the purpose of reaping domestic social and political gains (Meehan 1993: 68–9). Toward the latter part of the 1960s, this undertaking on the part of unions led to charges from governments that "the Commission was using trade unions as pressure groups against them" in order to infringe upon the national control over social policy-making (Meehan 1993: 69). As a consequence, it was not long before governments resorted to reprisals against the Commission, deciding to greatly limit its power of initiative in social affairs as well as imposing restrictions on its collaboration with organized labor (Meehan 1993: 69–70).

If this modifies the mechanistic, or purely "economistic" interpretation, it also points to the presence of a conflict between the Commission and the member states with regard to the role and scope of supranational social and welfare policy (see Collins 1975: 32–3, 99). As we shall see ahead, this struggle and conflict over the aim and scope of Community social policy would resurface in conjunction with the economic downturn in the 1970s, as well as during both the Single Market reforms in the 1980s and the negotiations of the Maastricht Treaty in the early 1990s.

Failing to gain a hearing for its larger social policy objectives, much of the Commission's efforts in this area during the 1960s and 70s would thus focus on obtaining substantial social rights for internal labor migrants and their families.[3] This became apparent in the numerous initiatives, programs, and new supranational legislation emanating out of Brussels, all of which aimed to facilitate the migrants' situation both at and outside their new workplaces. The migrants were not only to be treated in exactly the same way as domestic workers with regard to wages, working conditions, information rights, dismissal, and trade union rights; they were also to receive equal social welfare, equally favorable social insurances, and equal or even prioritized access to housing. The Commission also devoted much energy to ensure the right to family reunification for labor migrants, and that the families of labor migrants were given the same rights as nationals concerning working life and social benefits.

Even though the term "integration policy" (directed at migrants) had not been coined in the European context at the time, several of the Community social policy measures targeting internal labor migrants assumed the character of what subsequently in the 1980s and 90s would come to belong under that policy heading (Collins 1975: 101). According to the Commission's recommendations and the supranational provisions that gradually were adopted, labor migrants and their families were thus to be offered the best possible practical preparations for their move to another member state. They were also to be provided with assistance to psychologically prepare for work and life in a new country, and encouraged to keep in touch with family and friends who did not join them. Another priority was to make sure that migrants were given sufficient information about their social rights in the new country. While language courses should be offered, migrants should also be assisted by personnel who spoke their language so as to guarantee that all information was properly conveyed. Such personnel were also to facilitate migrants' acquaintance with the new country's culture and traditions as well as put them into contact with social and cultural associations.

As is evident, Community policy took pains to prevent a situation where member-state citizens would be degraded to second-class citizens when they moved to and started work in a member state other than the one where they held national citizenship. If this would be the case, the reasoning went at the time, intra-Community labor migration would hardly stand a chance of gathering the type of momentum necessary to meet the demand. Most actors were also practically in agreement that the free movement of labor migrants should not be allowed to lead to (what is today termed) social dumping, whereby richer member states and their corporations would start to use migrants from poorer ones for the purpose of lowering salary and welfare levels for the domestic labor force (see Collins 1975; Flanagan 1993; Geddes 2000a: 213).

More than a "Manifesto for Capital"

Given the Rome Treaty's strong emphasis on growth, economies and production bases of scale, internal free trade, free circulation for capital, and competitiveness, it is little wonder that many scholars have likened the Rome Treaty to a "manifesto for capital" (Williams 1994: 181). In many ways this is an appropriate simile (see further Carchedi 2001; Cocks 1980; Holland 1980; Mandel 1970; Moschonas 1996); or as the first European Commission President, Walter Hallstein (1972: 29), put it: "the basic law of the European Economic Community, its whole philosophy, is liberal. Its guiding principle is to establish undistorted competition in an undivided market." But if we are to understand the concurrent and rather successful work that the Commission carried out to ensure intra-Community migrants and their families' social rights (i.e. their social citizenship), the "manifesto for capital" simile needs to be qualified historically. During the first three postwar decades, capitalism and capital interests stood in a different relation to labor and welfare than they have done since the profound political-economic changes that began to transpire in the 1970s and 80s. For reasons of both a functional and political nature, this meant that capital accumulation and the power of corporate interests were embedded within and in many respects subordinated to the building of welfare states in Western Europe. To a large extent this was made possible by the "embedded liberal" postwar Bretton Woods system; an international political-economic regime, which bound states accountable to an international system of fixed exchange rates and capital controls (Ruggie 1982). European integration was in large parts both a result of and a response to this international regime's way of functioning. Characteristic of embedded liberalism was that it admitted, and in some sense had its basis in, a relative compatibility between international economic liberalization (i.e. multilateralism) and the build-up of national welfare states (i.e. social stability) in Western Europe (Ruggie 1982).

Such a relative compatibility was also built into the Community project from its commencement in the 1950s. It is thus through the conceptual lens of embedded liberalism that we can appreciate how the Rome Treaty and European integration could make up both a "manifesto for capital" *and* a springboard for internal labor migrants' social rights. As we will discuss more ahead, the imposing of transition arrangements by the old members on the free movement for the new member state citizens in 2004 and 2007 respectively, and the fact that this was largely motivated by an unwillingness on the part of the old member governments to grant new member labor migrants the social rights belonging to free movement, is just one of many cases verifying the diminishing role played by embedded liberalism in the current European political-economic order.

Different Regimes of Migration and Migrants' Unequal Rights

Despite the efforts that were invested to stimulate the labor mobility between the member states, it soon became apparent that intra-Community labor migration was far from keeping pace with the Community's great labor demand in the 1950s and 60s. As a consequence, the majority of migrant labor would instead come and be recruited from countries outside of the EEC. To be sure, from the end of the 1950s to the beginning of the 1970s intra-Community migration almost doubled in size. Yet, this increase was modest when compared to the growth of extra-Community labor migration to the EEC. Up until the early 1960s internal and external migration grew at approximately the same pace, with the former slightly ahead. Toward the end of the decade, this relationship had been entirely reversed; now the external side was supplying over 80 percent of the Community's labor migrants (Ascoli 1985; Flanagan 1993; see also CEC 1976 [1974]).

It was thus extra-Community migrants who would fill the brunt of the great postwar demand for labor, and, by so doing, also maintain the high growth rates achieved during the period (Williams, 1994: 43). To a large extent these migrants were recruited via the member states' different guest worker programs, and mainly came from Europe's poorer Mediterranean countries—that is, Greece, Portugal, and Spain—and from Yugoslavia and Turkey. But this migration also bore the stamp of both colonial and neocolonial relationships, where many migrants would come from Belgian, French, and Dutch colonies and former colonies. Colonial, but soon foremost neocolonial relationships, were, in this sense, not only advantageous for the EEC in terms of trade and supply of raw materials, advantages which had been procured through the association agreements established at the outset between the EEC and member states' colonies and former colonies (i.e. the Yaoundé, Lomé and, today, the Cotonou agreement); they were also to prove beneficial in providing the Community with a source of much needed labor (MacLaughlin, 1993).[4]

As noted earlier, migration from countries outside the EEC was to remain an area of national responsibility, governed and regulated by the respective governments and their, among themselves, very different and (historically) path dependent policy regimes of admission, recruitment, and incorporation (or "integration") of migrants. A bifurcated, or *dualized*, system for the regulation and handling of migration to the member states was thus established almost from the outset, whereby the Community's *internal* respectively *external* migration were to sort under different policy regimes and legal frameworks.

As it turned out, moreover, the Rome Treaty's clause on free movement was to apply exclusively to member state citizens, thereby excluding the external migrants, or the third-country nationals (TCNs), from the right of free movement within the Community. Interestingly enough, this exclusive application was not stipulated by the treaty itself; the treaty's articles on free movement only referred to "workers" and did not make any explicit distinction between member state citizens and TCNs (Geddes 2000a; Hoogenboom 1992; Kostakopoulou 2001). Rather, it was the member-state governments that, through legislation in the Council of Ministers in the 1960s, decided to restrict free movement to only include member-state citizens (Geddes 2000a; Hoskyns 1996: 169).[5] Given the strong economic motives behind the endeavor to stimulate intra-Community labor mobility, such a curtailment is difficult to explain with reference to a simple cost-benefit calculation. We raise this in view of the fact that the inclusion of TCNs in the free movement regime clearly would have served to increase labor mobility within the Community. According to Theodora Kostakopoulou (2001: 183), the decision instead needs to be viewed in the light of an increasingly negative attitude toward migration from less well off and, most of all, non-European countries that was to take shape in the 1960s (see also Steedman 1979). Indirectly, therefore, the decision contributed to the institutionalization of a perception of who did and who did not belong to the European Community. By excluding TCNs from the free movement provisions, Kostakopoulou (2001: 184–5) goes on, the prospects were also thwarted for the institution of criteria other than nationality, or formal citizenship in a member state, for an individual's belonging to and membership in the Community.

In addition to this, it was also decided early on that internal migrants (i.e. member-state citizens) should have preference over external migrants to employment in the Community—a rule that was upheld in the first stage completion of the free movement scheme in 1968 (Swann 1988:

161). The rule was foremost reflective of an Italian interest to facilitate as much as possible the outflow of its labor surplus to the other member states. Initially this was met with opposition from the West German government, which, owing to its large labor demand, wanted a free hand to recruit labor also from outside the Community. But since it soon became apparent that the intra-Community labor migration would come nowhere near meeting West German labor demands, Bonn's requests were never challenged; thus, the conflicting Italian and West German interests would not have to come to a head. It should be noted though, that the Commission was a warm advocate of these preferential rights for member-state citizens, and for long it clung to a conviction that these rights would indeed impact intra-Community labor migration positively in relation to external migration (Collins 1975: 104–5, 114–5).

As we shall discuss further ahead, the dualized order is still in place, although in a slightly modified form, and since the mid-1980s its ever more conspicuous consequences have been the subject of an equally ever-growing debate (see e.g. Ireland 1996: 136).

Crisis and a Search for Alternatives

The years spanning the late 1960s to the mid-1970s are often pinpointed as the starting point for a period of structural crisis and transformation for continental Western European models of capitalism. A general economic downturn, triggered initially by skyrocketing oil prices and characterized by mounting stagflation, growing unemployment, and decreasing wage shares in national income, ignited a fierce ideological battle between monetarists and Keynesians on how to best manage the changing conditions of the West European political economy (Boyer 1990).

This battle was further complicated by the changing structural conditions of the global political economy, as continental European states were pressed to formulate policy responses to the U.S. and U.K. pole position in abandoning the international compromise of embedded liberalism through "the liberalization of independent finance from Keynesian controls" already in the late-1960s (Holman and van der Pijl 1996: 63; see also Helleiner 1994). Heightened capital mobility and the "vocabulary" of "interdependence and competitiveness" (Cox 1992: 27) that accompanied it raised uncertainties about the future sustainability of continental Europe's models of welfare capitalism and their extensive social citizenship regimes. All in all, as Stockhammer (2005–6: 195–6) notes, it is important to emphasise that the actual effects of the crisis of the 1970s were experienced unevenly by the various social classes within Europe. The rising tide of joblessness and wage stagnation can indeed be regarded as nothing short of a crisis for Europe's working classes; one which they have yet to recover from. But for the capitalist classes, the downturn of the 1970s is best thought of as a temporary lull in performance whereby brief and modest dips in profit incomes were soon restored to their postwar "Golden Age" levels.

The general weakening of Western Europe's overall economic performance in this period also contributed to the activation of the Community-level as a forum for new discussions on how to meet and amend the crisis. Much of this discussion would center on social issues, on the future of welfare, and the question of citizenship (Hoskyns 1996: 79; Williams 1994: 182). The initiative also formed an integral part of an effort to increase popular support for European integration and, as it also was expressed, to put a "human face" on the European Community (Meehan 1993: 70–2; Williams 1994: 182). In the aftermath of the student revolts of 1968 and on the initiative of Willy Brandt's West German government, the Community launched grand plans for a "European Social Union" and a set of social issues was placed on the agenda (Carchedi 2001: 240; Meehan 1993: 70–1). At the Paris European Council in 1972, Community leaders gave their support for a strengthening of Community social policy, and two years later the first ever Community Social Action Program was adopted (see Council EC 1974). The program was extensive and called for action to eliminate unemployment, improve living and working conditions, reinforce employee codetermination and gender equality in the labor market. But the program also indicated a new approach in that intra-Community migrants no longer made up the sole target group for supranational social policy. Community social policy was from then on also to target the unemployed, women, the disabled, youth, *and* extra-Community migrants.

The Formation of a Discourse on Citizenship at the Supranational Level

The new social initiatives were also to trigger the first explicit discussions as regards a Community or "European" citizenship. Although "Citizenship of the Union," or a formal EU citizenship, was not to become part of the treaty until 1993—with the ratification of the Maastricht Treaty—the idea of creating such a citizenship for the EEC and subsequently the EC had been discussed off and on for many years (Wiener 1997: 537–8). References to "the citizens of Europe," "Community citizens," and a "Citizens' Europe" were thus frequent long before the legal category "citizen of the Union" had been established.[6]

The first tangible initiatives toward the creation of the present EU citizenship were taken at the Paris summit between the Community's heads of state and government in 1974, where a working group was set up for the purpose of studying what was referred to as "special rights" for member states' citizens (CEC 1993b: 1; see also CEC 1996a: 5). Prior to the 1974 summit the Copenhagen foreign ministers' meeting in 1973 had put forth a "Declaration on European identity" that (although it did not bring up the concept of a Community citizenship in the explicit) incorporated a discourse that to some extent would fit subsequent articulations of "European citizenship." Among other things, the "Declaration on European identity" spoke of the urgent need to focus on the shared "heritage" and "to ensure the survival of the civilization" which the Community countries and the potential new members were said to have in common (CEC 1973).

In 1976 the Tindemans Report[7] to the European Council would develop and expand on these interventions and link them directly to the idea of a "Citizens' Europe." Under this heading the Tindemans Report argued that in order for the Community to "be close to its citizens" the "values which are their common heritage" had to be safeguarded (Tindemans 1976: 26). It also explicated that "we," the peoples of the European Community, "must build a type of society which is ours alone and which reflects the values which are the heritage and the common creation of our peoples"; a society "which respects the basic values of our civilization" (Tindemans 1976: 12).

But the grounding of a "European citizenship" in these self-assured views on heritage and civilization was only part of the story. Given its favorable inclination toward social reform during these years (Hoskyns 1996: 78–83; Hantrais 1995: 1, 5; Rossilli 1999), the Community also included social and economic issues in its discussion of citizenship. In the 1976 Tindemans report, for instance, the goal of full employment together with ideas of economic and industrial democracy were discussed as part of the citizenship agenda (see Hoskyns 1996: 78–83).[8] As the powers over economic policy gradually moved to transnational arenas, it was argued, "this problem should be solved at the European level by increasing worker participation in the management, control or profits of business" (Tindemans 1976: 25). The "security of the workforce, ... and their participation in company decisions and company profits" were seen by the Report as policy objectives to be managed at the "European level" in order to "restore to us at Union level that element of protection and control of our society which is progressively slipping from the grasp of State authority due to the nature of the problems and the internationalization of social life" (Tindemans 1976: 24, 28). "[E]conomic and social rights," as citizens" rights, were thus seen as matters which should be managed by empowered Community institutions. As a consequence, intergovernmental arrangements were ruled out as unable to deal with "our collective needs" and the future social dilemmas of economic and corporate transnationalization (Tindemans 1976: 26, 29).

Community Citizenship and Migration

In conjunction with these developments, there were also some tentative signs that issues pertaining to external migration and resident TCNs were beginning to receive some consideration at the Community level. The growing attention being directed at social welfare and citizenship can thus be said to have been conducive to bringing also the situation for external migrants on the supranational agenda—and this for the very first time. The matter was not only touched upon in the 1974 Social Action Program; that same year the Commission also presented a proposal for an action program exclusively focusing on the question of migration, entitled "Action Program in favour of migrant workers and their families" (CEC 1976 [1974]). It should be said that the program chiefly focused on the situation for internal, free moving migrants, whom at this moment still were spoken of and categorized as *migrants*. But also external migrants, and particularly those domiciled, were given quite some consideration.

By discussing the situation for internal and external migrants in the same breath, the Commission also put the finger on what it took to be an ever more problematic and embarrassing division within the Community between two groups of migrants; two groups who despite being bound by basically the same obligations nonetheless lived under very different and unequal circumstances when it came to the enjoyment of rights and freedoms. As noted by the Commission (1976 [1974]: 14) at the time: "[T]he legal situation of migrant workers coming from third countries depends on the status accorded to them by the host country…. The result is that migrant workers from third countries are generally treated less favourably than workers coming from the Member States, and the situation of these third country migrants varies considerably from one country to another." Furthermore:

> [T]he social conditions of the migrant do indeed give cause for serious concern—especially in the case of third country migrants, who have no Community protection and rely solely on often restrictive national legislation… For this reason solutions in common must be found, not only to the problems of Community migrants but also for those from third countries. These solutions must take account of the migrant

workers' needs and their rightful place in a society to whose prosperity and well-being they contribute. As the migrant population increases, and they remain longer in the Community, so their interests in the affluent society around them increases and their sense of exclusion from it can become more acute. (CEC 1976 [1974]: 12)

On this view, the Commission called for measures to improve migrants' lot in general, and to gradually phase out the discrepancies with regard to rights and legal status between internal and external migrants. The fact, for instance, that TCNs ran an unwarranted high risk of being deported was addressed, and the Commission criticized the member states for the ways in which they were utilizing the deportation instrument. However, the Commission would not go as far as proposing that the right of free movement, and the rights and entitlements belonging to it, be granted to TCNs. Nonetheless, for its time these were still quite forcible formulations, and as is evident from the unfavourable depiction of the "restrictive" member states they also marked a certain divergence of opinion between the Commission and the member governments as concerned migration policy.

In connection with this, the Commission went on to caution that unless migrants' predicaments were alleviated this would contribute to a climate that was conducive to a growing racism and xenophobia. Therefore, measures were needed to enhance migrants' "integration" (this was probably the first time the term was used in the EU context) into society; and member states were asked to begin a coordination of their, among themselves, very dissimilar migration policies toward countries outside the Community. In addition, governments were requested to work out common measures to come to terms with "illegal immigration," which the Commission saw as a large and fast growing problem. In sharp contrast to its future outlook on the matter, which we will discuss ahead, the Commission was mostly concerned about the situation for "illegals" as such: that they lived under an impending danger of being deported; had little or no access to medical care and social services; and that they were exposed to exploitation from employers (CEC 1976 [1974]: 21).

In summing up the European Commission's work in the 1970s, we have seen that a significant portion of it was to coalesce around the question of rights, in general, and of social rights of citizenship, in particular. Firstly, the established citizenship rights for member-state citizens needed to be safeguarded, developed through the addition of rights of economic democracy, and adapted to a transforming economic environment by way of more powers and responsibilities vested at the supranational level. Secondly, albeit not formulated in these exact terms, the free movement–induced transnational citizenship for intra-Community migrants needed to be fully developed and on a par with rights of national citizenship, so as to simultaneously stimulate factor mobility and avoid migrants' degradation to second-class citizens, a prospect that was seen as putting a break on people's readiness to migrate. Third, and finally, the Commission had also begun to broach the issue of extra-Community migration and the problems facing TCNs; and, in addition to this, it had begun to lift the lid on the issue of "illegal immigration." In this context most of the attention was directed at TCNs' lack of many of the rights associated with national citizenships, on the one hand, and their exclusion from the (transnational) rights of free movement, on the other. To cite an indignant Commission yet again:

> In fact, after more than a decade of benefit from migrant labour, the Community finds itself with a large unassimilated group of foreign workers, who share almost all the obligations of the society in which they live and work but, more often than not, have a less than equal share in its benefits and rights. This situation is in the long term intolerable—degrading for the migrant and dangerous for the Community. (CEC 1976 [1974]: 12)

Conclusion: Slouching Toward "Euro-pessimism"

Despite the work invested in the many initiatives by the Commission and other actors in the 1970s, the concrete outcomes would be meagre indeed; and this was true of supranational efforts in both the fields of social and migration policy (Dinan 1999: 421; Hoskyns 1996: 82–3). The European Parliament continued to push for the ideas behind the concept of a "Citizens' Europe," but here too the tangible results were very few, which was partly due to a reluctance on part of the Council (CEC 1993b: 5; Hoskyns 1996: 83). Over and above that, practically nothing was done to expand the supranational mandate and authorities within the policy areas at hand. Rather, member states remained in control and the Council of Ministers made sure to water down the various Community programs on social and migration policy so that they mostly would come to function as mere consultative assessments, instead of gaining binding status (see Geddes 2000a, 2000b: 157–8). Expanded supranational powers demanded that all member governments agreed to such a transfer of authority, and as the development in the 1970s was to make clear governments would prove far from inclined to set about to negotiate such a consensus (Hoskyns 1996: 80–1). With the exception of the social and migration policy belonging to free movement, these policy areas would thus remain within member state purview.

If adding to this that the member states also thwarted Community efforts to expand the supranational mandate within economic policy, we can sense why the development from the mid-1970s and onward often is described as a period marked by "Euro-pessimism," "Eurosclerosis," and Community stagnation (Dinan 1999: 57–80). The picture gets accentuated by the fact that the supranational level was denied any instruments able to mitigate the consequences of the economic downturn and crisis whose full effects would not become visible until the latter part of the 1970s (Williams 1994: 5). In retrospect, therefore, the Paris European Council in 1972 represented a set of delusive hopes for those forces advocating more of supranational influence over measures to remedy weak economic growth, high unemployment, social problems, and obstacles facing extra-Community migrants. Among the many proposals and initiatives tabled by the Commission and other like-minded actors in the 1970s, it was those in favor of enhanced gender equality that, by far, would fair best (Hoskyns 1996: 78; see also Mazey 1988). As for extra-Community migration and the situation for TCNs, these issues would basically be dormant on the supranational agenda until the launching of the Single Market was to resurrect them in the latter part of the 1980s. The same was to apply to the question of "European citizenship."

Yet, what had been demonstrated with some force in the 1970s was that many Community policy makers, members of the European Parliament, but also member state actors had become convinced that if the integration project was to progress it could not afford to sidestep the question of a Community citizenship. They were, in other words, convinced that for the project to be able to enthuse the general public, which was seen as a requirement for further integration, it had to find a new and strong mobilizing appeal that went beyond the one concerned solely with the alleged benefits of economic and market integration. By the mid-1980s, a dual consensus was therefore starting to foment. On the one hand, it was increasingly accepted that the range of national responses to the over a decade-long transformations in European capitalism were no longer adequate, and that a "relaunch of the EU integration process" was the only response to ensure the strength and competitiveness in an increasingly integrated world economy (see Grahl and Teague 1992). On the other hand, it was recognized that the successful deepening and widening of the European project could not proceed without the concomitant fostering of a sense of belonging within the nascent supranational political community. As we reach the time period for the launch of the Single Market this, what we may call, legitimacy argument for "European citizenship" was to reverberate yet again; and it has done so ever since.

Notes

1. For a similar account, see for example Sassen (1999: 152–3).
2. While Britain and Ireland did not enact transition rules for the EU's new members in 2004 (although they did introduce restrictions on social welfare entitlements for the new EU citizens, something Sweden did not), they did impose such rules for Bulgaria and Romania in 2007.
3. The other priority area, besides internal labor migration, for Community social policy during this time period was made up by gender equality (see further e.g. Hoskyns 1994; Mazey 1988; Meehan 1993).
4. For an exhaustive account of postwar migration to countries in Western Europe, its driving forces and consequences, see Castles and Kosack (1985) and Castles and Miller (2003). For a specific account of the different types of guest worker systems employed by Western European countries, see Castles and Miller (2003: Ch. 4).
5. Indirectly TCNs were provided with some limited possibilities to enjoy the right of free movement, as in cases where a TCN was married to a member state citizen who made use of the right of free movement.
6. See for example Tindemans (1976); and CEC (1984).
7. Commissioned by the Community's heads of state and government at the Paris summit in 1974, the Tindemans Report was drawn up by Belgium's prime minister Leo Tindemans.
8. Similar statements reflecting such a reform-minded agenda are found in the "Council Resolution of 21 January 1974 concerning a social action programme" (Council EC 1974).

CHAPTER 3

A Citizens' Europe for Whom?
Social Citizenship, Migration, and the Neoliberal Relaunch of European Integration (1980–1995)

Introduction

With the aim of breaking the deadlock of "Euro-pessimism" and resuscitating European integration, the late 1970s and early 1980s would witness a newly awakened activity at the Community level. Already in 1979 a new monetary and exchange rate cooperation, the European Monetary System, was established (by some seen as reviving the dream of a common currency for the Community), and two years later a discussion got underway concerning a felt need for reform of the Community's institutions and decision-making procedures. In 1984 the European Parliament followed up on this and adopted the Draft Treaty Establishing the European Union, which called for institutional reforms and the need for a new treaty. Later on that same year the Fontainebleau European Council appointed an Ad-hoc Committee on Institutional Affairs. The Committee was given the task to inquire into a set of problems that demanded—the member states now seemed able to agree—common solutions within the Community framework. Among these problems counted economic matters concerning competitiveness, growth, and technological development. At the meeting in Fontainebleau, moreover, an Ad Hoc Committee on a People's Europe was created for the purpose of drawing up strategies specifically addressing how an eventual relaunch of the European integration project would be able to win popular support and legitimacy, and so promote the formation of a European citizenship and identity (see Hansen 2000; CEC 1985a).

The flurry of activity to at once reshape and infuse the Community with new life that marked the early 1980s, and where the Commission's (1985b) *White Paper on the Completion of the Internal Market* supplied the finishing touch, was to culminate in the signing of a new treaty, the Single European Act (SEA), in 1986. The SEA, which was ratified in 1987, constituted the first sizeable revision of the Community's founding treaties. Laying the foundation for the subsequent Economic and Monetary Union and equipping the Community with a policy in the field of science and technology, the SEA also strengthened and expanded the Community's competence in other important ways. As we will survey below, moreover, the SEA included measures to equip the Community with a "social Dimension" by seeking to boost the compass of social policy at the supranational level.

Most of all, however, the SEA was instrumental in setting in motion and providing the institutional, decision-making, and legal framework for the completion of the Single Market Program (anticipated to be accomplished by 1992), which the Commission's new president Jacques Delors— drawing on the blueprint contained in the abovementioned White Paper— had spearheaded in 1985. Despite the fact that the internal market and the free movement of goods, capital, services, and persons formed part of the Rome Treaty, these objectives were still far from fully realized. A row of national barriers and other obstacles still prevented the Community from constituting a single internal market. The institutional, decision-making, and legal reforms that the member states agreed on in the Single European Act were thus specifically designed to enable a swift implementation of the Single Market. With the purpose of facilitating the removal of the many national market barriers, the member governments decided to remove the national veto in a number of political-economic areas tied to the Single Market's function and logic. Hereby the right of veto was replaced by decision making with qualified majority voting in the Council of Ministers. This was indeed a big step, both in a real and a symbolic sense, and it is often cited as one of *the* most critical provisions overall agreed upon in the Single European Act (see Garrett and Weingast 1993: 191).

The Single European Act and the Single Market Program marked the beginning of a new era for European integration, and as such they were both reflective of and instrumental for the reconfiguration of Western Europe's ideological and political-economic landscape in the late 1980s and early 1990s. In this chapter we set out by unpacking the Single Market conversions in terms of their ideological, political-economic, and social content and driving forces. As part of this we scrutinize their impact on the EU's concurrent attempt in the late 1980s of equipping the supranation with a substantial social dimension, thus rekindling the project of a "social Europe" which had laid in fallow since its foiling in the 1970s. In particular, we attend to the Delors Commission's balancing strategy of making use of the Single Market–driven integration as a vehicle for transferring elements of the national welfare state to the supranational level; and through the conceptual and theoretical lens of *negative integration* we discuss some of the causes and consequences of the serious debacle this strategy would suffer. Taking the discussion into the 1990s and the culmination of the "Euro-optimistic" relaunch in the signing of the Maastricht Treaty in 1992, we go on to examine the changing outlooks on the EU's "social dimension" that emerged in the post-Maastricht era. Such reversals would, among other things, go hand in hand with a marked shift in the EU's understanding of the concept of *social exclusion;* a shift, we evince, that was indicative of an endeavor in Brussels to come up with a social and welfare policy formula more in tune with the sustained neoliberalization of the EU project that followed in the wake of Maastricht.

If the Single Market would revive (and soon recast) the vision of a "social Europe," it would also, as we discuss at length in this chapter, induce a relaunch of the vision of a "Citizens' Europe." And what is more, with the ratification of the Maastricht Treaty in 1993 a formal EU citizenship—or "Citizenship of the Union"—was born and bestowed on every person holding a national citizenship in a member state. From the mid-1980s, then, "citizenship" became a prestige word within EU policy making, and references to a "Citizens' Europe" and "European citizenship"—often coupled with calls to boost a popular feeling of "European identity"—grew at an exponential rate. However, and as with the concept of "social Europe," the Single Market's political-economic constitution would yield a significant alteration of the notion of a "Citizens' Europe," as compared to the one that surfaced in the 1970s. As we argue below, the EU's adoption of a neoliberal agenda (and the restraints it would impose on a vision for the EU project modeled on the 1970's welfare state) would both force and enable EU policy makers to tap into other sources than those harboring the traditional social citizenship provisions in order to articulate a citizenship formula for the European Union. Such a formula, however, would not only feed on neoliberal precepts of the *individualized* "market citizen," as is sometimes tacitly inferred in the political economy–oriented literature. As we show, in tandem with the Single Market reforms and Maastricht's corroboration of the neoliberal order, Brussels also supplemented the "market citizenship" with a *collective,* ethno-cultural articulation of European citizenship, founded on the claim that what amalgamates a citizenry is a shared sense of belonging to a historic community endowed with a common civilization, cultural heritage, and religion. This provided, our discussion proceeds by addressing the excluding implications of such an ethno-cultural articulation of EU citizenship for ethnic minorities with migrant background living in the European Union.

Finally, this merges into a discussion concerning the wider issue of how the Single Market conversions would impact on migration policy in the EU. As we demonstrate, the market-making measures introduced under the banner of the Single Market, particularly those pertaining to the free movement of persons and the associated goal of abolishing internal border controls, would have profound consequences for the EU's activity and role in the area of external migration and asylum. Put differently, the future dismantling of border checks between member states was generally perceived as intimately related to the compensatory development of coordinated control measures at the Community's external frontier. But since the free movement provisions came to apply only to member states citizens, the implementation of the Single Market would also come to hinge on the development of new measures on the internal control of third-country nationals (TCNs), and particularly those deemed to be "illegal immigrants," "bogus asylum seekers," and those involved in international crime.

From the outset, then, the endeavor to coordinate and harmonize migration and asylum policy in the Community was to have both external and internal repercussions on the "frontier-free Europe." With more and more harmonized perceptions and policies on migration starting to take shape among member-state governments and within the European Commission, this signaled the true emergence of migration as a common "European" concern, "problem," and "crisis," thus calling for common action and solutions which increasingly were to couch external migration in terms of control, security, and crime. As part of this development, assurances from governments and the Commission to do their utmost to stem the tide of extra-EU migration and to combat "illegal migration," in particular, were also articulated as integral to the new EU citizenship, thus serving to reassure EU citizens that migration harmonization and a relaxation of national borders (within the EU) in an ever more mobile EU economy by no means would imply less protection from external as well as internal threats.

This chapter scrutinizes the impact, ramifications and logic of this *double movement*, that is, the crucial nexus of external and internal repercussions. In addition, the chapter surveys and analyzes EU activity with regards to the internal dimension of migration policy that by now also had begun to address migrant integration and the situation of ethnic minorities of migrant background. Most of all, however, we focus in on the often contradictory ways in which EU citizenship policy was articulated in the context of migration policy, in both its external and internal dimensions.

The Politics of "Euro-optimism"

With the relaunch of European integration in the mid-1980s, "Euro-pessimism" gave way to a strong sense of "Euro-optimism" among the parties involved in the process. As already noted, this revival of the European integration project was contingent on the changing political and ideological climate that surrounded a variety of developments during the 1980s. In large parts, the reforming zeal walked hand in hand with the neoliberal change of wind that was to permeate many of the political changes during the 1980s and onward (Grahl and Teague 1989; Turner 1993). Such changes were to revolve around what Kathleen McNamara (1998) identifies as the formation of a "neoliberal European policy consensus" (see also Rhodes 1991; Holman and Pijl 1996). The European Community of the 1980s came to constitute both an arena offering new opportunities for political and ideological restructuring and an organ which itself took advantage of the new neoliberal atmosphere (see Goodman 1997: 173, 195). This was in glaring contrast to the development in the early 1970s. As we saw in the previous chapter, the (stifled) attempts at relaunch and reform in the 1970s were in large part driven by a (social democratic) political ambition and vision that wanted to vest the supranational level with more social clout in order to safeguard and develop the achievements of the welfare state and labor in a time of increased economic internationalization. In the 1980s this was turned topsy-turvy as neoliberal forces, both within politics and the economy, instead wanted to utilize the Single Market project in order to extend the scope of capital and market forces at the expense of the welfare state and labor.[1] This was, not least, evident in the expanding lobbying efforts by capital and industrial interests in Brussels during the 1980s. Also, it was there for everybody to see in the Delors Commission's close collaboration with the influential lobby organization The European Roundtable of Industrialists (see van Apeldoorn 2002; Bornschier and Ziltener 1999; Garret and Weingast 1993: 190–1; Goodman 1997: 173, 195; Hines 1997).

In sum, what spurred the relaunch of European integration in this period owed much to western Europe's emerging embrace of American deregulatory policies, the budding partnership between the Commission and Europe's chief manufacturers, and the mounting support for the Single Market among capital interests in general[2] (Dinan 1999: 82; see also Bornschier and Ziltener 1999; Carchedi 2001; Garrett and Weingast 1993; Kapteyn 1996: 63; Streeck and Schmitter 1996).

One of the most important factors that contributed to the deregulatory nucleus of the SEA was "a new ideological compromise" between Britain and France, which took shape in the middle of the 1980s (Hix 1999: 232). In brief, the compromise coalesced around Britain's belief that the Single Market constituted an opportunity to impart Thatcherite neoliberalism to the other member states, whereas France—after the reversal of Mitterrand's Keynesian reflationary project in 1981 and 1982—

approached it as holding out the prospect of enhancing the Community's competitiveness vis-à-vis Japan and the United States (Hix 1999: 232; see Delors 1992: 30). This compromise also took the West German government's fancy, since its potential result was seen to offer great advantages for West German capital (Garrett and Weingast 1993: 190).[3]

Closely resembling the Anglo-French compromise, the Single Market project was also made possible by the combination of large corporations' aspirations for competitive advantages vis-à-vis American and Japanese capital on the one hand, and elites at the state level intent on regaining the political authority they had lost as a result of intensifying international interdependence on the other. What seems to have enabled these two groupings to join forces was the willingness of corporate capital to concede national industrial protection schemes in exchange for state elites' commitment to phase out market regulations imposed by political bodies in the member states, as well as to ensure that these were not to be restored at the EU level in the future (Streeck and Schmitter 1996: 184–5; see also Ross 1992). On this account, the Single Market project was predicated on an ability to deliver watertight guarantees to capital that the new supranational powers would be used solely for "the *external reassertion of,* as opposed to *internal intervention in,* the European economy" (Streeck and Schmitter 1996: 185, italics in original; see also Grahl and Teague 1989). In turn, this not only meant that European integration became "bound up with a deregulatory project," but also implied that it had settled for the particular type of integration which, as we explain below, often goes under the name of negative integration—what in this context constituted the deregulatory project's institutional and legal facilitator (Streeck and Schmitter 1996: 185).

Negative Integration

According to Hooghe and Marks (1999: 71), one of the main dislocational effects brought about by the SEA stemmed from its institutionalization of "a double shift of decision-making away from national states—to the market and to the European level." In order to grasp the consequences of this "double shift," we need to introduce the concept and working of *negative integration*. The concept of negative integration not only offers essential guidance to our understanding of the Single Market reconfigurations in broad terms; it also provides an illuminating analytical framework with which the uneven, or asymmetrical, relationship between the EU of advanced market integration and the EU of limited welfare integration can be analyzed.

Negative integration, as it emerged in the Single Market context, refers to "measures increasing market integration (by eliminating restraints on trade and distortions on competition)," whereas positive integration implies the establishment of "common European policies to shape the conditions under which markets operate" (Scharpf 1998: 157). Undoubtedly, it is negative integration that has had the upper hand, and, historically speaking, has stood to gain from the legal and institutional arrangements of European integration from the outset. As Scharpf (1998: 157) elucidates, the logic of negative integration was in many ways inscribed in the Rome Treaty's "primary law," and from here "liberalization could be extended, without much political attention, through the interventions of the European Commission against infringements of treaty obligations, and through the decisions and preliminary rulings of the European Court of Justice" (see also Ross 1992). The latitude for positive integration, by contrast, lacked anything resembling these auspicious conditions, and was left at the mercy of the concurrence between national governments in the Council of Ministers (Scharpf 1998: 157).

Moreover, even if it is possible to identify ways in which the EU could have given rise to certain forms of positive integration, it is important to show why and how the realization of such positive integration has faced a number of significant obstacles. Perhaps the most important obstacle has to do with the "fundamental institutional difference" (Scharpf 1999: 51) or "asymmetry" (Scharpf 1998: 159) between negative and positive integration. Again, the roots of this difference are to be found in the Treaty of Rome and its clearly stated pledge to eliminate tariffs and other trade barriers, "as well as the rudimentary principles of a European law of free and undistorted market competition" (Scharpf 1999: 50). Under the auspices of treaty and European law, and with the Commission and the European Court of Justice as effective overseers, liberalization has thus been able to proceed and advance without much inhibition, implying, as it would do from the mid-1980s and onward, a "'constitutionalization' of competition law" along neoliberal lines (Scharpf 1999: 54; see also Jessop 2002: 209–10). As for positive integration, or policies that would reinstall at the EU level what liberalization detracts from democratic political bodies at the national level, practically none of these institutional and legal structures apply. Instead, such positive integration has remained in the hands of national governments in the Council of Ministers, where it readily falls prey to the principle of unanimity and consensual decision making (Scharpf 1999: 50–1, 72; see also Streeck 1995: 395). Given that negative integration has been endowed with such institutional and legal privileges, this is also why Scharpf (1998: 172) goes as far as to speak of "the imperialism of negative integration."

As a consequence of the logic of the policies and the institutional and legal framework established under the SEA and the Single Market, Streeck (1995: 395) argues, "the act of defending a country's sovereignty in the councils of Europe and the act of defending the freedom of 'market forces' in the integrated European economy thus came to be one and the same, with the objectives of liberal deregulation, or nonregulation, and of nationalist defence of sovereignty inextricably intertwined." Contingent on the logic of negative integration, Streeck goes on, neoliberalism and nationalism would, in fact, make up two mutually reinforcing developments, both being augmented by the transformations set in motion in the Community during the 1980s (see also Crouch and Streeck 1997; Hooghe and Marks 1999). In this sense, Streeck (1995: 395–6) speaks of a "historical convergence of nationalism and economic liberalism" as sitting at the heart of the political agreement that was to restart the process of integration in Europe in the mid-1980s. This point is also brought out by Crouch's (1998: 241) line of reasoning whereby, in a nutshell, the European Union, since the onset of the relaunch, is perceived as "experiencing simultaneously a globalization of economic processes but a reassertion of the nation state (against supranational political entities) at the political level." But, as Crouch is quick to add, one must keep in mind that there is one crucial pursuit that has been exempted from this development, namely, "policy to deregulate markets":

> The deregulatory part of the European integration project, the pursuit of the European Single Market, has met with universal applause, no government being more supportive than the Conservative, neo-liberal British one which in all other respects was fully opposed to further integration. This is because deregulation is a form of integration that immobilizes the scope for further political action. (Crouch 1998: 241)

As will be discussed below, a failed attempt of the European Commission to link firmly a "social dimension" to the accomplishment of the Single Market by the late 1980s is the most pungent illustration of Crouch's succinct point on the "immobilizing" dynamics of deregulation, and, we may add, of negative integration.

The Failure of Delors' Social Europe

In this context it is of the utmost importance to remember that the mid- to late 1980s also would witness a reborn activity in the area of supranational social policy. To a large extent, calls for a "social dimension" and a "social Europe" resulted from concern within the Commission and elsewhere that a one-sided focus on market liberalization could have negative consequences for labor and social welfare (Hix 1999: 227; Lange 1992). It needs to be kept in mind, too, that the most influential architect behind the Single Market and the SEA, Commission President Jacques Delors, could not accurately be described as a "rabid neoliberal" (Ross 1992: 61). On the contrary, Delors had a different plan for and outlook on the end product of all of that which was set in motion in the mid-1980s. For Delors, a champion of "regulated capitalism"[4] whose background was in the French Socialist party and trade union movement, the SEA and the Single Market constituted merely the first steps toward a set of "'state-building' policies" whereby the EC level would attain more authority in such areas as social policy, the macroeconomy, industry, the environment, and regional policy (Ross 1992: 61–2). For Delors and his allies the "goal was to create 'organized space' at the European level, regulating European capitalism in line with European Social-Democratic and Christian-Democratic traditions" (Hooghe and Marks 1999: 79). Or, as Delors (1992: 39) put it himself referring to the Single Market:

> It would make no sense if competition were to develop at the expense of the social protection and working conditions which are the basis of the European model. Europe will not be created if the workers do not feel involved in it, and if it does not have social progress as its ultimate aim.

As the Delorist plan managed to gain some political impetus in the late 1980s, it also created what many took to be a new window of opportunity for social policy at the EC level (Dinan 1999: 424–6). This was soon to result in the adoption by all the member states, except Britain, of the Community Charter of the Fundamental Social Rights for Workers (or Social Charter) in 1989. Although the twelve categories included in the Charter offered much on paper, its actual impact would be meagre indeed. This had much to do with its lack of binding legal force, and once the Commission sought to amend this its efforts were often stalled by the Council's failure to achieve unanimity, thus falling victim to the logic of negative integration. This could be seen too in the subsequent adoption of the Protocol on Social Policy—expanding on the provisions in the Social Charter—at the Maastricht summit in 1991, which, due to British opposition, was attached to rather than incorporated in the Maastricht Treaty. The Commission portrayed the Protocol as part of the efforts to come to terms with social exclusion by means of a strengthened social dimension for the EU project, and argued that this also made up an important aspect of "European citizenship" (see CEC 1993c, CEC 1994a). But although the Protocol opened up for majority voting in such policy areas as working conditions, health and safety in the workplace, and information and consultations of workers, it kept the rule of unanimity in those areas particularly sensitive to the interests of capital (Carchedi 2001: 241–2; see also Bornschier and Ziltener 1999: 46).

This provided, it soon became apparent that whereas agreement could be reached on the deregulatory provisions of the Single Market Program, "social Europe" and Delors' larger ambitions clearly failed to draw sufficient support. In trying to piece together an explanation for this predicament, Bornschier and Ziltener (1999) argue that even though the social dimension was the "weakest part" of the collection of measures incorporated into the SEA and the Single Market, it nonetheless constituted one of the cornerstones of the project. In this sense Bornschier and Ziltener (1999) go against the common belief that "the social dimension of 1992 came as an afterthought to legitimate the *fait accompli* of market liberalization" (Lehning 1997: 2). Rather, the failure of the social dimension, Bornschier and Ziltener emphasize, had less to do with Delors' basic position than with the particular method or strategy applied in the launching of the Single Market. Hence, if deregulation and neoliberal principles clearly were for Delors the means and "the sole undisputed core of the new thrust towards integration" (Bornschier and Ziltener 1999: 40), they were by no means, as they were for so many of the other actors and forces involved, ends in themselves. Instead, they constituted what was perceived as the necessary first phase in Delors' "'step by step' strategy." A strong social dimension was downplayed at this juncture because of the Commission's firm belief that this was the only way to secure a swift agreement on an equally swift launching of the SEA and the Single Market program. To insist at this stage on linking the Single Market to binding supranational social policies would thus have put the Single Market at risk. In other words, such linking would have clashed with one of the Single Market's enabling consensual sentiments among actors in Brussels and member-states' governments, who were calling for "as much deregulation as possible at the national level coupled with as little reregulation as necessary at the Community level" (Dinan 1999: 96; Bornschier and Ziltener 1999: 42). Instead of first endeavoring to amend "the structural weakness of the sociopolitically progressive actors at the European level" (Bornschier and Ziltener 1999: 42), Delors settled for what turned out to be counterproductive pragmatism.

Powerful neoliberal forces both outside and inside the Commission, were, of course, vehemently opposed to Delors' larger plan, and played an important part in ensuring that once the first *market-making* steps had been achieved no matching *welfare-making* steps were to be taken. However, the ditching of Delors' plan cannot be attributed solely to resistance from the neoliberal camp. Strong opposition also came from the confederalists (particularly of the French sort) who, even if they might have favored more decision making at the EU level, much preferred striking intergovernmental agreements (based on unanimity) to Delors' supranational solution (Ross 1992: 62). In addition, potential allies to Delors' agenda, such as Continental social democrats and labor unions, failed to rise to the occasion, bogged down as they were in trying to deal with problems brought about by social fragmentation and economic transformation at the national level. As Ross (1992: 64) goes on to argue, "[u]nion movements, representing the constituencies that the new flexibilizing Europe threatened the most, had lost their footing," and, from a position of weakness, "union movements virtually everywhere concentrated their dwindling resources on defending themselves within their national contexts" (see further Streeck and Schmitter 1996).

Social Europe after Maastricht

As a consequence of the many aforementioned obstacles that were to challenge, and contribute to the eventual undermining of, Delors' and others' more far-reaching (social dimension) objectives, the impetus for a supranational "social dimension" waned in the period after the Maastricht Treaty, experiencing an even greater setback than its counterpart of the 1970s (Bornschier and Ziltener 1999: 46). As Ross (1995: 386) suggests, this meant, among other things, that "market building" won out over "market correcting," leaving little or no room for the development of a strong social policy agenda at the EU level (see also Streeck 1995: 395; Ebbinghaus and Visser 1997: 199; Lehning and Weale 1997: 2). Those who had hoped that the 1990s—starting with the Maastricht Treaty—would break with the neoliberal pattern established in the 1980s and embrace a serious attempt to make economic objectives compatible with social welfare were thus quickly disabused (Ebbinghaus and Visser 1997: 198). In this context the adoption of the austere convergence criteria tied to the EMU project proved to be a major source of disappointment, since these severely limited the scope of social policy provisions in the member states, including measures against a mounting unemployment problem (Meulders and Plasman 1997; Coates 1998; Woollacott 1996). Moreover, the criteria were unaccompanied by any mitigating measures at the supranational level. If, as shown above, the Delors Commission in the 1980s had demoted the social dimension in favor of the Single Market Program, Delors' stalwart promotion of the EMU in the 1990s would yet again put the prospects for positive integration in welfare policy on the back burner (Bornschier and Ziltener 1999: 46).

Nevertheless, these developments in no way implied a corresponding flagging of supranational activity *as such* in the area of social policy. On the contrary, Brussels would continue to engage in it with unabated energy. But, as signaled earlier, the social policy regime promoted in the 1990s would differ in many significant respects from its predecessors. Based less on traditional welfare policy measures and more attuned to the alleged requirements of economic globalization, the new social policy regime that was launched in the wake of Maastricht could be seen as an (rhetorical) attempt to make the EU's twin goals of simultaneously enhancing capital accumulation *and* social protection more mutually compatible. As the Commission had it, the Union now needed to find a middle course or a "compromise" between the "extremes" of neoliberalism and the tradition of welfare state policies (CEC 1996a: 2).

If not relegation, then, it was rather adaptation or "modernization" that came to characterize supranational social policy in the post-Maastricht period. In this process of "modernization," "the fight against social exclusion" soon emerged as the favorite catchphrase. In contrast to the Commission's pre-Maastricht understanding of social exclusion as foremost an expression of weakened social citizenship rights, however, the post-Maastricht Commission would come to perceive of social exclusion as something that primarily resulted from a lack of "paid work" (see Schierup 2003). Already in the Commission's *Green Paper* on social policy from 1993 this change of tone was made apparent:

> There is a consensus in Europe that all citizens should have a guarantee of resources but social policies now have to take on the more ambitious objective of helping people to find a place in society. The main route, but not the only one, is paid work—and that is why employment policies and social policies should be more closely linked. (CEC 1993c: 21)

The Commission's (1993d) commanding White Paper on "Growth, Competitiveness, Employment" illustrated the EU's changing view of "social Europe" to the point. Thus, while the White Paper was not wanting in statements supportive of "[a]n economy characterized by solidarity," "the fight against social exclusion," unemployment and poverty (CEC 1993d: 15–6), it also firmly established that these aims in no way complicated the White Paper's overarching neoliberal stance. Prepared in close collaboration with the European Roundtable of Industrialists (Hines 1997), the White Paper comprised calls for a flexible labor market, a set of "more enterprise-friendly" regulations, reduced labor costs and unemployment benefits, lower taxes, cutbacks in welfare systems and overall public expenditures, as well as increased privatization (CEC 1993d; see also Levitas

1998; Leibfried and Pierson 1995: 49–50). This outlook would also find expression in the Commission's subsequent White Paper on social policy (CEC 1994a), where, as Bob Deacon (2001: 70) describes it, "a juggling act was going on with the Commission which wished to support social protection policies, but only insofar as these policies were adapted to the perceived requirements of increased global economic competition."

In capturing, finally, the state of the EU project as it emerged from the Single Market relaunch and the Maastricht agreement Bastiaan van Apeldoorn's concept of *embedded neoliberalism* provides an apposite aid in making sense of the seemingly contradictory enterprise on part of the EU of embracing neoliberalism while at the same time unabatedly nourishing a notion of a "social Europe." Embedded neoliberalism, van Apeldoorn (2003a: 156, italics in original) explains,

> is neo-liberal inasmuch as it emphasizes the primacy of global market forces and the freedom of transnational capital. Yet, as a result of such processes, markets become increasingly *disconnected* from their post-war national social institutions. Embedded neo-liberalism is thus "embedded" to the extent that it recognises the limits to laissez-faire, and thus to the disembedding process, and accepts that certain compromises need to be made; hence at least a limited form of "embeddedness" is preserved.

It was, van Apeldoorn (2003a) argues, embedded neoliberalism that emerged as the dominant ideological force in the shaping of the EU's trajectory from Maastricht onwards. This was contingent on the collapse of the Delors Plan and the failure of "transnational social-democratic forces" to set in motion a positive integration and supranational harmonization of welfare policy in the EU, and so put social policy on a par with the Single Market and the EMU (van Apeldoorn 2003a). As seen, however, the career of "social Europe" did not come unstuck with the closure of the Delors Plan. Rather, and in line with van Apeldoorn's position concerning the upholding of "a limited form of "embeddedness," it was set on a new course, leaving its old welfarist habitats behind for adaptation to more variable surroundings. As we shall see below and in chapters ahead, this evolving European order of embedded neoliberalism would also leave its mark on the future career of the "Citizens' Europe."

EU Citizenship in the Wake of the Relaunch

After the initiatives in the 1970s it would take almost another decade before the time proved ripe again for the question of "European citizenship" to be seriously prioritized on the Community agenda (see CEC 1993b). As previously noted, what set it off, formally speaking, was the European Council meeting at Fontainebleau in 1984, which emphasized the importance of developing a "People's Europe," a "Citizens' Europe," and a "European identity." For this purpose the Council appointed what was to become the influential ad hoc Committee on A People's Europe, led by Pietro Adonnino (CEC 1988: 22).

If we compare the EU's perceptions pertaining to European citizenship as they were articulated in the 1970s with those put forth from the mid-1980s and onward, there are at least two developments that need to be examined. Firstly, during the 1980s the grounding of European citizenship in a discourse of European civilization, culture, and heritage got more firmly established—a development that we will come back to in sections ahead. Secondly, whereas in the 1970s the Community held the door open to what we may term a federalism for social citizenship and was prone to emphasize collective social needs and rights, greater workers' participation in economic decision making, and other ideas of economic democracy, the 1980s would be practically void of such currents. As stated by the Commission (1988: 22) in 1988:

> In a Europe without frontiers, where increased competitiveness and cooperation will go hand in hand, the individual and his actions will carry far more weight, both economically and socially ... At the same time, awareness of a Community based on common values and cultures will be boosted and will gradually reinforce the idea of European citizenship.

Hence, within the Community discourse on citizenship that emerged from the mid-1980s "collective needs" came to refer less to the social domain and more, as we shall elaborate on below, to the domain of culture and identity. Equally important, the professionally mobile "individual" and the "Community citizen as consumer" appeared in the limelight (CEC 1985a: 11). "The goal," the Commission affirmed, "should be an easing of rules and practices which cause irritation to Community citizens" (CEC 1985a: 9), and then pointed to architects, engineers, lawyers, accountants, and tax consultants as groups that needed certain obstacles removed when they sought or moved to jobs outside their countries (CEC 1985a: 13). With the Single Market the European *market citizen* (Lehning 1997: 179–80, 195) started to eclipse the European *social citizen* that had been envisioned by many in the 1970s.

The coalescing of EU citizenship with the neoliberal agenda came to the fore most forcefully in the strong emphasis that the EU began to place on the relationship between Union citizenship and intra-EU mobility. To be sure, and as we discussed in the previous chapter, increased cross-border mobility had always been the central driving force behind the granting of transnational rights in the EU, and thus for the de facto transnational citizenship regime in the EU. However, prior to the Single Market and the neoliberal offensive, the modus operandi behind the call for an increase in cross-border labor mobility was closely bound up with the expansion of transnational social rights for the workers who moved. People were encouraged to move on the precise guarantee that they did not have to fear for their social rights being devalued when they settled in another member state. With the consensus around the strong welfare state on the wane from the early 1980s and onward, this mobilizing argument for mobility also changed. The opportunity to jump borders to pursue work was now no longer framed in terms of social protection; it was rather articulated as an opportunity to reap the benefits of a more open EU market, less and less hamstrung by (welfare) state regulations.

This market-prone understanding of citizenship found expression in numerous EU policy documents and citizen-targeted information campaigns at the time. As set forth by the Commission (1993a: 15), "[t]he first and foremost of the rights conferred on Union citizens is the right to travel and reside wherever they wish in any of the 12 Member States." The Commission also specified that "[p]erhaps the most important innovation is the free movement of persons: Union citizens are entitled to travel, reside, study and work wherever they want in the European Union" (CEC 1994b: 57). Subsequently, as part of the EMU-campaign from the mid-1990s and onward, "European citizenship" was also (symbolically) coupled with the monetary union and the euro, giving rise to statements such as the following:

> Thanks to the complete elimination of foreign-exchange transaction costs, it will lead to savings and simplifications in the lives of European citizens. The general public must be prepared now for this change so as to pre-empt any fears it might arouse. In addition to its economic and monetary aspects, the introduction of euro notes and coins should provide hundreds of millions of Europeans with a material and concrete symbol of their common identity. (CEC 1998a: 13)

As part of this the Commission also urged the member states to have their schools campaign for the euro. As the Commission contended, the EMU-project "offers a unique opportunity for the development of European citizenship." "Teaching the euro in schools is a formidable opportunity to anchor the idea of European citizenship … showing its importance as a symbol of peace and economic well-being" (CEC 1998b: 5).

Rather than construing of EU citizenship as an added social rights and economic democracy dimension serving to protect the achievements of the EU's national welfare states at the supranational level, as had been suggested in the 1970s, the EU citizenship that was endorsed in the wake of the relaunch was in many ways promoted as something that was resulting from the achievements of market deregulation: a stepping stone for the professionally mobile Europeans with marketable skills on an open, transnational job market. The frequent and calming characterization, during this period, in policy documents and elsewhere of the EU citizenship as not altering or replacing the status and modes of national citizenships, but as simply "complementing" and adding "extra rights" for "all" national citizens, thus needs some important restating. Examined in the 1980s and 1990s context of retracting and socially de-universalized national citizenships, EU citizenship might be better designated as a force that possibly amplified or at least was symptomatic of the social fragmentation in the Union. Kofman's (1995: 135) cautionary remark can thus be brought to bear on this development: "Multiplying the sites of citizenship may seem ... attractive, but we must be wary of producing a two-tiered system of citizenship: one for the 'poor,' who are locked into restricted spaces with second-class rights, the other cosmopolitan and encompassing all of the levels for the dominant groups in Europe."

The EU citizenship was therefore not, as was common (and still is), to be written off as an empty concept unable to create a new social purpose and content. Instead, we should take note of the fact that the new purpose that emerged with the relaunch in the 1980s mostly catered to certain elite groups and not to a larger whole. As Wiener and Della Sala (1997: 605) argue, what surfaced was "a fragmented citizenship policy establishing special rights, not for Europeans as a people, but for special groups of Europeans in the process." This provided, we can then talk about the emerging EU citizenship as one that granted new privileges for those who had been affluent enough to, in some sense, opt out of a reliance on and faith in public welfare provisions and so depend less and less on a national social citizenship, while this same EU citizenship had very little to offer those who could not but continue to depend on devaluated national social citizenship.

The late 1980s and early 1990s should therefore prove disappointing for those who had hoped that the reborn integration process would nurture the supranational social citizenship objectives of the 1970s. In this sense, as Pierson and Leibfried have argued (1995: 450), "the reinvigoration of European integration depended precisely on the emergence of an anti-social democratic consensus on economic policy within the major member states." To contextualize further, it is of crucial importance to note that constitutive of the ideological battle waged from the New Right in the late 1970s and 1980s was the attempt to gain control over and thereby change the meanings tied to the concept of citizenship. As Moore (1992: vi) emphasizes: "if there has been one central target for the New Right it has been the idea of citizenship." In evaluating the outcome of this attempt, it was unquestionably the case that neoconservative and neo-liberal forces would gain the upper hand, consequently generating an increasingly individualized and market-oriented perception of citizenship, where private interests were seen as better equipped to manage public assets and services, and where notions of "active citizenship," volunteerism, and charity were starting to replace commitments to universal and collectively financed citizenship entitlements (Smith 1995: 191–2; Bottomore 1992: 70–1; Mouffe 1988; Rose 1996; Kymlicka and Norman 1994). With the appropriation of the vocabulary of citizenship by forces on the right in the 1980s and 90s, Yuval-Davis (1997: 16–17) argues, "[t]he balance of citizenship rights ... shifted away from social rights of welfare towards civil rights of an economic kind."

Finally, in discussing the social restraints and the narrow popular appeal that became characteristic of EU citizenship in the 1990s, Streeck (1995: 413) perceived of this as a natural, even a functionally necessary consequence of the political-economic course onto which the EU project was set, starting in the mid-1980s:

> A free European market, if this is all that it is to be, does not "require" a "Europe of the citizen"; in fact, citizenship makes markets less "free." As far as the completion of the internal market is concerned, it does not matter that European citizenship ... has remained limited to freedom of movement and contract within the integrated market.

A Crucial Addition: EU Citizenship and the Ethno-Cultural Dimension

Although Streeck and others had a strong case for contending that the logic inherent to EU integration as it evolved from the Single Market reforms could do without a redistributive social citizenship at the EU level, it would be a premature conclusion to view citizenship policy in the Union as being solely pinned to the type of market citizenship outlined above. Much research only emphasizes the dynamic between these two ways of construing citizenship in the EU, and when concluding, correctly, that the social dimension gets marginalized, it also tends to conclude, incorrectly, that the entire notion of "European citizenship" is reducible to an individualized market citizenship.

An analysis of the flow of statements, policy documents, and information campaigns addressing the issue of "European citizenship" that Brussels began to disseminate in the mid-1980s clearly suggested that the EU was urgently seeking a citizenship formula that would supplement the individualized market citizenship. In other words, the EU was clear that market integration and the participation in market relations across borders by no means could constitute the only manifestations of European citizenship. As the European Parliament (1993: 10) put it at the time: "the European message must concern Europeans both in their professional dimension, in terms of new opportunities and better living standards, but also in their historical and cultural dimension, in terms of values, outlook and a commonly shared identity." Time and again Community policy documents were (and still are) spelling out the need "to assure citizens that 'Europe' is not about economics alone"; that the Union "depends for its very legitimacy on its citizens" (CEC 1993a: 15); and that "[p]enalty for failure" to gain the citizens' confidence "is that citizenship of the Union may appear to be a distant concept for citizens engendering confusion as to its means and objectives even fuelling anti-EU feelings" (CEC 1997a: 1). Thus, as these passages indicate, market integration was seen as needing some type of popular legitimacy if it was to progress smoothly. As the turbulence preceding the ratification of the Maastricht Treaty demonstrated, EU institutions seemed aware of the fact that there was a limit to how much popular obstruction and scepticism the EU project could muster; or as Jacques Delors once said: "You don't fall in love with a common market; you need something else" (quoted in Naudin 1994).

It is therefore of utmost importance to take cognizance of the fact that the Single Market relaunch also would carry with it a strong collectivist articulation of "European citizenship"; an articulation which appealed to a popular sense of rootedness in a shared European culture, heritage, history, and civilization. Rather than locating the quest for popular legitimacy in a discourse organized around the rights of social citizenship and a new transnational welfare regime, as had been the case in the 1970s, the EU came, starting in mid-1980s, to put its faith in an ethno-cultural citizenship discourse in which membership came to hinge upon descent and ties to a historical community (Hansen 2000; Kofman 1995: 128; Martiniello 1995; Shore 1993).

According to the then Commission President Jacques Santer, the "sources" of the European "common cultural heritage—the heritage of the Western mind and tradition"—are "Greek, Latin and Judeo-Christian" (quoted in Lundgren 1998: 136–7). Similarly, the European Parliament

(1991: 13) outlined present-day European culture as derived from "classical culture and Christianity." These sentiments were also fundamental to the vision laid out by the subsequent Commission President Romano Prodi. In a speech delivered before the European Parliament, Prodi maintained that Christianity constitutes the common consciousness upon which European integration is founded (Prodi 1999b). Convinced that "culture and citizenship go hand in hand" (CEC 1997b), the Commission repeatedly called attention to the need of creating a stronger sense of cultural awareness among the citizens, and to have "culture" constitute "a privileged field of action" (CEC 1996b: V, 3). According to the Commission, special measures needed to be taken in order to "improve access to heritage and the supply of information on it for the public at large so as to contribute to the affirmation of a European citizenship through greater knowledge of heritage" (CEC 1995a: 13). "[C]ultural heritage," the Commission went on to affirm, plays an important role in augmenting "the feeling of European citizenship" (CEC 1996b: part II, 17).

Essential to the ethno-cultural configuration of citizenship emerging after the relaunch, however, was not only the conception of culture and the community it denoted as something self-contained and objectively given. Engrafted upon the European citizenry was also an assumption of cultural superiority. In the Commission public relations booklet *A Citizen's Europe*, for instance, Europe is portrayed as "the cradle of critical reasoning" and "cultural creativity," thus making today's "European citizens" the beneficiaries of "the intellectual resources they have inherited from a cultural tradition going back 2000 years or more" (CEC 1993a: 45, 32). This, in turn, it is argued, makes Europe better equipped to ward off a decline similar to that of history's other "great civilizations" (CEC 1993a: 31). Romano Prodi would subsequently embrace this theme as part of his program, arguing "that Europe in the course of its history has had a great heritage to live up to, a heritage which still forms the richest store of culture and knowledge amassed by mankind" (Prodi 1999a).

Premised, as it was, on ties to a European ancestral estate, Christianity, and other ethno-cultural markers, the definition of "European citizenship" that came to light in the wake of the Single Market and Maastricht made up a highly exclusive construct. It promoted, by default, an understanding of membership of a Union citizenry as something reserved (however unintentionally) for white populations, hence ostracizing the millions of EU inhabitants who could not lay claim to the ethno-cultural heritage in question (see further Martiniello 1995; Painter and Philo 1995: 112–3; Kofman 1995: 128–9; Hansen 2000). Indeed, as Shore (1996: 487) points out, numerous EU statements pertaining to this issue resound of old-time anthropology, thus perpetuating "the idea of a distinctive, bounded region set apart from others by race, religion, language and habitat."

This ethno-culturalist bias in EU citizenship discourse was hardly a bolt from the blue, though, and neither was the development unique for the EU organization. Rather, it needs to be understood as having formed part of the general turn toward cultural explanations of socio-political ills, combined with self-fulfilling prophecies of Huntingtonian clashes of civilizations—increasingly pitting Europe and the West against an alleged Muslim peril—that came to permeate much of political discourse in the West, particularly as we entered the post–Cold War period (see Delanty 1995; Marfleet 1999; Patterson 1997). The trend manifested at many different levels and in many different contexts. In a speech in 1991 the then mayor of Paris, Jacques Chirac, diagnosed France as suffering from an "overdose" of immigrants (*The Economist* 1993), and then went on to distinguish between European and non-European immigrants:

> That there were more foreigners before the war is probably true, but they were not the same type and it makes a difference. Having Spaniards, Poles and Portuguese working in our country certainly poses less problems than having Muslims and blacks.... Imagine the average French worker who, with his wife, earns around 15,000 francs a month, and who sees across the landing of their council flat, all piled up, a family with a father, three or four wives and twenty children, who earns 50,000 francs of social benefit without lifting a finger. Add to that the noise and smell and, well, the French worker will go crazy. And it's not being racist to say that. (quoted in *Times Online* 2005)

Around the same time Pope John Paul II started to make repeated appeals to people in Europe to unite as Christians, since, as he phrased it, "Christianity is at the very roots of European culture" (quoted in Kettle 1990). Along similar, although more explicit, lines then Dutch foreign minister, Hans van Mierlo, voiced his fear of an alien religious intrusion into the European Union, stating: "A large Muslim state would pose a problem. Do we really want such a state in Europe?"[5] (quoted in Jönsson 1998). The emerging exploitation of Islam as constituting Europe's ultimate "other," even enemy (see further Haddad 1993; Rees 1997), also found an outlet in the then NATO secretary-general, Willy Claes, who professed that so-called militant Islam had succeeded the role of the former Soviet Union in posing "the gravest threat to western security" (quoted in Rees 1997: 32). It is worth noticing too that the conservative party group in the European Parliament, EPP, at the time justified its opposition to Turkish membership of the EU by claiming that Turkey did not belong to the "European cultural community"[6] (quoted in Boqvist 1997; see also Kinzer 1997).

This is certainly not to suggest that the EU institutions necessarily had any intentions of fuelling a growing hostility toward people born outside of the ethno-culturally defined European "stock." Rather, the gravity of the matter lay in the fact that the EU came to embrace the same basic categories, definitions, and general outlook on "Europe" and what should constitute its "natural" citizenry as those forces who did not stop short of defining the included—as was mostly the case with the EU—but who also explicitly designated *those who should be excluded*. Where the former failed to acknowledge the excluding consequences of an ethno-cultural framing of Union citizenship, the latter both acknowledged and endorsed them.

Migration, Market, and Citizenship: From the Single Market to Maastricht and Beyond

A Changing Outlook on Migration

The Single Market project and its concomitant citizenship project would also play out directly in matters of external migration and the situation for resident third-country nationals (TCNs). The development, whereby more and more policy areas and future challenges to the member states took on a "European dimension" and started to conform to the new and increasingly commanding logic of European integration, would thus by no means sidestep the question of migration. As a result, increasingly harmonized perceptions and policies on migration were starting to take shape among member-state governments around this time.

Up until the mid-1970s, the Commission had treated both internal (free movement) and external migration and migrants as within the purview of migration policy, and, as we observed in Chapter 2, the Commission had become increasingly anxious about the differential treatment of migrants. In the proposals of the 1970s, the Commission saw the solution to this problem as one related to a *social rights dimension* for TCNs, one that aspired to put external migrants and resident TCN on the same footing with internal migrants with regards to social rights. Yet, as we enter the Single Market era the internal migrants were no longer viewed as migrants as such, but became "European citizens," at first informally and later formally as a result of the Maastricht Treaty's institution of an EU citizenship. Meanwhile, the social rights dimension for external migrants and TCNs was toned down and replaced with a policy discourse—at both national and supranational levels—which saw external migration more and more as an issue and problem of security, "illegal immigration," and "bogus asylum seeking." Here, the Commission began to frame European citizenship as a means to "protect" EU citizens from risks, threats, and other problems associated with external migration. Yet, at the same time—perhaps paradoxically—the Commission launched a bid to work for the enhancement of the sociocultural integration of resident TCNs and external migrants, as well as pledging to combat the increasing tide of racism and xenophobia throughout the Union.

Why the Single Market Made External Immigration an EU Issue

The main reason and structural driving force behind external migration's ascent on the EU agenda are to be found in the Single Market's logic and design (Butt Philip 1994; Monar 2001). If focus in the past had been on the elimination of national barriers for a free, yet highly regulated, movement of *labor* within the Community, the Single Market was to expand on this to also open up for a more spontaneous free movement of *persons*. Since the Single Market's ultimate objective was the elimination of all border and passport controls, and thus, in the end, also the elimination of much of the physical borders as such between member states, this was quite a radical shift in focus. In order to make the abolition of internal borders possible, however, it was made utterly clear that this would altogether depend on a parallel, compensatory reinforcement of the Community's external border controls. Otherwise, the reasoning went, free movement could be exploited by anyone who succeeded in penetrating one single border; that is, one of the EU's insufficiently guarded external borders. In that way, the migration movements toward those member states bordering on nonmember states would also become a common concern for all member states. In turn, this meant that the conception of the EU as a territorial entity was reinforced and thus constructed in intimate relation to the issue of migration and asylum. In particular, it would manifest in the 1980s' and 1990s' ever-growing focus on illegal immigration to the EU. It was, in other words, the issue of migration that equipped the external border—a phenomenon that had played a minor role up until the launching of the Single Market—with a concrete and policy-relevant meaning.

But migration policy's new EU–European dimension did not confine itself to the question of external border management. Since TCNs, whether they were permanent residents, asylum seekers, or undocumented, still were barred from the free movement provisions, the Single Market would also induce common measures as concerned the internal control of TCNs. As such, then, the Single Market's strong impact on migration policy would give rise to a number of externally as well as internally directed policy responses in the new, and purportedly "frontier-free Europe."

Much of this arrangement, however, ran counter to the European Commission's plans for the development of migration policy in the EU following the relaunch. Early on, the Commission had instead made plain its aspirations to supranationalize immigration and asylum, seeing it as a necessary and logical part of the Single Market's larger framework. It was equally necessary and logical, in the eyes of the Commission, that the freedom-of-movement entitlements should embrace all Community residents, irrespective of whether they were member state nationals or ("legally" resident) third-country nationals. Without such a universal arrangement, the reasoning went, the abolition of internal border checks would be unfeasible (Geddes 2000b: 70). It immediately became apparent, however, that such a transfer of competencies to the Community level would not be attainable, since member states proved far from ready to surrender their sovereignty in this policy area (Geddes 2000b: 70–1; Hoskyns 1996: 172–3). Not surprisingly, the universalist approach to freedom of movement suffered the same fate, with member states refusing to abandon the henceforth even more decisive discrimination between member-state nationals and third-country nationals. As Geddes (2000b: 71) puts it, "[u]nequal treatment persisted and was sanctioned by EC law" (see also Guild 1999). Rather than a supranational solution, then, it was *intergovernmental* "cooperation," "coordination," and "harmonization" that became the new watchwords in the member states' migration policy.

Such intergovernmental cooperation—which was characterized by secret diplomacy and a lack of democratic accountability and thus subjected to much criticism (Den Boer 1995; Flyghed 1998; Hentges 2002)—got off to a quick start. Already in 1985 the first Schengen Agreement was signed by five of the member states, followed by the establishment of the Ad Hoc Group on Immigration in 1986, and the Co-ordinators' Group on Free Movement of Persons two years later. The Schengen Agreement, which was the most important and influential among these, aimed to abolish border controls for people within the Schengen area while at the same time seeking to establish a common policy for the control of the area's external border. As Emek Uçarer (2003: 297) has it: "Schengen's primary objective was to develop policies that would apply to the Community's external borders, with the aim of making it easier to remove the EC's internal borders." In this sense, Schengen made up a necessary complement to the internal Single Market; it was set to complete, through intergovernmental means, that which the Single Market required but which its otherwise supranational structure had not been assigned the competence to carry out and administer.

After its initiation in 1985, the Schengen cooperation would come to extend its focus toward common measures aspiring to attain the following: free movement for persons; strengthened external border controls; build-up of the internal surveillance of people's movement; cooperation in policing and intelligence; harmonization of the fight against crime and narcotics; judicial cooperation; harmonization of visa and asylum policy; and common measures to fight illegal migration and stay. From the outset, the work with the various matters within Schengen was to progress at very different speeds, and in 1990 a new agreement was signed—the Schengen Implementation Agreement, or Schengen II—which did not gain legal force until 1995. Although Schengen suffered from some difficulty in cooperating, the work in several areas got off to a quick start, and the results were not long in coming. Asylum and visa policy made up two such areas. The imposition of fines, or so-called carrier sanctions, on transport companies carrying asylum seekers without valid identification documents was one of many measures resulting from the Schengen cooperation. Schengen also facilitated the member states' signing of the Dublin Convention (ratified in 1997) in June of 1990, which coincided with the signing of the Schengen Implementation Agreement. Designed, in large part, to develop a common framework and course of action for the combating of illegal immigration and the management of asylum matters in the Community, both of these interlinked intergovernmental schemes would serve to gradually weaken the asylum institute and the Geneva Refugee Convention during the 1990s (Guild 1999; Hentges 2002; Joly 1999; Lavenex 2001; Overbeek 1995; Ward 1997).

Although this intergovernmental manner of proceeding in the post-SEA period clearly ran counter to the Commission's supranational scheme, the Commission's response never came close to all-out rejection or confrontation. Instead it opted for a "pragmatic stance," deciding that it could have more say in the matter, however hamstrung, by accepting a subordinate role inside the intergovernmental arrangements than by maintaining a principled opposition from the sidelines (Geddes 2000b: 72). It should be noted, though, that strong voices from within the European Parliament *did* challenge not only the form but also the content of the intergovernmental cooperation on immigration and asylum, claiming, for instance, that the intergovernmental groups

> treat migration and refugee matters very much as related to policing. And this has a very negative effect on public opinion. Associating migrants and refugees with police and national security could well feed racist ideas and could be used to legitimize certain forms of racist behaviour (extra identity control of those who are or look like "foreigners") (European Parliament 1990: 133).

To a significant extent, then, the notion and practice of the Single Markets' free movement goal came to revolve around the question, or "problem," of immigration and asylum. Its prized realization and promise, as well as its feared impracticability and demise, were thus inevitably projected on to the success or failure of controlling and containing the admission and movement of asylum seekers and third-country migrants. In this scheme of things, migrants and asylum seekers became, as it were, the potential party poopers of Euro-optimism, the Single Market Luddites. With the freedom of movement for *some* inextricably bound up with the containment of *others*, it is not surprising that immigration and asylum increasingly emerged as a "problem," a nuisance, in need of a swift resolution.

The Impact of Maastricht: The Contradictions of External Migration Control and Internal Migrant Integration

The growing salience of migration as an EU issue was further underscored by the Maastricht Treaty (or Treaty on European Union), which formalized intergovernmental cooperation on migration and incorporated it into the treaty's newly established Third Pillar of Justice and Home Affairs (JHA). As far as transparency and democratic accountability were concerned, this formalization offered few, if any, improvements. From here on, on the contrary, immigration and asylum were best construed as matters located "outside the procedures of the EC's institutions, but under rules linking it to the EC," or "inside the Union, but outside the European Community"; and as such they continued to be "cloaked in considerable secrecy" (Commission for Racial Equality 1994: 16, 22; d'Oliveira 1994: 261).

Besides immigration and asylum, the JHA third pillar also contained cooperation on police and judicial matters, including the fight against international crime, terrorism, and the traffic in narcotics. As d'Oliveira (1994: 261) notes, these were all issues to be regarded as "'matters of common interest' to the Member States in their efforts to achieve the objectives of the Union." This meant that immigration and asylum became thoroughly entrenched in the policy realm of international crime prevention, policing and security. Indeed, as we reach the early 1990s external migration was increasingly perceived and discussed as naturally related to serious international crime, drug trafficking, and terrorism—not only in the member states but also, and increasingly so, at the EU level (Anderson et al. 1995; Den Boer 1995; Huysmans 1995; Martiniello and Rea 1999). Hence, if the framing of certain forms of migration as problems, even as threats against social stability, had been prevalent at the national level for many years, Maastricht formalized the duplication of this securitized approach at the EU level.

Accordingly, the European Commission now came to share many of the elements that structured the hegemonic discourse on migration and asylum—emanating from the various national contexts—which treated migration as a "problem" and migrants and asylum seekers as "floods" about to destabilize the Union unless checked through vigorous security measures at the external borders, as well as within the EU (see Hathaway 1993; Maier 2002: 94; Ward 1997). After Maastricht, the Commission's message thus became more pronounced on migration matters, particularly as regarded so-called illegal immigration and bogus asylum seeking. In a voluminous 1994 Commission policy document titled *On Immigration and Asylum Policies*, the issue of illegal immigration was now viewed as one of the most urgent:

> Rigorous controls at the external frontiers and visa policy will also play their part in discouraging and combating illegal immigration.... Preventive measure and more systematic border controls ... will be important in combating illegal immigration, but cannot be completely effective in stopping it. Measures which permit the identification of persons within the Community in an irregular situation will therefore continue to have an important role to play as well. This issue has been touched upon by the 1993 Recommendation on expulsion policies which mentions, inter alia, the importance of internal checks. This is undoubtedly sensitive territory since the location of migrants in an illegal situation is generally a police matter which needs to be set in the context of a wide range of other priorities, of which the general fight against crime is probably the most important. (CEC 1994c: 28)

The Commission also elaborated on a "comprehensive approach" to migration (originally drafted in 1991), consisting of a three-pronged strategy, which called for: (1) "taking action on migration pressure"; (2) "Controlling migration flows"; and (3) "strengthening integration policies for the benefit of legal immigrants" (CEC 1994c: 11). As the third item in the strategy indicates, the period around the Maastricht Treaty also marked the establishment of a policy discussion on migrant integration at the EU level. The first steps were taken already in conjunction with the commencement of the Single Market in the mid-1980s (see CEC 1985c), but it was not until after Maastricht that the Commission began to formulate a more coherent policy discussion on migrant integration. This development was interwoven with a mounting debate in the EU over migration and asylum, a budding support for political parties of the extreme right, and an outburst of racist violence against migrants and asylum seekers. Such integration efforts crucially included discussions and policy initiatives on how to come to terms with racism, social exclusion, and other obstacles confronting ethnic minorities of migrant background residing in the Union. In this spirit, the Commission broached issues of cultural identity and multiculturalism, calling for the fostering of greater tolerance and "intercultural" understanding between majority and minority populations (Hansen 1997; CEC 1994d). In this context, the Commission (1994d) affirmed that it had become high time not only to acknowledge but also to appreciate the fact that all member states had developed into "immigrant countries" and "multicultural societies." This transition, the Commission argued, had also generated a number of challenges which could not be met solely by amplified national responses but which also required coordinated action at the EU level. The Commission concluded that it was necessary to confront the increasingly common and too often overlooked obstacles facing the EU's migrant communities.

Although the Commission promoted its integration policy as an antidote to the growing racism and anti-immigrant sentiments in the EU at the time, a closer look at the Commission's reasoning gives at hand a number of contradictions, most of which were related to the EU's increasingly restrictive and securitized position on asylum and external migration. As the Commission's abovementioned "comprehensive approach" to migration makes plain, the benevolent goals vested into migrant integration was clearly subordinate to the Commission's uncompromising call for ever more restrictive measures to control external migration and refugee movement. Unmistakably, one of the key assumptions in this approach rested on the postulate that unless migration was greatly reduced integration would be unfeasible. To put it in an incisive wording, the achievement of greater tolerance, migrant integration, and diminished racism were made to hinge on a migration policy that perceived of migrants as being detrimental to the EU. To use the Commission's own formulation (1994c: 11): "It has, for example, become clear that an indispensable condition for successful integration policies with respect to third country nationals resident in the Union is control of migration flows." And further: "society's readiness to accept the inflow of new migrant groups depends on how it perceives government to be in control of the phenomenon" (CEC 1994c: 32).

In the 1990s, this emphasis on an assumed European citizenry that was said to demand that governments curb migration became one of the most commonplace ways for the Commission and EU governments to disguise their own populist readiness to talk tough and impose restrictive migration policies as simply reflecting the mood of European citizens (see Miles 1993: 201, 206). An equally imperative aspect was the Commission and governments' unremitting failure to recognize that once migration had been identified as an ill-boding "problem," this would scarcely promote the desired integration of migrants or decrease the obstacles for those migrants residing in the EU who already suffered from various forms of discrimination. In conformity with migration policies targeting the external frontier, moreover, the calls to integrate "legal migrants" were also tinged with references to security, control, and ominous scenarios (see further Hansen 2000). What emerged in the 1990s was thus an EU policy discourse that on the one hand denigrated migrants and asylum seekers as "problems" and potential threats, and on the other hand pleaded for the integration of migrant ethnic minorities on the basis of intercultural understanding and stressed the need for measures to remove the numerous discriminatory barriers faced by migrant communities.

For the Commission, however, the enterprise harbored no such conflict. Nonetheless, the Commission *did*, in fact, emphasize the importance of enforcing in its handling of migration affairs this very same division between measures to reinforce the external frontier and to crack down on internal "illegals" on the one hand, and measures to integrate "legal" immigrants on the other. Once combined, moreover, and presented as two sides of the same coin—the former said to epitomize "realism," the latter "solidarity"—these two approaches, rather than spelling incongruity, were promoted as a mutually reinforcing pair of outlooks and policy programs. As the Commission (1994c: Foreword) put it:

> The deepening of the European integration process calls for an integrated and coherent response, which combines realism with solidarity, to the challenges which migration pressures and the integration of legal immigrants pose for the Union as a whole. Failure to meet those challenges would be to the detriment of attempts to promote cohesion and solidarity within the Union and could, indeed, endanger the future stability of the Union itself.

EU Citizenship in the Migration and Security Nexus

As intimated in the foregoing, the EU's securitized framing of external migration and its commitment to combat "illegal immigration" would also exert a heavy influence on the framing of EU citizenship in the post-Maastricht era. Beside its pronounced references to the new opportunities proffered by the internal market and the sense of community presented by a rich European cultural identity, EU citizenship policy would also become bound up with external migration and asylum policy. By articulating EU citizenship as a bulwark against various external as well as internal threats, among which international crime and illegal immigration figured prominently, EU citizenship was increasingly utilized as an instrument to amend the EU's popular legitimacy after Maastricht. To be sure, the explicit coupling of citizenship with the migration and security nexus was by no means a recent appearance. Rather, it should be analyzed as part of a larger development, starting in the member states in the 1970s, in which international crime and immigration increasingly were framed as making up "threats" and security problems of equal magnitude; and consequently something which the "citizens" had to be protected from (Den Boer 1995; Huysmans 1995).

The way in which the articulation of European citizenship unfolded in relation to migration and asylum thereby disclosed another exclusionary strand within the EU's policy discourse on citizenship. Here the underlying assumption conveyed that the EU citizenry, in order to consolidate, needed to be assured that migration, together with other matters brought forth as assertively related to public safety, were effectively checked at the external borders. To cite the Commission: "the problems of immigration and asylum, drug trafficking and other aspects of international crime are matters of increasing concern to the citizens of Europe" (CEC 1995b: 62). Likewise, in an information booklet, which specifically addressed the "European citizen" and the issue of citizenship in the EU, the Commission points out that since many "are concerned about immigration, especially illegal immigration, thinking that this could increase once internal border controls have been fully swept away," the problem of immigration must be solved in a way that satisfies everyone (CEC 1996c: 13–14). A related concern among EU citizens, according to the booklet, found the following formulation: "Will the eventual dismantling of all internal borders lead to an increase in levels of immigration to my country, both from inside and outside the Community?"; to which the Commission could give a calming answer: "No, it should not. The fundamental point about dismantling the Community's internal borders is that this process must be accompanied by the synchronized tightening of all external borders" (CEC 1996c: 15).

It goes without saying that the promotion of European citizenship as a bulwark against extra-European or non-Western migrants risked to legitimize and so aggravate discriminatory perceptions and practices toward people with migrant background who were already residing in the EU. This not least since, as demonstrated above, those held up as ill-suited for admission into the EU upon entry would fall into the same domestic category that had been screened from ethno-cultural membership in the European citizenry.

Conclusion

In this chapter we have argued that once the Single Market and the Single European Act set out to restrain regulatory powers at national levels, the prospects, scope, and relative strength of policies tied to the welfare state would, from the mid-1980s, increasingly come to hinge on the compensatory capacities and regulatory competencies at the supranational level. But as has also been shown, mainly because of the prevalent political disinclination at the time—that is, "the neoliberal European policy consensus" (McNamara 1998)—the supranational level was never invested with such compensatory authorities. To the detriment of the Union's welfare states and the original vision of a "social Europe" set to protect and develop the achievements of national social citizenships, it was rather negative integration that prevailed, hence endowing the EU with an institutional, decision-making, and legal framework and dynamic that would come to work in aid of a deregulating *market integration* but at the expense of a positive *welfare integration*. This provided, the political and social consequences of the Single Market transformations were to become both extensive and lasting. As we shall see in the chapters ahead, these transformations continue to cast their shadow on today's developments and, as such, they remain essential when we seek to comprehend the current situation.

If the original 1970's "Social Europe" vision was altered as a result of the Single Market, this held equally true for the original conception of a "Citizens' Europe" (as discussed in Chapter 2). This, of course, was no coincidence since both concepts had social citizenship as their moral-political basis in the 1970s; and in this sense Social Europe and Citizens' Europe were largely synonymous and easily amalgamated into a concerted, yet failed, push for a *European Social Citizenship*. Thus, when the initiative for a supranational social citizenship ran out of steam in the 1980s, this would also force an alteration of the original Citizens' Europe vision. The general thrust of the argument developed here has been that European citizenship, as it emerged from the mid-1980s, mainly was recast to serve as an intermedium between a neoliberal economism and a newly awakened ethno-culturalism.

As such, EU citizenship came to comprise, firstly, a rights dimension which largely, although not completely, was tailored to the demands of the Single Market, and which de facto confined its appeal to the stratum of resourceful inhabitants for whom the freedom of movement (and, therewith, attached rights) proffered real and ramifying opportunities; often bypassing constricted national outlooks. Secondly, the new EU citizenship incorporated an identity dimension chiefly couched in an ethno-cultural idiom, which crystallized around ingrained narratives on Europe's allegedly unitary and undefiled historical legacy and cultural heritage. Herein citizenship and descent community were conflated, thus implicitly delimiting EU citizenship to be inclusive only of those with primordial ties to a prescribed historical, cultural, and religious community. Correspondingly, and likewise implicitly, EU citizenship barred from membership the millions of EU inhabitants—many of whom were, in fact, formal EU citizens—who could not lay claim to the European ethno-cultural community in question. Since, as also attended to above, Maastricht's formalized EU citizenship was not bestowed on long-term resident TCNs—the formal EU citizenship being open only to nationals of a member state—the ethno-cultural delineation of EU citizenship added to the marginalization of many migrants and minority communities in the Union. To be sure, this ethno-cultural turn was not unique to the EU, but rather walked hand in hand with a larger and much more deliberate North Atlantic tendency bent on designating Islam as the West's new (post–Cold War) threat, calling on Western leaders and publics to rally around their common European and Judeo-Christian culture and civilization. If less deliberate in its ethno-cultural mobilization, the EU—at least the European Commission and Parliament—could arguably also be said to have contradicted its ethno-cultural message by adopting, in parallel, an integration policy position which urged member states to embrace multicultural and intercultural measures in order to promote integration and foster tolerance between majority and migrant minority populations.

Finally, the period surveyed in this chapter also marks the emergence of the EU as an important structural force, as well as a nascent actor, in the area of migration policy, taken as whole. As we have explained, this had much to do with the changing regime for the management of the EU's internal and external borders brought about by the Single Market Program and the Maastricht agreement's quest for competitiveness, deregulated economies, and more flexible labor markets. The logic engendered hereby was one of making the relaxation of the Union's internal borders for European citizens depend on the reinforcement of the EU's external borders and internal surveillance in order to combat the entry and movement of "illegal migrants," "bogus asylum seekers," criminals, and terrorists.

If we have pointed to the detrimental effects that this securitization of migration would have on the asylum institute in the EU, a crucial addition with regards to the relation between the EU's stated objective of fighting illegal migration, one the one side, and its neoliberal political economic objectives, on the other, needs to be made here so as to introduce a discussion that will be developed further in the chapters ahead. This concerns the fact that the latter objective's translation into more competitive and flexible labor markets, which often were made to rely on a steady increase of cheap and casual labor, acted to offset the former objective. That is to say, the EU economy's growing demand for cheap labor, starting in the 1980s, would frequently prove to be tantamount to a demand for "illegal," or irregular migrant labor. In the early 1990s, more and more research started to attend to this condition and was able to demonstrate that many EU governments that claimed to be fighting "illegal immigration" in actuality were quite aware of, even content with, the fact that their economies were profiting from and thus becoming increasingly dependent on the cheap labor performed by "illegal" or irregular migrants (Overbeek 1995: 31–2).

But if the Commission and member-state governments kept quiet about the nexus between neoliberal economic policy and irregular labor migration, they never missed an opportunity to publicly highlight the nexus between security and migration. Not only that; we have also shown how Brussels' policy discourse on EU citizenship got enmeshed in the security and migration nexus, whereby asylum seekers and, above all, "illegal immigrants"—that is, precisely those migrants contributing to making EU labor markets more competitive—were staged as potential security threats. By alluding to a presumed fear of external as well as internal "illegals," EU citizenship was promoted as a ticket to an increased sense of security and stability in the Union.

In keeping with other major reshufflings, however, the development discussed in this chapter would neither follow an inherent or predestined course, nor be devoid of internally as well as externally induced discords and stumbling blocks. As explained above, the European Parliament's unrelenting criticism of some of the proposals and objectives advanced by the Council and the Commission, including even allegations that these could foment racist sentiments, serves as a poignant illustration. But voices and groups from within the European Parliament, as well as from within the academic community, were far from the only actors who were turning their critical attention toward the EU-level's migration and citizenship agenda around this time. On the contrary, the post-Maastricht era would see a plethora of NGOs, migrant and ethnic minority associations, human rights organizations, religious groups, and various social movements increasingly taking their respective cases to the supranational level. This contributed to the establishment of Brussels as a focal point for all sorts of causes and lobbying efforts relating to migration policy.

In all, the years following the inauguration of the Single Market would witness a great conversion of the actual working, conduct and articulation of citizenship and migration policy in the EU. But if the political and institutional landscape was being transformed, so was the political-economic map on to which questions of citizenship and migration were being projected. In the chapters ahead, we turn our attention to how this complex development was to unfold from the mid-1990s and onward.

Notes

1. For a thorough account of this shift, see van der Pijl (2006).
2. For an in-depth account of the European Commission's cooperation with transnational corporations and other capital interests, see Bornschier and Ziltener (1999) and Holman and Pijl (1996).
3. For a detailed inquiry into the French, British, and German governments' pivotal roles in enabling the SEA through their concurrent convergence on least-common-denominator preferences of (neoliberal) deregulation and market liberalization, see Moravcsik (1991).
4. For elaboration on the concept of "regulated capitalism" in the context of the Delors plan and beyond, see Hooghe and Marks (1999).
5. Our translation from Swedish.
6. Our translation from Swedish.

PART II

The Current Trajectories of Citizenship Politics in the EU

CHAPTER 4

"No Rights Without Responsibilities"
Adapting Citizens for the New European Economy

Introduction

Forming part of what is often referred to as the integration project's "extended relaunch" (1985–1999), developments in the latter half of the 1990s would build upon the momentum of the Single European Act, the Single Market Program, and the Maastricht Treaty. Perhaps most significant during this period was the move toward the European Economic and Monetary Union (EMU), culminating with the official introduction of the euro currency in most of the Union in 1999. The formation of the EMU involved the creation of a highly controversial monetary policy framework of low interest rates governed by the European Central Bank (ECB) and a set of restrictive fiscal policies known as the Growth and Stability Pact; a synthesis of the Maastricht convergence criteria devised in 1997 to rein in state spending by limiting annual budget deficits and accumulated debt to 3 percent and 60 percent of GDP respectively (Cafruny and Ryner 2007). This period also witnessed a new wave of enthusiasm toward enlargement following European Council meetings in Copenhagen in 1993—which established liberal democratic institutions and competitive market economies as the minimum criteria for accession—and in Essen in 1994—which outlined the need for institutional reform in line with any future enlargements (Holman 2001: 178–9). This paved the way for the accession of Sweden, Finland, and Austria in 1995, and set in motion preparations for the EU's "big bang" enlargement into the former Communist states of Central and Eastern Europe (CEE) to be realized within the next decade.

As centrepiece initiatives from this period, monetary union and enlargement did not stray far from the logic of negative integration and the ideological hegemony of embedded neoliberalism of the Maastricht era.

Yet, a distinguishing feature of the latter half of the extended relaunch was the unprecedented proliferation of various forms of *resistance* arising to challenge the deepening and widening of EU integration. To a large extent, this was prompted by the "French winter of discontent" in 1995–6 (Singer 1999)—when approximately two million French workers took to the streets to protest against persistent unemployment and welfare state cutbacks, attributed primarily to the government's plan of deregulation, privatization, and fiscal tight-fistedness that was being instituted to meet the criteria of EMU. In many ways setting a new tone for political and social agency in the EU, the French demonstrations were followed by different forms of popular manifestations against what the late Pierre Bourdieu (1998: 129) called the "social costs of economic violence," involving both new types of social movements, such as Attac, organizing among the unemployed (Bourdieu, Lebaron and Mauger 1998; Singer 1998), and more traditional labor movements coordinating trade union initiatives at trans- and supranational levels (Bieler 2006). With the global shock waves from the East Asian and Russian financial crises in 1998 generating increasing skepticism toward neoliberal austerity and free market orthodoxy, all these events provided additional testimony to the seeming destabilization of neoliberal hegemony in the EU and the wider world.

Crucially, however, it must be emphasized that alongside these progressive movements, resistance to the EU project also came from the resurgence of the extreme right in several member states—a force that, although for the most part ardently anti-EU, could never be claimed to be anti-European in the ethno-culturalist, identitarian sense, as is often falsely assumed (see Betz 2002). While the former was manifested in imagery of the white, brown, and black faces of strikers and protesters in France and elsewhere rallying around claims to the social dimensions of citizenship in ways that cut across ethno-cultural divides, the latter, bolstered by electoral successes by the extreme right-wing parties in France, Austria, Belgium, the Netherlands, Italy, and Denmark, lambasted the "Brussels bureaucracy" for compromising popular will and destroying national identities (MacShane 1998; Frey and Hall 1999).

When considered alongside the continuing apathy toward European Parliament elections (*The Economist* 1994; Norman 1999), the forms of resistance that arose in the latter half of the extended relaunch served to illuminate the failures of market-based supranational citizenship in fulfilling its intended purpose of fostering legitimacy for the EU project; leading many political and academic commentators to label it "an embarrassment" (Weiler 1997: 499). Of all the movements that emerged in response to the EU's crisis of legitimacy in the mid- to late-1990s, the one serious contender for hegemonic status was a reinvigorated transnational social democratic project, claiming to offer a plausible alternative to the "embedded neo-liberal" order and its concomitant market citizenship model. Social democratic parties had by this time come to power in nearly all EU member states—yet in order to secure this hegemonic challenge, the project as a whole would have to first overcome its own internal divisions, with the faction of "modernizers" of the "Third Way" led by Tony Blair and Gerhard Schröder gradually winning out over the traditionalist camp associated with figures such as Oskar Lafontaine. In the words of its primary academic proponent, Anthony Giddens (2000: 2), the Third Way movement was to offer a modernized social democracy better equipped to address the "advent of global markets and the knowledge economy," introducing "a different framework, one that avoids both the bureaucratic, top-down government favoured by the old left and the aspiration of the right to dismantle government altogether." Central to this modernized form of social democracy would be a recasting of the relationship between state and citizen—one declaring that there would be "no rights without responsibilities" (Giddens 1998, 2000; cf. Ryner 2002).

In the EU political arena, the Third Way's influence was felt early on in the Amsterdam Treaty (1997): first, through its inclusion of "people issues" (environment, health, and anti-discrimination) in the treaty text, and the expansion of European Parliament powers through the extension of co-decision into all areas of social policy (Warleigh 2001: 28–9); and second, through its efforts to formulate multilevel political solutions to the region's persistently high unemployment rates, where the treaty vowed to bring together member states and EU institutions to develop a "co-ordinated strategy for employment." Later that same year leaders at the Luxembourg European Council meeting would elaborate on these plans by unveiling what is now known as the European Employment Strategy (EES), an EU-coordinated set of "soft law" governance mechanisms involving relevant supranational and national institutions, as well as the social partners, in the identification of "optimal" policy practices that would be used to devise "jointly set, verifiable, regularly updated targets" upon which member state employment policies would converge (Luxembourg Presidency Conclusions 1997).

However, the apex of the Third Way's ideological ascent in the EU would come in 2000 at the Lisbon European Council, where calls were made for a "radical transformation of the European economy" to make the EU into the most "competitive and dynamic knowledge based economy in the world" by 2010 (Lisbon European Council 2000). Hailed as the harbinger of a new era of EU integration, the Lisbon Agenda, as it is now commonly known, was developed with the intention of "balancing" the overriding goal of economic competitiveness with a strong commitment to fostering a meaningful EU-level "Social Policy Agenda" (SPA), captured by the pledge to create "more and better jobs and greater social cohesion" (Lisbon European Council 2000). This social dimension of the Lisbon Agenda was to be attained primarily through refinement and extension of "new modes of governance" or "soft law" mechanisms, now rebranded as the "Open Method of Coordination" (OMC), into other realms of social policy (e.g. pensions, social inclusion, and healthcare). The social dimension of Lisbon was subsequently greeted with enthusiasm by political and academic commentators who claimed that it could potentially represent "Europe's Maastricht for Welfare" (Rhodes 2000). Most importantly for our purposes here, the Lisbon Agenda was also welcomed for bringing new life to the EU's citizenship model, bridging "the traditional concerns of egalitarians and conservatives by embracing both the individual and collective rights and responsibilities of citizens" (Rhodes 2000: 2–7), and "nesting" EU-level social rights as a counterweight to negative integration (Ferrera 2005). More than a decade after the defeat of Delors' vision of a Social Europe, it now appeared as though positive integration of social welfare policy had finally been given crucial political impetus under the Lisbon Agenda, which, in its pledge to transform the Union into a prosperous new knowledge-based economy (KBE), garnered support from a wide array of social forces ranging from the European Roundtable of Industrialists (ERT) to the European Trade Union Congress (ETUC).

Our purpose in this chapter is to analyze how the form and content of EU citizenship has developed since the late 1990s and especially since the launching of the Lisbon Agenda—an anchor of a new era of the integration project. Whereas Chapters 5 and 6 are concerned mainly with what Castles and Davidson (2000) identify as the status of "becoming a citizen," the analysis here is concerned with EU citizenship politics as it relates to the status of "being a citizen" (see Chapter 1). To this end, we seek to uncover the extent to which the Lisbon Agenda reform strategy actually deviates from the "embedded neoliberal" hegemonic order and socially thin market citizenship model of the Maastricht era (as examined in Chapter 3). Contrary to enthusiastic assessments outlined above, we argue that the form and content of EU integration in the Lisbon era does not mark a positive turning point for EU-level social citizenship, but instead remains firmly grounded within the framework of embedded neoliberalism (see van Apeldoorn 2008). Crucially, however, we are careful to emphasize that the Lisbon Agenda does not merely signify "more of the same" in the historical development of EU integration, especially as it pertains to the development of EU citizenship. We argue in particular that the Lisbon Agenda's espousal of a highly contradictory *neoliberal communitarian*[1] citizenship model that focuses almost solely on citizens' responsibilities or duties to make themselves employable (Bieling 2003), is above all an attempt to legitimate the further disembedding of the neoliberal project, and thus the further dismantling of social citizenship rights in line with what Bob Jessop (2002) calls "Schumpeterian Workfare Regimes" (see also Ryner 2002, 2008).[2] As an important component of our overall argument, we explain how this has been further intensified since the shift in early 2005 to a streamlined "growth and jobs" agenda under the Barroso Commission. This shift, and the contradictions it entails, is invariably bound up with a recent resurfacing of legitimacy crisis.

As far as the exposition of our argument is concerned, the chapter begins by tracing the Third Way's multilevel rise in the EU in the late-1990s as it first surfaced nationally and through intergovernmental dynamics of the European Council. The discussion then turns to analyze the Third Way's emergence in the supranational arena, first by way of its subtle influences on the Amsterdam Treaty in 1997 through to its pinnacle as the hegemonic ideological framework underpinning the Lisbon Agenda, the defining initiative of EU integration and governance under the Commission of Romano Prodi (1999–2004). It is during this period that we identify the initial emergence of neoliberal communitarianism within EU citizenship politics; building upon rather than diverging from the more one-dimensional "market citizenship" of the Maastricht era (see Chapter 3). While socially thin market citizenship emphasized foremost the labor mobility rights of European elites in the context of market deregulation, the discourse of neoliberal communitarianism under the Prodi Commission sought to render EU citizenship more compatible with the Lisbon Agenda's twin goals of economic competitiveness *and* social cohesion. As our analysis suggests, the Prodi Commission's dedication to a supposedly "balanced" approach between these two goals was based on ambiguous appeals to social citizenship, and concrete commitments to redefining the "social" away from the unconditional social rights of the welfare state toward a focus on citizens' responsibilities to make themselves "employable" and "adaptable" in the transition to a globalized knowledge-based economy (KBE). This move, though paying lip service to a "European Social Model" (ESM), not only follows embedded neoliberalism in subordinating the social to the supposed exigencies of global competitiveness, but also further disembeds it by placing the burden of socioeconomic restructuring on the shoulders of EU citizens (Ryner 2002).

We then turn our attention to the shift to a more "streamlined" Lisbon Agenda under the current Barroso Commission (2004–). In its narrow focus on "jobs and growth," the streamlined Lisbon Agenda represents a more explicit subordination of the social to a logic of competitiveness, and by extension a purer expression of neoliberal communitarianism putting more emphasis on the "active" dimensions of its citizenship model. It is in fact the Barroso Commission's streamlined Lisbon Agenda and accompanying citizenship model that approximates what transnational capital has been pushing for since the Lisbon Agenda was unveiled at the turn of the millennium. This leads us to identify a private/public pattern of authority at the heart of the neoliberal trajectories of the Lisbon Agenda. On the one hand, it finds civil society expression in the transnational capitalist cadre of business think tanks, such as the prolific ERT and the lesser-known Lisbon Council for European Competitiveness (LCEC). On the other hand, it finds institutional—and therefore hegemonic—expression in the policy machinations of the EU Commission. Finally, we conclude the chapter by further fleshing out what we see as the social contradictions of neoliberal communitarian citizenship, placing this within the context of resurfacing forms of resistance to the EU project (e.g. the French and Dutch rejections of the EU Constitution in 2005), and the EU's new campaign to "reconnect" with its citizens.

The Specter of Keynesianism?
The Social Democratic Challenge of the Late 1990s

Popular dissatisfaction with neoliberal orthodoxy in the EU in the late 1990s had given rise to a host of antagonisms and controversies around what constituted "realistic" and "sound" economic policy and its bearings on the social. As one commentator put it in seeking to capture the sentiment in the EU at the time: "A specter is haunting Europe—the specter of John Maynard Keynes" (Hedström 1998).[3] To be sure, from within the ranks of the EU's newly elected social democratic governments proposals and discussions now emerged which indicated that the long reign of a neoliberal policy consensus perhaps was on the verge of coming apart.

Oskar Lafontaine, Germany's minister of finance in the newly elected red-green coalition government, immediately took the European Central Bank (ECB) to task, challenging the rigidities imposed by the Maastricht convergence criterion of price stability, as well as calling for lower interest rates in order to stimulate the economy and reduce unemployment in the EU area. Italian prime minister Massimo d'Alema made a similar intervention, pleading for a relaxation of the restraints imposed on member states' budgetary policy. He thereby called into question yet another convergence criterion laid down in Maastricht and the Stability Pact (Wahl

2002: 46–7). Aiming to stave off the problems of wage and overall social dumping in the Union, Lafontaine also made a case for coordinating economic policy and for harmonizing social policy and taxation in the EU, trying to safeguard political space to maneuver that otherwise would be lost to the market and a monetarist ECB (Wahl 2002: 47; Svenning 2000: 124–7). "We Social Democrats," Lafontaine (1998: 74) contended,

> insist on the mistaken nature of neoliberalism's response to the increasing world-wide integration of trade—making nations participate in a competition to sink costs even lower. At root it signifies a farewell to politics, leaving it all up to the market. But Social Democrats insist that politics must be put back in its rightful place. Wage dumping, tax dumping and welfare dumping are not our response to the globalization of markets!

By and large, Lafontaine had an ally in the French prime minister, Lionel Jospin, whose platform, promising as it did to tackle head-on *la fracture sociale*, even resonated with some of the sentiments embraced by the movements behind the "winter of discontent." Taking up the Polanyian dictum of condoning a market economy while firmly opposing the development of a market society (for further elaboration on Karl Polanyi, see below), Jospin too presented himself as being convinced that neoliberalism had been a mistake and that the political space at both national and EU levels had to be expanded at the expense of the market and the orthodoxy of inflation control. For the purpose of better regulating and controlling the whims of global capitalism politically, Jospin tabled the idea of establishing an economic government for the EU, which, among other things, should be in charge of the harmonization of taxation and social policy in the Union (Svenning 2000: 20; Jospin 2000).

On the whole, however, it was the effective tackling of the member states' common problem of unemployment that the EU's incoming social democrats took on as their prime task and responsibility. These indications of a joint inclination to launch a concerted effort to confront joblessness in the Union, together with the fact that social democracy for the first time ever was able to style itself as "the party of Europe" (Moschonas 2002: 262), were soon to create a widespread sense that the prospects for a Social Europe had once again been invigorated with fresh blood. In addition, the social democrats had potential popular allies among the advancing social movements, including many labor unions, which since the mid-1990s had increasingly been gravitating toward the EU project as such, manifesting their discontent with neoliberal policies and calling for an EU with a strong social dimension.

Undoing the Challenge: The Rise of the Third Way

But hopes, as well as apprehensions, that the social democrats of the EU actually were prepared to challenge the neoliberal orthodoxy and set the Union on to a more socially progressive course were quickly dashed. Rhetoric apart, it is arguably questionable whether there were any real grounds for such hopes to start with. When the EU's confident social democratic leadership gathered in Malmö, Sweden, in 1997, for instance, many expectations could in fact be seen to have been nipped in the bud when Tony Blair decided to parade his neoliberal credentials, expressing an unconditional espousal of capitalist globalization and calling for further liberalization of labor markets in the EU (Panitch and Leys 2001: 275). According to Blair, it was now high time for social democracy to adapt to the "corporate culture," to realize that the "European Social Model" had failed the cause of "social cohesion," and, not least, to look to the American example for inspiration and guidance (Svenning 2000: 19).[4] At about the same time, in one of his first actions as prime minister, and despite campaign promises to the contrary, Jospin for his part went ahead and upheld, more or less unconditionally, the EU's Stability and Growth Pact (Moschonas 2002: 196–197). As *Business Week* reported jubilantly, it was not long before Jospin "begun injecting the concept of 'modernizing France' into his speeches" (Edmondson 1998), a change of tone that soon was translated into multiple privatization schemes and policy reshufflings favorable to business (see further Budgen 2002).

During the Brussels meeting of the Council of Ministers of Finance in 1998, moreover, Lafontaine and other dissenting social democrats received a firm telling-off from the ECB and the European Commission over their attempt to tamper with the stipulations laid down in Maastricht and the Stability Pact (Wahl 2002: 47). "Globalization," the Council declared, "requires economic reforms with the aim of creating a just and socially acceptable system," to which it added: "to achieve this, the economy must be made more effective, the market must rule, and the obstacles for free trade must be removed" (cited in Wahl 2002: 48). Lafontaine's (coerced) resignation in 1999 (Moschonas 2002: 269; Callinicos 1999: 93), which was warmly greeted in stock markets and Downing Street, as well as occasioning a surge in the euro (Wahl 2002; Ali 2000), not only underscored "the left's powerlessness to construct a social democratic Europe" in general, but also buried the prospects for "the neo-Keynesian project conclusively" (Moschonas 2002: 197). As Wahl (2002: 48) puts it, referring to Lafontaine's resignation: "the balance of power in Europe was made crystal clear. The social democratic project of creating a 'social Europe' from above had run aground." As such, the "Lafontaine affair" constituted "a moment of great symbolic import" (Moschonas 2002: 268n21). However, the import should not be seen as stemming from the shunning of any alleged radicalism on the part of Lafontaine. In fact, it was exactly the other way around. The significance of the moment, therefore, rather lay in the fact that Lafontaine could be framed as a political liability among his own for merely sticking with a set of very traditional social democratic policies and values. "In this sense," Moschonas (2002: 268n21) argues, "the 'Lafontaine affair' is a moment of assertion and confirmation of the identity of the new social democracy: Oskar Lafontaine was a potential destabilizing factor in a political family that has made macroeconomic stability its standard-bearer."

As far as relations with grass-roots movements were concerned, the message from the social democratic establishment was equally unambiguous. Hence, and despite initial signs of some receptiveness (Svenning 2000: 48–9; Swardson 1998), the conspicuous resurgence of activism from a motley crowd of old and new movements was soon to become a thorn in the side of the EU's (social democrats and) political establishment. Choosing the summits of the European Council as one of their main sites at which to voice criticism against a number of EU and member state policies, these gatherings soon degenerated into de facto police states in miniature. Here the EU's political leaderships barricaded themselves behind an unprecedented muster of police, while simultaneously unleashing some of the harshest and most extensive crackdowns ever witnessed in postwar western Europe (see Busch 1998; Panitch 2002). Taking advantage of the possibilities for incursions on civil liberties engendered by September 11, the Council of the EU decided in the spring of 2002 to incorporate future surveillance activity and crackdowns at EU summits and similar gatherings into "the Framework Decision on combating terrorism" (Council EU 2002a).

The European Commission Follows Suit

All in all, it was the "modernized" social democracy of the Third Way that emerged victorious from the late 1990s neo-Keynesian intermezzo. This was, of course, also facilitated by the fact that the Commission under Jacques Santer and, subsequently, Romano Prodi had positioned itself firmly within the camp of the "modernizers" (see Prodi 1999a, 1999b, 2000a, 2000b).

With an ever-growing accent on the need to combat unemployment and social exclusion in the EU, the influence of the Third Way would be initially felt in the Amsterdam Treaty which made this plain by incorporating a new title on employment, heralding the subsequent European Employment Strategy, which promised to "place employment and citizens' rights at the heart of the Union" (CEC 1997c: 1; Council EU 1997a). In addition, with the new British Labour government assuming office just prior to the Amsterdam summit, this resulted in the incorporation of the Social Protocol into the Amsterdam Treaty. Yet despite these and other new provisions in the social field, their actual substance showed few signs of altering the post-Maastricht trend of growing skepticism toward *thoroughgoing* and *harmonized* social policy measures at the EU level. As such, Dinan (1999: 429) argued at the time, the Amsterdam Treaty provided additional testimony to a continued "toning down of EU social policy." Introduced alongside the title on EMU rather than social policy, moreover, Amsterdam's title on employment effectively steered clear of traditional social democratic methods of fighting joblessness. This provided, Dinan wrote (1999: 429), "the [British] Labour government's acceptance of the social protocol was an easy way to repudiate the previous government's EU policy without endorsing a radical social policy agenda." What resulted from the Amsterdam Employment Title was thus, as Barnard and Deakin (1999: 359–60) explain, a lack of meaningful EU-level social policy response to the crisis of structural unemployment, and instead set its sights on promoting, for the first time in any systematic way, the citizen's *duty* to become "employable" and "adaptable" in the face of labor market flexibility.

The Lisbon Strategy and Third Way Hegemony under the Prodi Commission (1999–2004)

Although the nascent emergence of the Third Way in the post-Amsterdam EU did not give rise to a "radical social policy agenda," Dinan's assessment would, nonetheless, soon prove to have been somewhat premature. As it turned out, the years around the turn of the millennium in fact marked the beginning of new and unprecedented EU activity in the social field. With the Employment Title, the Employment Strategy, the Social Protocol, and Amsterdam's stated goal of combating "social exclusion" on board, then, it would not be long before the EU also launched a Social Policy Agenda (SPA). The agenda, drawn up by the Commission and adopted at the Nice European Council in 2000, was set to cover the time period 2000–5, whereupon a new was adopted for the period 2006–10.

The Third Way modernizers' decisive opportunity to "deliver the goods" on social policy in the EU political arena would come when the SPA was incorporated into the strategy devised at the Lisbon European

Council in 2000, which set out the lofty goal of transforming the EU into "the most competitive and dynamic knowledge-based economy in the world capable of sustainable economic growth with more and better jobs and greater social cohesion." Now adapted to a Union of twenty-seven members, the Lisbon Strategy, the Lisbon process, or the Lisbon Agenda as it is now commonly known stands out as the boldest move made by the EU since it embarked on monetary union in the 1990s. Given its overarching objective of putting the EU at the top of the world economy, and as seen in the immense flurry of activity that has followed in its wake, the Lisbon Strategy is unprecedentedly comprehensive and has left few policy areas unaffected. However, and notwithstanding its comprehensiveness, the Lisbon Strategy is also characterized by simplicity and straightforwardness, and so does its utmost to benefit from a set of clear goals and courses of action.

In many respects, the ambitiousness of the Lisbon Strategy's social and economic goals can be attributed to the optimism in the late-1990s and early-2000s surrounding the EU's transition to a knowledge-based economy, comprised of a new growth model based on Internet Communications Technology (ICT) (for an overview, see Boyer 2004), and the acceleration and deepening of financial market integration in the EU, which would "play an essential role in fuelling new ideas, supporting entrepreneurial culture and promoting access to and use of new technologies" (Lisbon European Council 2000). Thus taking cues from the successes of the ICT growth in certain areas of the U.S. (e.g. Silicon Valley), and the upswing in the American stock markets right before the turn of the millennium (Duménil and Lévy 2004: 64), many held faith that the EU could rival and overtake the more competitive economies of the U.S. and East Asia, while at the same time promoting "capitalism with a human face" underpinned by the values of the so-called European Social Model (ESM) (van der Pijl 2006). This sentiment is best captured by members of the Prodi Commission, who held that with the proposed Lisbon Strategy reforms, the EU was prepared to encounter the "quantum shift" resulting from increased globalization (Diamantopoulou 20000). Indeed, Commission President Prodi (2000c) even went as far as to associate the Lisbon Strategy with a new "renaissance for Europe." This optimistic tone was reinforced by the fact that the Lisbon Strategy garnered fairly broad-based support from social forces ranging from the ERT to the ETUC and social NGOs, who all embraced an encouraging blueprint for fairly balancing social and economic policies in the EU.

Coalescing around economic, employment, and social policies, and subsequently adding an environmental dimension, the Lisbon Strategy was set to operate in accordance with what we may term a three-stage rocket philosophy, whereby a growth-friendly economic policy—characterized by macroeconomic stability, competition promotion, wage restraints, and further liberalization—is said to generate more and better jobs[5] which, in turn, will spawn social inclusion, increase social cohesion, and combat social exclusion (see CEC 2003b: 12). On many occasions, however, this more or less linear causality or chain reaction is exchanged for, or complemented by, a vigorous emphasis on the need to set in motion a dynamic interaction, streamlining, and coordination between economic, employment, and social policies; this in order to engender innovative "policy mixes" and "virtuous circles." Of this the much-discussed Open Method of Coordination (OMC) forms an integral part, being instituted to provide the means to guide and move the "dynamic" policy process forward. Limited, at first, to EU employment policy (as a result of the Amsterdam Treaty), the OMC was later officialized, revised, and generalized at the Lisbon European Council, and from then on was set to cover a range of other policy areas, including social policy and immigration (see Chapter 5).

The OMC constitutes "a method of policy delivery," "an instrument improving EU governance" (CEC 2003a: 6) in politically tricky areas where supranational competence and harmonization have not been forthcoming. More specifically, the Open Method has "its core domain ... in precisely those areas of employment and social policy in which the European Union has not traditionally proven able to legislate under the Community method" (Wincott 2003: 296). Rather than through binding legislation and harmonization, then, which was the goal during much of the Delors era, policy delivery under the OMC is to be procured through an intricate ensemble of jointly agreed commitments, objectives, policy guidelines, targets, and indicators, which, in turn, are to be continuously developed and refined in a process of mutual learning, benchmarking, peer group evaluation, exchange of good practices, partnerships, and so on. In this "iterative" procedure of "'soft law' governance" (Trubek and Mosher 2003), the European Council occupies a principal position (Chalmers and Lodge 2003), while the Commission assumes the function of overseer, hence performing "a key coordinating and monitoring role" (Wincott 2003: 296). The Commission keeps track of the activities of the various "stakeholders"; it monitors measures adopted by the member states with regard to the Lisbon goals, points to progress made and objectives not met concerning implementation; it provides updates on the economic, employment, and social situation in the EU and from there goes on to address new challenges and necessary action. The Commission then brings this together in a massive number of recurrent recommendations, general as well as country-specific policy guidelines, annual reports, reviews, and scoreboards on implementation.

In trying to assess the merits of the OMC, it is clear that much of the initial enthusiasm directed toward the Lisbon Strategy was reflective of what many saw as the great promise of this new mode of governance. As Martin Rhodes argued in the immediate aftermath of the Lisbon European Council meeting, the OMC's innovative refining of "soft law" mechanisms in areas of social policy appeared to offer a balanced compromise between "EU intervention via directives and the alternative (given the long history of blockages in the Council) of leaving policy instruments in the hands of the member states"; hence his hinting that Lisbon could potentially mark a "Maastricht for Social Europe" (Rhodes 2000: 2–7). In a similar vein, Zeitlin (2003: 5) argues that "[b]y systematically and continuously obliging the Member States to pool information, compare themselves to one another, and reassess current policies in light of their relative performance, the OMC appears to be a highly promising mechanism for promoting crossnational deliberation and experimental learning across the European Union." While this enthusiastic view largely tallies with the one nurtured by the Commission and other participant actors, Zeitlin (2003: 6) adds a proviso as to how the OMC will operate, more precisely, and how effective it really can be short of any powers of enforcement.

This problematic is also taken up by Wincott (2003: 297), who argues that since "the OMC does not impose substantial sanctions on states that fail to achieve the targets set by the common policy, this might mean that the OMC amounts to little more than a 'merely' symbolic policy or sloganeering." But instead of leaving things there, and getting bogged down in meticulous descriptions of the procedures surrounding the OMC, or, for that matter, in attempts at figuring out methods to make the OMC function as intended—which preoccupy so many of the scholarly interventions in the field—Wincott also touches on some of the broad political and ideological implications of the OMC. In a general assessment, he argues that "the OMC could once again move 'Europe' in the direction of an 'Anglo-Saxon' policy regime" and thus "be part of a process of Americanization, facilitating US style workfare" (Wincott 2003: 297, 299). This is not to exclude the possibility that the OMC could engender alternative policy paths or, for that matter, simply not engender very much to speak of at all. Most importantly, however, and as the significance that the British government attributed to the OMC and its considerable influence on the shaping of the Lisbon Strategy serve to underscore, Wincott's account demonstrates that the OMC's impact upon employment and welfare policies in the EU cannot be reduced to a question primarily about technocratic efficacy but needs to be analyzed as contingent on the political and ideological context in which it is set to operate.

In an edifying piece on the Open Method of Coordination, Chalmers and Lodge (2003) pick up on this critical yet infrequently undertaken task. When viewed "as a strategy for reincarnation of the European Welfare State," they argue, the "OMC is subservient to the ideologies, path-dependencies and structures of Economic and Monetary Union, as institutionalised in the Broad Economic Policy Guidelines (BEPG)." This provided, the Open Method "is not a coherent strategy, for all its rhetoric, but a tactical response with limited manoeuvre to the new political economy of the Euro-zone" (Chalmers and Lodge 2003: 2). A look at the content of the BEPG from 2002, for instance, reveals proclamations derived from Third Way rhetoric—emphasizing yet again the necessity to retain and nurture "a culture of entrepreneurship," "a culture of stability," and "a culture of enterprise" (CEC 2002b: 6, 19)—establishing "paid work" as a panacea for a number of social and economic ills in the Union (CEC 2002b: 9). In line with this, the Commission called upon the member states to do more to "make work pay and encourage the search for jobs." Member states were advised to devote further attention to "incentive effects of benefit schemes, including conditionality of benefits, eligibility, duration" and the like; all for the purpose of making "the systems more employment friendly" (CEC 2002b: 20, 16, see also 2003b). In this context Sweden was reprimanded by the Commission for its "very high tax burden combined with relatively generous benefit schemes," since these are said to "reduce the incentives to work," while Britain received praise for having established one of the "best-performing" labor markets in the EU (CEC 2002b: 63, 65). With reference to the labor market in the EU, moreover, the Commission lauded the fact that recent years had seen "a greater use of temporary and part-time contracts": a development that "has contributed to making labour markets more flexible and inclusive" (CEC 2002b: 14). This mantra is repeated in the BEPG for the 2003–2005 period. Here it was emphasized that Europe needs a "more flexible economy," which means that Europeans partly have to adapt to U.S. standards and work more hours, retire later and receive "greater opportunities for part-time work and flexible working hours" (CEC 2003b: 3, 6).

By way of elucidating the preeminence of the BEPG, Chalmers and Lodge (2003: 5) also point to the fact that, although these emanate from a process that share features with the OMC, they are not grounded, as is largely the case with the social objectives and employment guidelines, in the OMC and Lisbon, but rather in Maastricht and the Growth and Stability Pact. This imbalance is also reflected in the fact that the EU's employment policy and the accompanying employment guidelines—that is, the European Employment Strategy (EES)—"are required to be compatible with the BEPG" (Chalmers and Lodge 2003: 6). In a 2003 Council decision "on guidelines for the employment policies of the Member States," this stipulation is repeated time and again. "In addition to the employment guidelines," the Council (2003a: 16) underlines, "Member States should fully implement the broad economic policy guidelines and ensure that action is fully consistent with the maintenance of sound public finances and macroeconomic stability." Since the EES is explicitly prevented from intervening in key areas for employment, such as monetary, fiscal, and wage policy, it has developed "largely as a supply-side strategy focusing on altering structural impediments to unemployment" (Trubek and Mosher 2003: 41). For the most part, this supply-side strategy has been preoccupied with reforms that would make social and welfare policies in the EU more "employment-friendly" and conducive to job creation; something that is evidenced most forcefully in the EU's Social Policy Agenda (SPA).

The Social Policy Agenda and the "Modernization of the European Social Model"

To begin with, and reflecting the aforementioned supply-side strategy on employment, when one surveys the SPA one can be in no doubt that it is largely modeled on the EU's Employment Strategy. When the Commission (2000a: 2) first outlined the SPA's three main fields of action in 2000, employment, not social policy, was at the top of the list. Characteristically enough, moreover, it is the goals of the EES that head the SPA's catalogue of "Objectives and actions"; thus, they call for macroeconomic stability, highlight the need to "remove all remaining barriers to the development of the services sector," and attach great weight to the promotion of "employability," "adaptability," "entrepreneurship," and "equal opportunities" (CEC 2000a: 15–6). Likewise, in its *Mid-term Review of the Social Policy Agenda,* the Commission (2003a: 3) defines the SPA as "the roadmap for employment and social policy." The almost undivided attention given to employment and the next to magical qualities assigned to "paid work" recur in the Commission's OMC-driven *Social inclusion strategy,* which makes up a key component of the SPA. Here, the Commission (2002c) defines the OMC on *Social Inclusion* as a complement to the Employment Strategy and whose primary challenges and objectives are "participation in employment" and "employability." Similarly, in a communication with the illuminating title *Modernising Social Protection for More and Better Jobs: a comprehensive approach contributing to making work pay,* the Commission declares that "[i]ncreasing participation in employment, particularly among most disadvantaged people, is also seen as the main safeguard against drifting into poverty and social exclusion" and, further, that "the best safeguard against social exclusion is a job as it was stated in the Lisbon conclusions" (CEC 2003c: 3).

But if the SPA is a "roadmap" for employment, the Commission (CEC 2004b: 3) also points out that "[t]he social policy agenda is the EU's roadmap for modernising and improving the European social model." Indeed, "[a]t the heart of the Agenda is the modernisation of the European social model" (CEC 2000a: 2). Since the launching of the Lisbon reform agenda, the called-for "modernization" of the European Social Model (ESM) stands out as one of *the* most prominent watchwords in EU policy discourse. As spelled out in the Lisbon Strategy, the modernization of the ESM is set to facilitate the "dynamic interaction of economic, employment and social policy." Moreover, since it is alleged that "[m]ore and better employment in a dynamic and competitive economy strengthens social cohesion," the modernization of the ESM "is required to underpin economic dynamism and pursue employment generating reforms" (CEC 2000a: 2, 7, see also 2004d).

It is also important to note that the modernization of the ESM taking place within the SPA does not entail an attempt to harmonize the welfare systems of the member states. Given the widespread reluctance to contemplate it, the insufficient EU competence and, not least, the significant (institutional) differences that exist between the various social systems in the EU—differences that have widened even further with eastern enlargement (see CEC 2004c: 21–2)—such harmonization is deemed unfeasible for the foreseeable future. Rather than harmonization, a modernized ESM is to emerge from a set of commonly agreed upon objectives, benchmarks, scoreboards, and indicators prepared within the framework of the OMC. Put differently, "it is no longer necessary to seek to harmonize the 'black box' of internal institutional arrangements, but instead, to articulate several main objectives at the European level, to be reached by each Member State" (de la Porte 2002: 290). What this means is that the EU's social model will thereby be embodied in and defined "by its performance rather than by its intrinsic qualities" (de la Porte 2002: 290). From the perspective of the Commission, then, social policy needs to be approached, first and foremost, as "a productive factor," its objectives firmly anchored "in the context of the internal market and the single currency," and always "sufficiently flexible" to face up to new challenges (CEC 2004b: 22, 2000b: 7).

Given its close reliance on performance, productivity and flexibility, thereby subjecting the ESM to an ongoing process of modification, the modernized ESM is not easily identified. But even if it proves difficult to present a lucid picture of what the ESM amounts to today, we can still provide an assessment based on what it *does not*, indeed *cannot*, amount to under present circumstances. Thus, while EU policy documents abound with general statements embracing a modernized ESM that is conducive to "a high level of social protection" and "an appropriate balance between flexibility and security," they appear rather noncommittal when juxtaposed to the out-and-out concurrence of the modernization process with the all-pervading economic policy guidelines that have been surveyed here. In the light of such acquiescence, there is little gainsaying de la Porte and Pochet's (2002: 292, italics in original) contention that the EU's social model is taking shape "in the shadow of an economic and monetary model that continues to constitute the *idée-force* of European integration." Due to these obvious limitations, "[c]ertain options in welfare politics are simply not open" (Chalmers and Lodge 2003: 10).

The Lisbon Agenda as Embedded Neoliberalism

In all, the Lisbon reform agenda represents a further alteration of the approach to the welfare state on the part of the EU, one that is almost exclusively preoccupied with growth and competitiveness while effectively steering clear of any serious attention to social citizenship entitlements. Here, economic policy encroaches upon social policy by way of seeking to extricate, or immunize, itself from those aspects of welfare policy that are deemed to impinge on growth, competitiveness, employability, and so on. To borrow from Chalmers and Lodge (2003: 10), this encroachment/extrication nexus now operating in the EU could also be likened to "a colonisation of the Welfare State by the economic policy-making process."

Despite such "colonization" and the patently neoliberal nucleus of the Lisbon process, we should not overlook the continual divergence of opinion over the actual meaning and scope of the endeavor to "modernize the European Social Model" under the Prodi Commission. At the EU level such contestation, albeit sotto voce and hardly ever made explicit, can be discerned between, for instance, the different Directorates General, and it shines out from various reports commissioned by the EU. A good illustration of the latter is found by juxtaposing the reports drawn up under the Prodi Commission by the Employment Taskforce (2003) and the High Level Group (on the future of social policy in an enlarged European Union) (2004).

While both reports represent a line of policy that is neoliberal at its core, they nonetheless emphasize quite different problems and potential hazards on the Union's journey to growth, competitiveness, employment, and social inclusion. Whereas the Employment Taskforce, whose report was candidly titled *Jobs, Jobs, Jobs*, launches a campaign for far-reaching flexibility, sizeable reductions of labor costs, hiring and firing, and emulation of the U.S., the High Level Group, although committed to "the concept that individual workers should show more responsibility" (2004: 29), proceeds more cautiously, recommending inter alia that social inclusion "must be developed as policy in itself" (2004: 28). Dissatisfied with the notion that employment somehow constitutes a universal remedy against social exclusion and poverty, the High Level Group also highlights the problem of the "working poor." Notwithstanding the Employment Taskforce's aggressive neoliberal approach, it is also important to note that its report, which was warmly praised by the Commission, also assigns a highly central role to governments, to public authorities and, in particular, to the "social partners":

> Governments need to ensure that educational attainment levels are improved and, as a matter of priority, all stakeholders must be mobilised to make lifelong learning a reality. The Taskforce urges each Member State to devise ambitious policies to raise educational levels and ensure greater participation in training throughout working life. (Employment Taskforce 2003: 10)

It is also noteworthy that the taskforce, for all its enthusiastically neoliberal counseling, still clings to a vague notion of social security, said to consist of "decent pay, access to lifelong learning, working conditions, protection against discrimination or unfair dismissal, support in case of job loss and the right to transfer acquired social rights when moving jobs" (Employment Taskforce 2003: 28).

The wavering disposition on the part of the Lisbon process could be seen as symptomatic of the difficulties inherent in the attempt to persuade a European public of the unmistakable merits of neoliberalism. The retention of rhetoric in defence of social protection, social cohesion and the ESM may then be construed as a strategy of appeasement—particularly directed toward organized labor—and a necessary move to generate enough consent around the Lisbon reforms. This seems, at least in part, to be borne out when considered in the light of Lisbon's heavy emphasis on the need to rally all "stakeholders" (and the "social partners" are often held up as tipping the scale) and to persuade European citizens that the necessary reforms are in line with their best interests.

Many features of the Lisbon reform agenda under the Prodi Commission are therefore captured well by the concept of embedded neoliberalism (see Chapter 3). The emphasis on a the crucial role played by the social partners testifies to this, as do the repeated calls for apt policies on cohesion, lifelong learning, training, education, R&D, anti-discrimination, gender equality, integration of immigrants, "active labor market measures," regional development and so on. Another case in point is the Commission's promotion of "corporate social responsibility," whereby corporations are encouraged to "integrate social and environmental concerns into their business operations" (CEC 2002c: 5). The embedded character of Lisbon's neoliberalism is also observable in its forthrightness about the key role to be played by the state, governments, and public authorities; something that clarifies the limits of what markets and corporations can do on their own. From the standpoint of the aforementioned Employment Taskforce, and regardless of its aggressive neoliberal advocacy, there is thus no compromise involved in its calls upon governments to invest heavily in human capital, education, training, and the updating of skills. Rather, and in order to remedy such problems as "[t]he vicious circle of low investment by business in training" (Employment Taskforce 2003: 10), competitiveness and growth are said to depend on such state intervention (see also CEC 2004d).

On one reading, then, Lisbon could be interpreted as based on an understanding that neoliberal restructuring in the EU should not be allowed to progress beyond certain limits. Here, a drive to remake the EU in the image of the U.S. would be out of bounds, not only because it is deemed politically unfeasible—or socially unacceptable?—but also, and perhaps more important, because such a transformation might be seen as unnecessary and even to be detrimental to growth and competitiveness in the EU area. Rather than being reducible to vague moral commitments motivated by nostalgia for the *European* Social Model, Lisbon envisages retaining some facets of welfare policy as a structural precondition for enhancing the EU's global competitiveness. A certain amount of welfare policy is thus to be maintained, indeed needs to be maintained, provided that the bulk of it serves the competitive advantage of European capital, subsequently producing a virtuous circle of more jobs and enhanced social inclusion. In a nutshell, arguably, this is how the Lisbon agenda endeavors to convert welfare policy into "a productive factor": one that upholds budgetary discipline, meets capital's demand for flexibility and, not least, ensures a steady flow of (re)skilled labor through investment in publicly subsidized training and education programs. This seems to be how a modernized yet "uniquely" *European* Social Model is set to provide the EU with an equally unique competitive edge in its quest to emerge as "the most competitive and dynamic knowledge-based economy in the world." In this sense, when Lisbon calls on the state, governments, public authorities, the "social partners," and welfare policy to perform certain tasks and duties, these are framed as indispensable primarily to the extent that they are targeted at growth and competitiveness.

Interpreted as such, the development that culminates in the Prodi Commission's steering of the Lisbon process can now be further qualified as representing a *limited form* of embedded neoliberalism (van Apeldoorn 2003: 160). As seen above, this means, simply, that while Lisbon necessitates (welfare) state intervention, the active participation of labor and a certain degree of social consensus, these elements are, in the final analysis, nonetheless "subordinated to the overriding objective of neoliberal competitiveness" (van Apeldoorn 2003: 160). Again, this reflects the structural imbalances in the strategy process: the imbalance between "a relatively incoherent set of welfare targets and a strong neoliberal policy dynamic" (Chalmers and Lodge 2003: 11).

Edging Toward Neoliberal Communitarian Citizenship

It is important to assess the ideological underpinnings of European integration during the Lisbon era, and from there to go on to broach the types of possibilities and restraints that these have imposed on the current trajectory of the EU. At the same time, we should not let such assessments conjure up a functionalist image of European integration as fettered by an unalterable logic. Though the Lisbon Strategy, with its attendant Third Way ideological underpinnings, is largely continuous with the embedded neoliberal project of the extended relaunch, this should not be misconstrued as an inevitable compromise, some form of equilibrium, between neoliberals and welfare state proponents that cannot be pushed in any other direction.

As indicated earlier in this chapter, with the increasingly conspicuous discontent toward neoliberal austerity that emerged in the EU during the 1990s, "[s]omething new [was] added to the struggle between ideological projects concerning the European political economy: a contest for endorsement by the public" (Hooghe and Marks 1999: 97). As far as the Lisbon Strategy is concerned, the significance of this novel public fact cannot be overstated. In illustrating this problematic, the assessment by the aforementioned Employment Taskforce (2003: 10)—whose "policy messages are shared by the Commission and the Council" (CEC 2004a: 3)—is symptomatic:

> To succeed [with the Lisbon reform agenda], it is essential that governments build up reform partnerships, by mobilising the support and participation of the various stakeholders, and securing public conviction in the need for reforms. Also, more efforts should be made to demonstrate to the general public why reform is necessary and why it is in the interest and advantage of all.

Once again, as with the initial relaunch of the integration process a decade earlier (see Chapter 3), EU citizenship would come to the fore as the key battleground through which this contest for endorsement by the public would be played out. Yet, as intensifying resistance during the extended relaunch made clear, embedded neoliberalism backed by a market citizenship model as its primary means to legitimacy was no longer a stable arrangement. With continued reliance on such a model a risky tactic at best, how was the EU to convince its citizens about the supposed necessity of Lisbon reforms, especially if the alternative of traditional Marshallian citizenship stood in direct contradiction to the strategy's subordination of social policy to exigencies of neoliberal competitiveness? In a statement that is indicative of the milieu of EU governance in the early 2000s, the European Roundtable of Industrialists (ERT) even went so far as to suggest that the EU would require "new Europeans" to match the "new European economy" envisaged in the Lisbon Strategy. Drawing from the analysis above, what then does being a "new European" entail? We suggest that addressing this question requires delving a step further into the Lisbon Strategy's Third Way ideology, revealing how it relies on the institution of citizenship to smoothen the process of socioeconomic restructuring.

In general terms, proponents of the Third Way advocate what can best be described as a neoliberal communitarian citizenship model, based on a fusion of neoliberal market citizenship with a communitarian element that attempts to countervail the most harmful effects of neoliberal deregulation and restructuring not by reinvigorating the social rights of the Keynesian welfare national state but through attempting to "activate the state" in strengthening (private) community networks (Bieling 2003: 53). Neoliberal communitarian citizenship therefore signifies a movement away from "unconditional social citizenship entitlements" (Ryner 2002: 15) toward an emphasis on providing Schumpeterian-style labor market policies that offer opportunities for skill upgrading and lifelong learning so that citizens will be "willing to *accept more public duties and social responsibilities*" (Bieling 2003: 65, emphasis in original). The citizens' role is thus contained within the mantra of "no rights without responsibilities," as opposed to the unconditional social citizenship entitlements of traditional social democracy which advocates "positive welfare intervention by a 'social investment state'" (Ryner 2002: 15). Arguing that "the relationship between individual rights and responsibilities was thrown out of balance from the late 1960s onwards," advocates of neoliberal communitarianism suggest that a situation of "moral hazard" has arisen among EU citizens, and that problems of social instability can be solved by fostering a society which gives more responsibilities and duties to individual citizens (Bieling 2003: 63, 65).

It is within such an ideological framework that, as van Apeldoorn (2003b: 114) notes, "'flexibility' and 'adaptability' on the part of the workforce have ... come to be seen as the panacea for Europe's unemployment problem." Unemployment is as a result regarded within neoliberal communitarian citizenship as "a moral problem of the individual who is unemployed" (Ryner 2002: 10), and who therefore has a personal responsibility "to make sure they qualify for employment (whatever the changes in the structure of the labour market)" (Overbeek 2003: 27). This view contrasts with a more social democratic (and Keynesian) view of unemployment as a societal problem that can be managed through economic intervention (Overbeek 2003; see also Albo 1994).

This type of citizenship discourse is rampant within the Lisbon Strategy policy documents of the Prodi Commission, where it is constantly argued that "a job is often the best protection against exclusion," and the only politically feasible option for securing social cohesion in light of the supposed exigencies of neoliberal global competitiveness (CEC 2002d: 12). Thus citizenship rights are given credence only to the extent that they equip citizens to take on their responsibilities to make themselves employable (e.g. via job training, skill development, lifelong learning). In a speech to the European Banking Congress in 2000, Commission President Prodi (2000d) expresses this view of citizen rights as he discusses the significance of Lisbon and the knowledge-based economy as they relate to European citizens:

> [The Lisbon Strategy] means educating our young people for the digital age, getting our schools and universities on line. It means training and retraining our workforce, giving them new skills for the new economy, filling thousands of IT job vacancies. It means cutting red tape for entrepreneurs, and giving bright young business people ready access to venture capital.

When gauging the overall significance of the Lisbon Strategy's emergent neoliberal communitarian citizenship model under the Prodi Commission, it is important to keep in mind that its narrow emphasis on labor market flexibility and citizen responsibilities at the expense of universally guaranteed social rights was intended not merely as a solution to the EU's widespread unemployment problem. Since increased labor market participation was also in turn narrowly regarded as the sole guarantor of social cohesion, it follows that increasing citizen responsibilities was to serve as the key solution to the contradictions between capital accumulation and social welfare that feature so prominently in Third Way ideology in general and in the Lisbon Strategy in particular. In other words "flexibility" and "adaptability" on behalf of the workforce also became *the* primary way to think about social policy. However, the "social" within social policy is no longer defined, as it had been in advanced industrial societies throughout the twentieth century, as an outcome of social struggles between capital and labor, but is instead viewed in individualistic terms, with the onus for reform falling on the shoulders of properly trained and educated citizens no longer reliant on the state to guarantee social cohesion.

Finally, it should be stressed that the historical movement from the market citizenship toward a neoliberal communitarian one was not abrupt and seamless. Still reeling from the effects of social-democratic infighting and the doubts raised by the traditionalist camp about the sustainability of neoliberal restructuring, the Prodi Commission was somewhat hesitant about advocating paid work as the exclusive guarantor of social cohesion. As a result, the Commission's embrace of labor market flexibility is tempered with constant, yet vague, pronouncements that "people need to be able to plan their lives, and should not be the victims of shock redundancy announcements" (Prodi 2000c). As was suggested in our analysis of the EU's Social Policy Agenda (SPA), this involves minimalist commitments to market-correcting social rights, yet only insofar as they are portrayed as "productive" or "positive economic" factors that mitigate against the worst social effects of socioeconomic restructuring (CEC 2003d; Diamantopoulou 2003).

On the one hand, these views on citizenship rights are consistent with our analysis of the Lisbon Strategy, which has revealed how Third Way ideology's concerns for social cohesion become incorporated into and ultimately subordinated to the imperatives of neoliberal competitiveness. On the other hand, if nothing else, these concerns also demonstrate reluctance on behalf of the Prodi Commission to commit itself too openly to a narrow workfare strategy. Perhaps even more so than a narrow market based citizenship model, this renders the neoliberal communitarian citizenship highly compatible with the EU's broader embedded neoliberal hegemonic project as it emerged during the extended relaunch and as it was fortified by the Prodi Commission through the auspices of the Lisbon Strategy. What remains to be analyzed is whether or not this compatibility between EU citizenship and the integration project forged under the Lisbon Strategy has steered the EU onto a stable, sustainable path. Has the "active" neoliberal communitarian citizenship model, committed to fostering citizen responsibilities while appealing rhetorically to social rights, held sway, and if so, will it do so in the long run? Alternatively, has this rhetoric been abandoned in favor of a more purely workfare citizenship model, or finally translated into political action in the form of EU social rights? An analysis of the Lisbon Strategy's evolution under the Barroso Commission (2004–) provides necessary insight into these questions.

Streamlining Lisbon: Jobs and Growth under the Barroso Commission (2004–)

In early 2005 the newly appointed Commission under José Manuel Barroso, acting in unison with member states in the conclusions made at the Spring European Council in Brussels, presented a plan to "relaunch" the Lisbon Strategy in a streamlined form focused on raising employment rates and boosting economic growth. The imperative for this revision was attributed to a myriad of factors: the September 11 terrorist attacks in the U.S., the challenges of eastward enlargement, the dot-com bubble burst, the general economic downturn in the Euro zone, as well as to the shortcomings of the previous Prodi Commission in taking the necessary steps to reform. Indeed, by the end of the Prodi Commission's tenure, even President Prodi himself was forced to admit that the Lisbon Strategy had been a "failure" (Barber and Parker 2004).

Although it was insisted that this relaunched focus on growth and jobs did not mean that the EU was abandoning its commitment to social cohesion and the ESM, the plan proved to be highly controversial and seemed to confirm suspicions of the newly appointed Commission, especially President Barroso, as too "business friendly" and bent of shifting the EU to the right (*Irish Times* 2004). More specifically, many observers regarded the move toward "jobs and growth" (via increasing emphasis on deregulation, privatization, and flexibility) as a means to strengthen the EU's neoliberal orientation at the expense of degrading the already weak "social dimension" (Buck 2005). This view was not easily quelled by the remarks of President Barroso who, already known for his hard-nosed neoliberal politics in his former role as Portuguese prime minister, declared that "for business, we need to roll out the red carpet" (cited in Eaglesham and Parker 2006). In what has proven to be perhaps the most controversial statement of his tenure thus far, President Barroso (2005e), in a speech to the EU parliament, made plain his views of the relaunch and its role in aiding the EU's "sickened" economy by equating the three Lisbon Strategy goals to his three children:

> It is as if I have three children—the economy, our social agenda, and the environment. Like any modern father—if one of my children is sick, I am ready to drop everything and focus on him until he is back to health. That is normal and responsible. But that does not mean I love the others any less!

Though such controversial statements have not been repeated in such a direct manner, a new sense of urgency, and indeed crisis, marks the turning point of the Barroso Commission's streamlined focus on growth and jobs; a shift that contrasts starkly with the initial optimism surrounding the EU's prospects in the "age of globalization" under the Prodi Commission.

Acting upon recommendations made by another EU-commissioned High Level Group—this time led by former Dutch prime minister Wim Kok to carry out an independent mid-term review of the Lisbon Strategy—the Commission claimed that in light of the EU's failures to move any closer toward reaching its Lisbon Strategy goals and to adapt to ever increasing competition, demographic challenges from an ageing population and slow growth, a shift in focus was needed to make the strategy relevant under changed circumstances. Indeed as the High Level Group made clear in its Lisbon review, "time is running out," and in light of the "new economic situation" that has developed in the EU since the Lisbon Strategy was launched in 2000, the EU needs to take drastic measures to update the Lisbon Strategy in response to current pressures (High Level Group chaired by Wim Kok 2004: 6).

The shift to growth and jobs has therefore involved further reinforcement and more explicit acceptance of the argument that higher employment and economic growth in and of themselves secure social protection and inclusion. This shift has two main interrelated implications for EU citizenship. First, we find an increased emphasis on the active dimensions of neoliberal communitarian citizenship, as the EU tries once again to rally public support for restructuring. In spearheading the streamlining, the High Level Group states quite clearly, and in somewhat paternalistic terms, how the EU's citizens' role needs to be rethought with Lisbon's relaunch:

> The need for reform has to be explained especially to citizens who are not always aware of the urgency and scale of the situation. "Competitiveness" is not just some dry economic indicator that is often unintelligible to the man in the street; rather, it provides a diagnosis of the state of economic health of a country or a region. In the present circumstances, the clear message must be: if we want to preserve and improve our social model we have to adapt it: it is not too late to change. In any event the status quo is not an option. Engaging and involving citizens in the process has two mutually reinforcing attractions: it in effect seeks public support by giving people elements for debate and it leverages that support to put pressure on governments to pursue these goals. (High Level Group chaired by Wim Kok 2004: 44)

The Barroso Commission, for its part, recognizes that the EU has "failed to mobilise support around the idea of what Europe can be" (Barroso 2005b), and addresses these criticisms in its documents and speeches related to the shift to growth and jobs. There is therefore a constant effort on behalf of the Commission to make citizens active participants in the Lisbon Agenda reforms, with the success of these reforms seen as hinging on the cultivation of "a real sense of ownership" (Barroso 2005c) toward the Lisbon goals so that citizens feel they have a "stake in the success of these reforms" (Barroso 2005a). The failure of Lisbon to this point is at least partly attributed to the Prodi Commission for falling short in actively involving EU citizens in the tasks of socioeconomic restructuring.

The second implication for EU citizenship of the shift to jobs and growth has been a more transparent subordination of the Lisbon Agenda's social goals to the supposed demands of neoliberal competitiveness. This is based on the argument that what the EU needs most of all is "a dynamic economy to fuel our wider social and environmental ambitions" (CEC 2005a: 4):

> Growth is a necessary condition for effective solidarity. Without growth, without a dynamic economy, there will be no sustainable development, no future pensions and no response to the pressures on our quality of life. (Barroso 2005a)

Bound up with the Barroso Commission's more open bias toward neoliberal competitiveness is a more refined position on the role played by social rights within the streamlined Lisbon Strategy; a subtle change of position that is best explained through the inclusion of social rights discourses within the latest "buzz concept" of EU policy making and governance: "flexicurity." While use of the term "workfare" was largely off bounds due to its politically risky associations with welfare state restructuring in the US, the Commission instead turned to "flexicurity," which seeks to combine labor market flexibility with job security, in order to render social and employment policy compatible with neoliberal competitiveness. The bundle of labor market flexibility and job security seems contradictory at first glance, and it would be if job security was defined in the traditional sense as guaranteed stable or long-term employment with a single firm or, in the case of redundancy, unconditional unemployment insurance provided by the welfare state. But, instead, what the Commission means by flexicurity is a combination of labor market flexibility (read "precariousness") together with a pledge to equip citizens with the necessary skills so that they can move from one job to another "in times of accelerating economic change" (CEC 2007a: 8).

Much like the Prodi Commission, the streamlined jobs and growth approach is still vague on the role of social rights within the Lisbon Strategy, but is clear that they should not go beyond temporarily assisting recently and unexpectedly unemployed workers in their search for new jobs. The provisions laid down for employment and social cohesion in the European Social Fund and the European Globalization Fund are thus focused on worker training and lifelong learning, confirming the EU belief that unemployment is foremost an individual, rather than structural, problem. As a result, the EU is thus tasked with the responsibility of providing an adequate supply of jobs to its citizens, and "maintaining a worker's ability to find a job" (Špidla 2005). Citizen rights become limited to the right to obtain more skills and better training and education, so that "workers and enterprises" alike "become more adaptable and labour markets more flexible" (Barroso 2005d). As the EU Commissioner in charge of Employment, Social Affairs and Equal Opportunities, Vladimir Špidla, puts it:

> The impact of changes can be limited by sustained investment in developing workers' skills, thereby enabling them to cope with change: a well-trained worker is better able to find a new job in the wake of *unavoidable* restructuring. (Špidla 2005; our emphasis)

Once again claiming to find the proper balance between rights and responsibilities, the "flexicurity" approach to social cohesion espoused in the streamlined Lisbon Agenda closely resembles the Third Way and its neoliberal communitarian citizenship model. Emerging initially under the Prodi Commission, neoliberal communitarianism has thus been firmly solidified as the dominant framework for EU citizenship under the Barroso Commission. This was achieved by promoting more explicitly the active engagement of citizens in Lisbon restructuring, while in turn removing some of the ambiguity surrounding social citizenship by casting social rights exclusively under the guise of labor market inclusion. When it comes to EU citizenship, the flexicurity approach of the streamlined Lisbon Agenda is more appropriately defined as a combination of labor market flexibility and citizen flexibility: the "security" element of "flexicurity" is simply reliant upon, and therefore impossible without, citizens taking responsibilities to adapt themselves to changing labor market conditions.

Neoliberal Communitarian Citizenship: At the Behest of Transnational Capital

It comes as no secret, nor conspiracy, that much of the substance of the Lisbon Strategy has been built directly upon the recommendations of the ERT's Competitiveness Advisory Group (van der Pijl 2006: 34–5). Together with other elements of transnational capital operating within what Kees van der Pijl (1998: Ch. 5) calls the cadre class (e.g. Lisbon Council for European Competitiveness (LCEC) and the World Economic Forum's Lisbon Review), the ERT has been front and center in lobbying EU institutions to its own particular vision of what the Lisbon Strategy reforms should entail. As one document tracking the chairmanship of Morris Tabaksblat exclaimed, the ERT (2005: 74) found it "very satisfying" to see that much of its lobbying efforts for structural reforms to make the EU more competitive in the global economy had been reflected in the Presidency Conclusions of the Lisbon European Council in 2000. Yet, it was the streamlining of the strategy under the Barroso Commission which was most enthusiastically embraced by the ERT and other business lobbies as the answer to the demands that they had been pushing for since the strategy's unveiling a half a decade earlier. Paul Hofheinz (2005), president of the LCEC, even went as far as to label critics who argued that Lisbon's relaunch would further jeopardize European welfare states as "dangerous demagogues" who make uninformed assumptions that "efforts to improve the economy will lead to a less social Europe."

At the center of the ideological similarities between transnational capital and the Barroso Commission is a "logic of no alternative" (Hay and Watson 2003) that regards the restructuring proposed within the Lisbon Strategy as the only effective response to a crisis induced by "globalization"; an inevitable and agent-less external economic constraint that limits the scope for EU policy making:

> The future prosperity of Europe is coming under enormous strain. Unless urgent action is taken on long awaited and long overdue structural reforms, Europe risks paying a heavy price in terms of future economic growth, job creation and its ability to compete successfully in global markets. (ERT 2003: 1–2)

> At the beginning of the 21st century, as we move from the industrial age to a networked, knowledge-based economy, our current Social Model is in desperate need of modernization. At a time when flexibility and speed are engines of economic growth and wealth creation, our current system breeds inertia and gridlock ... Our economy, too, has ground to a screeching halt, leaving us puzzled about Asia's and North America's ability to grow out of recession while we sputter along in endless debate, seemingly unable to return to the forefront of the global economy where we belong. (LCEC 2004a: 1–2)

In the words of the LCEC executive director Ann Mettler (2005a), the Lisbon Strategy should mirror the restructuring undertaken by the most successful EU member states, those "that have learned to meet the challenges, and reap the opportunities of globalization, rather than wage a futile and destructive fight against it." Here, the allegedly stubborn resistance of the EU (to technological innovation, labor market flexibility, and social welfare cuts) becomes a key factor in explaining the current crisis.

Furthermore, European citizens are seen as needing to play a key role in the realization of transnational capital's view of the Lisbon Strategy reforms. As noted by the ERT (2001: 6), "the education, personal qualities, attitudes and behaviour of Europe's citizens are essential ingredients for success." In appealing for "new Europeans" to accompany the "new European economy," transnational capital calls for citizens who accept that they "are not born with a God-given right to one of the world's highest standards of living" (LCEC 2004: 3), who realize that prosperity hinges on competitiveness in the global economy, and who acknowledge that "everybody has a vital stake in, and must make a significant contribution to, the economy and well-being of society" (LCEC 2004: 3).

In this way, the citizenship discourses of transnational capital represent the neoliberal communitarian model *par excellence*. Nowhere is this more apparent than in the ERT's campaign to encourage Europeans to:

> bring a spirit of enterprise to life as an employee and a citizen. Not necessarily in the sense of developing and pursuing business ideas, although Europe certainly needs more business entrepreneurs, but definitely in terms of developing a capacity for creativity, innovation, flexibility, team work and intellectual curiosity. Such an individual must be capable of taking charge of his or her employment destiny. Lifetime employment will not soon disappear, but it will be less relevant for many people. In pursuing other preferences and opportunities, they will need, among other things, to be able to identify emerging employment opportunities and to acquire necessary training for them. (ERT 2001: 4)

Accordingly, the ideal citizen is envisioned as a self-reliant "risk-taker," a "life-long learner," an "entrepreneur," and an "innovator." Those citizens who are unwilling to take this responsibility upon themselves to adopt more competitive attitudes are regarded as complacent, and too "[a]ccustomed to social safety nets and an assured standard of living" (ERT 2004: 6). Responsible citizens are those that take sight of their private individual interests by increasing their own "employability" so that they are no longer reliant on (Marshallian) social rights of the welfare state.

In the previous chapter we highlighted the fact that visions of the ideal European citizen were not reducible to a neoliberal market citizenship, but also steeped in an exclusionary discourse linking EU citizenship to a primordial European cultural heritage based on Christianity and other ethno-cultural markers (see Chapter 3). With the consolidation of neoliberal communitarian citizenship under the Lisbon Agenda it is not as if this ethno-cultural dimension has been swiftly replaced with this new emphasis on communitarian responsibilities. Rather, the ethno-cultural dimension now surfaces most prominently in the EU's migrant and ethnic minority integration policy. Furthermore, the ethno-cultural message contained within integration policy has been increasingly fused with neoliberal communitarian ideology, whereby migrants and minorities are expected to adapt not only to so-called European cultural values—what we term a neo-assimilationist approach to migrant integration—but also to norms of labor market flexibility. This nexus of the ethno-cultural and neoliberal communitarian dimensions will be explored in detail in the subsequent chapters, which focus on the increasingly important implications of migration and integration policies for citizenship politics in the EU.

Conclusion: The Social Contradictions of Neoliberal Communitarian Citizenship

Overall, we find that the Lisbon Strategy, with its attendant neoliberal communitarian citizenship model steeped in Third Way ideology, attempts to place the burden of socioeconomic restructuring squarely onto the shoulders of EU citizens. As a result, it appears as though "the entire weight of the social contradictions of modern capitalism is to be borne by the individual, who has no social rights at all to claim 'without responsibilities'" (Ryner 2002: 19). When viewed in terms of the historical power relations underpinning EU citizenship (see Chapter 1), this has the effect of empowering capital at the expense of labor. Thus it should come as no surprise that the content of the Lisbon Agenda, especially in its streamlined "jobs and growth" form, corresponds closely to the views of the transnational capitalist cadre. Though cast in the guise of "modernizing" the ESM, the discursive redefinition and ultimate subordination of traditional social democratic ideas—such as social solidarity, social rights, and full employment—to the commodifying logic of neoliberal restructuring starkly contradicts the assertions made by certain scholars that the Lisbon Strategy marks a sort of positive turning point for EU social policy. Nearing the strategy's deadline, we contend, in contrast to this initial optimism, that it is more accurate to view the Lisbon Agenda as largely in accordance with the embedded neoliberal hegemonic order, but that this order has been further challenged by the intensification of neoliberal restructuring since the move toward "jobs and growth." The same can be said for EU citizenship, as Third Way neoliberal communitarian citizenship fails to add substantive social rights to the socially thin market citizenship model of the extended relaunch, and in fact, reinforces neoliberal restructuring insofar as it places the burden of reform on citizens through calls to increased responsibilities.

When considered in light of the turbulent history of neoliberal restructuring in the EU since the mid-1980s (see Chapter 3), we should not expect the Lisbon Agenda to be free of new conflicts, tensions, and contradictions; the very notion of citizenship being based on neoliberal and communitarian principles is itself a contradiction in terms. In capturing these dynamics, it is worth returning to T. H. Marshall's thoughts on the centrality of social rights to modern capitalism (see Chapter 1). Despite all the relevant criticisms directed toward his original formulation (for naïve evolutionism, Euro-centrism, and patriarchal tendencies), Ryner and Cafruny (2007: 85) explain how Marshall did touch upon something crucial in suggesting "that it is only when risks of destitution and insecurity associated with industrial capitalist society are eliminated, or at least substantially mitigated, through the social rights provided by the welfare state that the broad mass of the population can fully obtain the status required to effectively exercise civic and political citizenship." Therefore the "active" element in neoliberal communitarian citizenship is not really active at all, in the sense that the subordination of social citizenship rights serves to also jeopardize the citizen's ability to exercise those civil and political rights that underpin the supposed "active" element implied within citizenship. Indeed, as Ryner (2002: 20) argues, it is hard to comprehend how one could expect that a citizen should be a "heroic, competitive, flexible and mobile individual who at the same time is a nurturing parent, rooted in a community, in which he/she has time and energy to invest civic involvement." By placing such unreasonable demands on citizens (Ryner 2002: 20) neoliberal communitarian citizenship risks inducing the "exhaustion of society," whereby the "organization of daily life" becomes "insecure and increasingly difficult" for the majority of the population (Bieling 2003: 59). As we shall see in Chapters 5 and 6 this development comes with even more dire consequences for the EU's migrants and ethnic minorities.

This argument has many parallels with Karl Polanyi's (1957) analysis of the breakdown of the liberal market order of the late nineteenth century; an era which Polanyi argued was the single instance where efforts to impose a self-regulating market on society became a historical reality. Polanyi is thus at pains to document the institutionalization of a self-regulating market, which he argued, contra neoclassic economics, was temporarily secured and sustained through conscious state planning. For Polanyi, the embedding of social relations in the economy rather than the economy within social relations was an inherently self-destructive process because it entailed treating humans and their natural environment as "fictitious commodities." Subjecting labor to the market imperatives of the price mechanism (Watson 2005a)—as is implied in the very notion of labor market flexibility—was of particular concern as he felt that "leaving people to the fate of the market would be tantamount to annihilating them" (Polanyi 1957: 137). Polanyi argued that a counter-movement clamouring for social protection and a re-embedding of the economy in social relations would ensue when commodification had reached a point at which society and nature could no longer bear its discipline.

With this in mind, and in spite of all the Third Way rhetoric, there is no reason to believe that a neoliberal communitarian conception of citizenship espoused in the Lisbon Strategy will render "the exhaustion of society as a consequence of intensified capital accumulation ... a thing of the past" (Bieling 2003: 71). Nor are there any guarantees that this citizenship model will be "internalized" by EU citizens. In the aftermath of the Barroso Commission's relaunch, the same trade unions and social NGOs that enthusiastically embraced the Lisbon Strategy as a route to EU-level social protection and cohesion began speaking out against the narrow objectives of the streamlined focus on growth and jobs (ETUC 2005; Platform of European Social NGOs 2005). These criticisms have been accompanied by calls for the strengthening of the social rights dimension of the Lisbon Agenda through the formation of transnational social policy initiatives ranging from pan-European "codetermination" rights for workers to a minimum citizen income to protect EU citizens against social exclusion and poverty.

The centrality of financial market deregulation to the Lisbon Strategy has also drawn the ire of key social forces, especially those emanating from members states of "Rhenish" capitalist lineage. Crucial here has been the recent striking down of the Lisbon-linked EU "takeover directive," which proposed the pan-European institutionalization of a "one share, one vote" rule across the Union and designed to facilitate shareholder power over corporate decision making (van Apeldoorn and Horn 2007). The rejection of the takeover directive is no doubt related to the simultaneous emergence of controversies over the role of hedge funds and private equity firms in European corporations, which have been branded as predatory "locusts" by various political and trade union leaders for purportedly stripping companies bare in their search for short-term profits, and threatening the consensual nature of firm relations within the "networked" systems of corporate governance in continental EU member states (see Watson 2005b). Yet these investors have been empowered by the European Commission, which in partnership with its "Expert Subgroups" on Hedge Funds and Private Equity, declared regulation of their investment activities undesirable because of their role in providing essential market liquidity necessary to the Lisbon Strategy's objective of instilling competition and dynamism in the new European economy (Hager

2007; Party of European Socialists 2007). At the same time, the skepticism toward the Lisbon Strategy's deregulatory thrust in finance has gained further momentum in light of the recent global economic downturn initiated by the collapse of the subprime housing market in the U.S. At the time of writing, the small gains in growth and employment that had been so proudly attributed by the Barroso Commission to the streamlining of the Lisbon Strategy are now being reversed due to stagflationary pressures from the global credit crunch, and also most importantly for the EU, from volatile swings in oil prices (Atkins 2008).

Thus it is no coincidence that the growing skepticism toward the Lisbon Strategy has developed hand in hand with a deepening crisis of legitimacy for the broader EU project.

The EU's own self-awareness of this crisis was dramatically provoked by the rejections of the EU's constitutional treaty referenda in France and the Netherlands in the spring of 2005. In response, the EU resorted to a "Plan D for Democracy, Dialogue and Debate," directed by Communications Commissioner Margot Wallström and vowing to give "new impetus to the debate on the future of Europe by encouraging new ways to draw citizens into the debate" (CEC 2006a: 3). Determined to get to the heart of the constitution's failure, polls conducted by the EU itself have made it clear that although the reasons for the "no" victory was multifaceted, a large majority of voters, especially in France, felt compelled to lend their support to the No campaign because of "the impression that the Constitution leant too much towards the liberal or not enough towards the social" (CEC 2006a: 2; see also van der Pijl 2006; van Apeldoorn 2008). Still, as we saw in our Introduction, these results have failed to move EU institutions and political leaders into any serious questioning of the overall social purpose of the integration project, as Plan D has pledged to "serve" EU citizens through the familiar recipe of neoliberal restructuring, together with, as we shall examine in Chapters 5 and 6, an increased emphasis on "protecting" European citizens from the perceived threats of "illegal migration," terrorism, and international crime.

In the wake of policy prescriptions offering "more of the same" when it comes to social citizenship, what Plan D essentially boils down to is a public relations strategy to open the channels of communication between EU institutions and citizens in order to make EU policies "understandable and relevant" (CEC 2006a: 3). This position suggests that, at least when it comes to substantive concerns over social policy in the EU, what is wrong is not the EU's inherent institutional bias toward market integration, but the citizens' perceptions of this bias; a problem to be resolved not through the extension of social rights (as has been called for by EU citizens themselves), but through the strengthening of "transparent" communication and information channels in order to enlighten EU citizens about their misguided views on the EU's social dimension. Yet, another string of disappointments for the EU elite stemming from Treaty and Constitution referenda No votes seems merely to confirm the suspicion that the problem of perception may not rest with EU citizens, but instead with EU institutions and political leaders, who would do well to return to T. H. Marshall's conceptualization of the relationship between social, political, and civic rights, and as well to Jacques Delors' oft-cited adage that people do not fall in love with an internal market.

Notes

1. We borrow this term from Hans-Jürgen Bieling's (2003) insightful analysis of employment policy in the EU.
2. For an elaboration of the notion of Schumpeterian Workfare Regimes, see Jessop (2002).
3. Our translation from Swedish.
4. Our translation from Swedish
5. The Lisbon Agenda pledged to boost EU average employment rate from 60 to 70 percent by 2010.

CHAPTER 5

A New EU Politics of Migration, a New Politics of EU Citizenship?
Analyzing the Amsterdam Treaty and Tampere Program

Introduction

The signing of the Amsterdam Treaty in October 1997 resulted from years of preliminary work and arduous negotiations, which had often centered on the issues of migration and asylum. The political mood in which Amsterdam took shape was characterized by a growing dissatisfaction with Maastricht's intergovernmental management of matters pertaining to migration (Lavenex 2001: 864). Hence, the European Commission had begun to depart from its earlier, rather pragmatic disposition (see Chapter 3) and had thrown in its lot with the European Parliament's more consistent criticism of the Maastricht era's allegedly opaque and democratically unaccountable conduct in Justice and Home Affairs (JHA) (see Hix 1999: 328). In order to come to terms with these problems, the Parliament and the Commission called for a supranationalization of migration and asylum policy. Unlike the political climate in which its predecessors—the Single European Act (SEA) and Maastricht—were moulded, however, the Parliament and the Commission were far from alone in championing a supranational solution. By the mid-1990s the case for some form of supranationalization had also gained support in all but a few of the national cabinets (Geddes 2000b: 115–8; Melis 2001: 14).

Another novel feature of Amsterdam's preparatory stages was the attendance of numerous NGOs, all advocating the cause of expanded protection and rights for refugees and immigrants. Forming part of the larger attempt to boost the EU's threadbare democratic credentials and to widen the scope of EU citizenship, and thus the EU's popular legitimacy, NGO representatives were invited to present their cases regarding the shaping of the Union's future migration and asylum policies (Geddes 2000b: 113–4). Being favorably disposed to transferring migration policy to the Community level (Hix 1999: 329), these NGOs' involvement provided an additional impetus to the supranational cause.

As it turned out, however, backers of further supranationalization were to be yet again frustrated (Geddes 2000b: 117). Even so, the Amsterdam Treaty did not, as had been the case with Maastricht, reject the supranational solution wholesale. What resulted was rather a type of half measure: while important parts of immigration and asylum policy were transferred from the EU's third intergovernmental pillar to the first supranational pillar, decision making in the area still had to abide by the unanimity principle. Thus, even though it assumed recognition as a "communitarized" area, immigration and asylum policy was not supranationalized and subjected to the traditional Community method of qualified majority voting (QMV) and the Commission's sole right of initiative. Instead, the exercise of the Commission's exclusive right of initiative was postponed until 2004 (Lavenex 2001: 865). A changeover to QMV was also anticipated for 2004; but such a decision was made dependent on a consensus among the member-state governments (Den Boer 1999: 312; Geddes 2000b: 123). However, a Council Decision (Council EU 2004d) in December 2004 settled the matter, thus making QMV applicable to the Amsterdam Treaty's new articles on immigration and asylum.

Despite the rather awkward "supragovernmental" setup, which drew criticism from many quarters (see Melis 2001: 51), the Amsterdam Treaty marked a historical shift toward a significantly augmented role for the EU and the supranational level. With the overarching aim of developing the European Union as an "area of freedom, security and justice," Amsterdam laid down the broad outlines for a future EU policy on migration and asylum. Upon ratification, the groundwork for such a policy was to be built incrementally over a period of five years (1999–2004). Some of these changes were spelled out in Article 61 under Amsterdam's new Title IV:

> In order to establish progressively an area of freedom, security and justice, the Council shall adopt: (a) within a period of five years after the entry into force of the Treaty of Amsterdam, measures aimed at ensuring the free movement of persons ... in conjunction with directly related flanking measures with respect to external border controls, asylum and immigration ... (b) other measures in the fields of asylum, immigration and safeguarding the rights of nationals of third countries. (Council EU 1997b: Article 61)

Further, Article 62 specified that measures should be adopted granting certain limited intra-EU mobility rights to "nationals of third countries." In addition, Article 63 outlined a series of measures on asylum and immigration, stressing the creation of a set "minimum standards" in the area of asylum. As part of this reshuffling, Amsterdam also incorporated the Schengen acquis into the treaty framework.

Unlike its predecessor, however, Amsterdam did not confine itself to immigration and asylum proper, but also introduced into the treaty explicit wordings concerning the Union's resident third-country nationals (TCNs) and ethnic minorities (see passage quoted above). Moreover, the treaty enacted an article to better equip the Union in its fight against racism and other forms of discrimination.

Owing to British, Irish, and Danish opposition, and in order not to derail the negotiations, it became necessary to allow these countries to opt out of these new provisions. Such opt-out, but also opt-in, agreements had to be codified in a series of complex protocols (see Hailbronner 1998; Hedemann-Robinson 1999; Melis 2001). In allowing for this intricate mix of opt-out and opt-in schemes, Amsterdam authorized a differentiated, multi-speed integration of greater flexibility (Hedemann-Robinson 1999). Since the literature sometimes, and the EU documents routinely, convey a bewildering impression to the contrary, it must also be stressed that by no means the entire policy area of migration and asylum was relocated to the first pillar (Hailbronner 1998). Thus, a number of significant areas—such as labor migration from third countries—were not subjected to the arrangements laid down in Amsterdam's new Title IV (Lavenex 2001: 866–7).

Following the signing of Amsterdam in 1997, some skepticism surfaced about whether member states actually would be willing to shoulder the ambitious goals set forth in the new treaty. At the Tampere European Council in 1999, however, much of this uncertainty was put to rest, at least for the time being. Here, at "the first ever European Council focusing on JHA matters" (Monar 2000: 125), the Council decided that "a common European asylum system" gradually should be put into operation (CEC 2001e: 3). As far as migration as a whole was concerned, Tampere "decided that a major focus of the EU's efforts should be on the more efficient management of migration flows, on more effective external border controls, and on combating illegal immigration" (CEC 2000b: 9). Tampere also "declared that a more vigorous integration policy should aim at granting" third-country nationals "rights and obligations comparable to those of EU citizens." Moreover, the Council undertook to "enhance non-discrimination in economic, social and cultural life and develop measures against racism and xenophobia" (CEC 2001a: 2).

The Amsterdam and Tampere agreements would set off a flurry of EU activity in the area of migration policy (Monar 2004: 127). In conjunction with migration policy moving up the EU agenda, moreover, this rapidly growing activity would expand well beyond the formal confines of the Amsterdam Treaty and Tampere Program. The Commission's bold move to declare an end to the era of "zero" labor migration from third countries (i.e. non-EU and non-OECD countries), as well as its call for expansion of the "externalization" of the EU's migration and asylum policies to third countries, are just two of several examples highlighting this dynamic development.

This chapter focuses on the development of EU migration policy after the Amsterdam and Tampere agreements. In this sense, together with the following Chapter 6, it examines the politics surrounding the status of *becoming a citizen* in the EU, including especially the obstacles and barriers to attaining the status of *being a citizen* (see Chapter 1; Castles and Davidson 2000). In terms of demarcations, it covers the development up until the conclusion of the Tampere Program (1999–2004), leaving off right before the launching of its multi-annual successor agenda, the Hague Program (2005–10), which will be the topic for the subsequent Chapter 6. Our examination can be said to proceed through a double movement, surveying and analyzing both internally and externally directed policies, as well as their intimate and often contradictory interplay. We set out by examining supranational initiatives in the fields of migrant and ethnic minority integration and anti-discrimination policy, focusing specifically on the strong interaction of these enterprises with labor-market policy and the issues of citizenship, social exclusion, and "European values." We then go on to explore the Commission's objectives and assumptions concerning its calls for a sizeable increase in labor migration from third countries. Besides relating this to the Lisbon Strategy and the internal requirements of the EU's transforming labor market, we also discuss the external ramifications of the EU's developing labor migration framework. The final sections scrutinize the EU's emerging asylum policy. They attend, inter alia, to the EU's ever-widening smorgasbord of security-oriented asylum and migration policies in the post-Amsterdam and post–11 September era (Huysmans 2006), which, as we go on to argue, together served to transform the right of asylum into a problem of "illegal immigration." Above all, this predicament is discussed in relation to the growing importance of immigration and asylum matters in the EU's external relations.

A New Deal for the Union's ("Legal") Third-Country Nationals?

The Meaning of Civic Citizenship

The pledge to improve the lot of the EU's "legal" and permanently settled TCNs was clearly one of the boldest declarations made in Tampere. By stating that "a more vigorous integration policy should aim at granting them [TCNs] rights and obligations comparable to those of EU citizens," the Council opened up for a revision of the legal restraints built into the EU citizenship that was instituted by the Maastricht Treaty. As was agreed upon in Maastricht (Part Two, Article 8(1)), "Every person holding the nationality of a Member State shall be a citizen of the Union" (Council of the European Communities, CEC 1992). To the extent, therefore, that the rights granted by the "European citizenship" altered the status of national citizenship, these alterations affected positively only the citizens of member states, and so created new hierarchies and cleavage structures between inhabitants in the EU area (see Balibar 2004; Kofman 2002). In this sense EU citizenship did not replace national citizenship but underlined its importance, since people residing in the Union could not acquire EU citizenship without first having acquired its counterpart in a member state.

As few could have failed to notice, the reluctance to incorporate the millions upon millions of resident TCNs into the new EU citizenship regime—and hence make residence rather than nationality the basis of membership—would be subjected to much criticism throughout the 1990s (see d'Oliveira 1995; Hansen, R. 1998; Kofman 1995; Martiniello 1995; O'Keeffe 1994). Besides the criticism being voiced from within academic circles and by various NGOs, the granting of extended rights to TCNs was also the subject of recurrent efforts on the part of the European Parliament and the Commission, particularly in order to redress the disparities between EU citizens and TCNs in the area of free movement.

It must be emphasized, though, that neither Amsterdam nor the declarations in Tampere indicated that permanently settled TCNs were about to become naturalized EU citizens any time soon, or, for that matter, that long-term residence was about to replace nationality as the determining principle of EU citizenship (Kostakopoulou 2002: 452). This provided, the strategy adopted by the Commission seemed rather to be geared toward making the most of Tampere's pledge to grant rights to TCNs that were "comparable to those of EU citizens."

According to Kostakopoulou (2002), the Commission's endeavor to address and expand the rights of permanently settled and "legal" TCNs should indeed be seen as an "important step towards equal membership and full political inclusion." Above all, Kostakopoulou (2002: 452, 454) contends, it makes clear that "[l]ong-term resident TCNs in the European Union are no longer invisible," and that a "rights-based approach centred on the principle of equal treatment ... and the granting of free movement rights has begun to emerge." On the word of the Commission, this rights-based approach forms an integral part of the larger objective of fostering a sense of "civic citizenship" among the Union's "legally" settled TCNs. According to the Commission (2000c: 19), civic citizenship is deemed a long-term goal, emerging out of the progressive "granting of civic and political rights to longer-term migrant residents." Comprising "a set of rights and duties offered to third country nationals" (2000c: 22), civic citizenship is said to epitomize the principles and values laid down in the "Charter of Fundamental Rights of the European Union" (European Union 2000), which was adopted at the Nice summit in December 2000 (CEC 2001a: 3). The Charter was later incorporated into the unratified and subsequently revised and renamed "treaty establishing a Constitution for Europe"—then renamed "the Lisbon Treaty" (ratified in November 2009) (Conference of the Representatives of the Governments of the Member States 2004: Part II, Titles I–VII). In terms of content, the Charter "sets out the civil, political, economic, and social rights of European citizens" (CEC 2001b: 21). Despite the Charter's explicit reference to "European citizens," the Commission has been eager to point out that this by no means precludes its (partial) application to TCNs.

Evidently, it is "free movement" that constitutes the core issue around which the Commission organizes and articulates its civic citizenship endeavor to expand the rights of "legally" resident TCNs. Consequently, whenever the Charter of Fundamental Rights is being brought to bear on the issue of civic citizenship, it is always its Article 45 (2) on "Freedom of movement and of residence" that appears in the foreground. "A genuine area of freedom, security and justice," the Commission (CEC 2001a: 8) asserts, "is unthinkable without a degree of mobility for third-country nationals residing there legally, and particularly for those residing on a long-term basis." With the adoption of a Council Directive in 2003 "concerning the status of third-country nationals who are long-term residents," the Commission gained (somewhat of) a hearing for its repeated calls and hence certain limited rights of intra-EU mobility and residence were granted to third-country nationals "who are long-term residents" (Council EU 2004c).[1] Yet, the mobility rights offered to TCNs by the directive come nowhere near those contained in EU citizenship; also, the directive was a far cry from the Commission's original proposal for such a directive (as tabled in 2001), which aimed to provide TCNs with more rights (Luedtke 2007).

The Political Economy of Free Movement

Granted that a possible upgrading of mobility rights for TCNs must be taken to be significant as such, the issue cannot rest simply as a structurally detached expression of the Commission's benevolent intention to use every means available to make "legal" TCNs more visible through their gradual "integration" as "civic citizens." This is not to suggest that civic citizenship is unworthy of our consideration. Rather, it is to stress the importance of linking it to the larger question of *the political economy of free movement*. The Commission's attempt to expand the scope of free movement to also incorporate TCNs must be understood in the context of its perpetual mission to stimulate the economically vital yet so far dormant labor mobility within the EU area. On this point, moreover, the Commission is crystal clear. Hence, it contends that to continue barring legally resident TCNs from the free movement provisions runs counter to "the demands of an employment market that is in a process of far-reaching change, where greater flexibility is needed" (CEC 2001a: 8). It goes on:

> The evolution of the employment market in the Union is highlighting employment shortages in certain sectors of the economy. Third-country nationals who are long-term residents may be ready and willing to relocate either in order to put their vocational skills to work in another Member State or to escape unemployment in the Member State where they reside. The mobility of long-term residents can thus make for better utilisation of employment reserves available in different Member States. (CEC 2001a: 8)

Explicitly tailored to the demands of a flexible labor market, the underlying rationale of devising a civic citizenship for TCNs should be seen as modeled upon similar market-making objectives as those shaping the EU citizenship for member state nationals.

It is in this larger context that we need to situate the objectives of civic citizenship and the Commission's attempt to extend selected free movement rights to TCNs. Permanently settled third-country nationals thus constitute an untapped labor reserve that, once unhampered by the EU's internal borders, could help remedy recurrent labor shortages in growth industries and other labor market distortions across the Union (CEC 2004f: 18; 2003e: 1). In this equation, moreover, unemployment appears to be a key variable. Since TCNs suffer disproportionately from unemployment, the Commission presumes they should be more open to intra-EU labor mobility than are member state nationals: hence the Commission's promotion of extended free movement rights as a means by which TCNs could "escape unemployment in the Member State where they reside" (CEC 2001a: 8).

Arguably, the articulation of civic citizenship is contingent upon the Commission's more general approach toward "social exclusion" as manifested in the Lisbon Strategy and reform agenda (see Schierup, Hansen and Castles 2006). As such, albeit explicitly designed for a different target group, civic citizenship also forms an integral part of Lisbon's neoliberal communitarian citizenship that we discussed in the preceding chapter.

The institution of civic citizenship thus rests on the Commission's basic premise that accelerated labor market deregulation and a more flexible and adaptable labor force hold the keys to the EU's allegedly *analogous* problems of unemployment and social exclusion. Promoted as a possible ticket out of unemployment for TCNs, in particular, and as a means to attain more flexibility within the EU's labor market as a whole, civic citizenship could then be seen as yet another attempt at reconciling social cohesion with market expediency.

But if the extension of mobility rights to TCNs constituted a core component in the Union's post-Amsterdam policy on civic citizenship in particular, and on integration policy vis-à-vis TCNs, in general, it was by no means the only one. As will be discussed below, since Amsterdam and Tampere numerous other policy initiatives were launched to promote the integration not only of TCNs but also of the EU's ethnic minorities as a whole.

Migrant Integration with "European" Obligations

EU integration policy was to experience some notable shifts and changes in the post-Amsterdam period. While still not altogether reducible to economic objectives, the Tampere Program's policy discourse on ethnic minority integration would find less and less application outside of the realm of market expediency and, in particular, of labor market policy. The Commission's comprehensive Communication *On a Community Immigration Policy* (2000c) thus markedly toned down the type of broader discussions which were commonplace in the pre-Amsterdam period and which often linked integration with the larger questions concerning the multicultural and multi-ethnic society (as discussed in Chapter 3). In the post-Amsterdam policy discourse, by contrast, the more elaborate discussion most often equates the integration of migrants and ethnic minorities with "their integration into the labour market" (CEC 2000c: 19; see also CEC 2003f: 1).

Another discernible modification of the Commission's post-Amsterdam integration discourse was to be found in the Commission's growing emphasis on migrants and minorities' own responsibilities in the area of integration. While underscoring the necessity of not only facilitating "their integration into the labor market," but also to create "a welcoming society," the Commission argued that it was essential

> to recognize that integration is a two-way process involving adaptation on the part of both the immigrant and of the host society. The European Union is by its very nature a pluralistic society enriched by a

variety of cultural and social traditions ... There must, therefore be respect for cultural and social differences but also of our fundamental shared principles and values: respect for human rights and human dignity, appreciation of the value of pluralism and the recognition that membership of society is based on a series of rights but brings with it a number of responsibilities for all of its members be they nationals or migrants. (CEC 2000c: 19)

Although the Commission's division of the Union into two clear-cut societies—one being the "host," the other being the "immigrant" society—begged a number of questions as to what made such a division a sensible starting point, it was, nonetheless, the assertion that these two societies must be made equally liable for the integration process that stood out as the most conspicuous ingredient, since it, by default, implied that the two societies have an equal, or symmetric, amount of social, economic, political, and cultural resources to bring to bear on the integration process in question.

Upon closer scrutiny, however, and once the question of "principles and values" entered into the picture, the "two-way process" quickly yielded to a one-way process where integration, in essence, became synonymous with an exclusive duty to adapt on part of the migrant society. This proceeds from the Commission's appropriation of the "respect for human rights and human dignity" as being constitutive of "our" particular values (see also CEC 2000e: 2). Although the Commission refrained from making any explicit statements about the possible content of the "immigrant society's" particular values and principles, Brussels position nevertheless intimated that it very well might champion values that contravene "our" "respect for human rights and human dignity."

It goes without saying that such a, what we choose to term, "neo-assimilationist" articulation of integration policy was drawing on the, from now on, even more prevalent sentiment, which holds that those migrants who are said to beget the Union's ever more culturally and ethnically diverse make-up are somehow more unfavorably disposed toward the specific values at issue. We find this reflected in the positions on migrant integration that started to germinate in many member states around the turn of the century (Carrera 2006); or, as the then British Home Secretary, David Blunkett, put it when seeking a formula to circumvent the outbreak of any future "race riots" similar to those that rocked Britain in the summer of 2001: "We have norms of acceptability and those who come into our home—for that is what it is—should accept those norms" (cited in Alibhai-Brown 2001).

It needs noting too that those values and principles that the Commission chose to define as "ours" now also were being grouped under the generic term "European values" as well as being incorporated into the Charter of Fundamental Rights of the European Union. In this context, the Commission (CEC 2001c: paragraph 3.4) speaks of the importance of providing migrants with "appropriate language training and information on the cultural, political and social characteristics of the country concerned including the nature of citizenship and of the fundamental European values." On this issue the European Parliament's position was to become even more emphatic, stating that "immigrants are expected to respect the community of values—as set out in the EU Charter of Fundamental Rights—and to show a willingness to integrate into society in the Member States" (2001a: 10). The Parliament would also call for stiffer "integration-related requirements" than those put forth by the Commission. In 2001, for instance, it contended that "[t]he award of long-term resident status" to migrants should not be a "substitute for successful integration; instead, an advanced degree of integration into the life of the Member State concerned is a precondition for the award of that status" (European Parliament 2001b: 6). It should also be mentioned that the Council took a favorable view of these proposals and sentiments (Council EU 2002b: 17).

In sum, this signaled that EU measures geared toward the specific problem of a trailing migrant integration increasingly were resorting to a moralizing, Third Way–type policy discourse, full of allusions to obligations, responsibilities, duties, and sanctions. If, as we argued in Chapter 4, the Third Way–inspired neoliberal communitarian citizenship model designed for EU citizens rests on citizens' responsibilities to adapt and make themselves "employable" in the new flexible labor market, the ultimate success (or failure) of the EU integration policy that comes into view here is, similarly, made to hinge upon the moral stature of the migrants themselves, on their "willingness to integrate," as well as on their ability to adapt to certain prescribed cultural and civic values. We should mention, finally, that this new (Third Way–oriented) outlook on integration also places a heavy emphasis on the prominent part to be played by "civil society" and on the benefits of "diversity management," whereby integration was held up as a potentially "profitable strategy" for corporations, "helping them to achieve their business goals through its focus on the commercial possibilities arising from increased diversity" (CEC 2003h: 20).

The New Anti-discrimination Agenda

In parallel with these integration policy developments, Amsterdam and Tampere would also give rise to some quite remarkable advances in EU policy-making on anti-discrimination and anti-racism. As such, the approach at the supranational level to the problem of racism was no longer to be confined to the merely symbolic responses that mostly characterized the pre-Amsterdam period (see Chapter 3). This change was first and foremost made possible by—to use the Commission's (CEC 2003g: 1) expression—the "groundbreaking" decision to incorporate a new anti-discrimination article (Article 13) in the Amsterdam Treaty. According to the Commission (CEC 2001d: 4), Article 13 "gave the Community for the first time the power to take legislative action to combat discrimination."

Article 13 was hardly a bolt from the blue, but was prefaced by an intensified supranational engagement with the problem of racism and xenophobia from the mid-1990s and onward. Such engagement was largely triggered by the growing electoral popularity of the extreme right (see Chapter 4). The European Year against Racism in 1997 and the decision to establish a European Monitoring Centre for Racism and Xenophobia in Vienna were just two of several developments that prepared the ground for and gave an impetus to the treaty amendment (see CEC 1995c; Council EU 1997c; CEC 2001d: 4).

After the Amsterdam Treaty came into force in 1999, the momentum continued, and it would not take long before this explicit anti-discrimination orientation began to take the form of mandatory directives and development programs requiring member states to combat racism and discrimination. Already in November 2000 the emerging policy agenda had been adapted to an ambitious six-year (2001–6) implementation scheme, spelled out in the "Community Action Programme to combat discrimination" (Council EU 2000b). Just before that, moreover, Article 13 had facilitated the adoption of a landmark Racial Equality Directive (Council EU 2000c). This directive aims to put into practice Article 13 and thus to give effect to "the principle of equal treatment between persons irrespective of racial or ethnic origin." Integral to this is the objective of creating "a socially inclusive labor market" and "a high level of employment and of social protection." This was soon complemented by the Employment Framework Directive (Council EU 2000e), which, among other things, added discrimination in the labor market on grounds of religion to the general framework for combating racism and discrimination.

In addition to these directives, EU anti-discrimination policy was also equipped with a plethora of "soft law" schemes corresponding to the EU's new policy-making style of the Open Method Coordination (as discussed in Chapter 4). As Soininen (2003: 45) has it, it was largely the Commission's astute utilization of soft-law policy making, starting in the mid-1990s, that paved the way for the Council Directives and thus for the introduction of binding EU legislation on anti-discrimination. "Soft law has contributed to establishing support for further action, and to 'softening up' the policy area in preparation for later action by the Commission" (Soininen 2003: 45). Particularly instrumental in this development has been the Commission's effort "to pursue a coherent strategy of integrating anti-racism into EU policies, known as mainstreaming" (CEC 2003g: 5). Mainstreaming has been part and parcel of the EU's anti-discrimination policy ever since the redoubling of activity in the field in the late 1990s. The strategy of mainstreaming has thus facilitated the incorporation of anti-discrimination measures into a variety of EU programs and policies, most prominently in employment and social policy (Soininen 2003).

Belonging under the Directorate-General for Employment and Social Affairs, the Equal Program (2000–6) was one of many policy schemes that was to operate in accordance with this strategy (see e.g. CEC 2001e: 9). Managed by the European Social Fund (ESF), the Equal Program tied together the new anti-discrimination and migrant integration agenda with the EU's social policy and employment agenda. In keeping with the objectives guiding parts of the integration policy examined above, as well as with the EU Lisbon agenda's neoliberal communitarian citizenship that we discussed in the previous chapter, the Equal Program combined a neoliberal and Third Way–type policy discourse. Hence it put a great deal of emphasis on *social inclusion* of disadvantaged groups through *employment*. This was supposed to take place through the collaboration of public administrators, NGOs, social partners, and the business sector within the framework of mostly local development partnerships (see CEC 2000d: 13, 2001e: 9).

Arguably, the new anti-discrimination policy framework constituted a significant development. For one thing, it put pressure on member states to adjust and upgrade their anti-discrimination policies and legislations. This also implies prospects for changes of a systemic nature whereby EU policy may alter the distribution of influence between various social actors over national policy making in the field (Soininen 2003: 46). As already alluded to, however, significant parts of EU anti-discrimination policy conform very well with neoliberal objectives, particularly as these have come to influence the EU's employment policy. Market expediency and anti-discrimination policy are thus framed as being mutually reinforcing. As Soininen (2003: 44) notes, for instance, when anti-discrimination policy enters the areas of the EU's Employment Strategy and social inclusion policy, "the rights perspective shifts over to perspectives such as the employability of the individual." When seen from this perspective, one needs to ask to what extent the development of EU anti-discrimination policy in the Tampere Program merely constituted yet another market-expedient employability instrument substituting for, rather than forming part of, an

EU commitment to the establishment of a structurally embedded social citizenship dimension.

Ending the Policy of "Zero" Labor Immigration from Third Countries

A New Realism for the EU's New Demand for Labor from the South

After this inquiry into the EU's post-Amsterdam policy approaches to the "integration" of TCNs and ethnic minorities of migrant background, we now turn our attention to the interrelated development in the areas of (labor and "illegal") migration and asylum, where the transformations induced by Amsterdam and Tampere have been even more momentous.

To start with, it did not take long for the Commission to decide to reverse its official stance on the question of extra-EU labor migration. In the communication *On a Community Immigration Policy* (2000), the Commission elaborates on this new outlook:

> [I]it is clear from an analysis of the economic and demographic context of the Union and of the countries of origin, that there is a growing recognition that the "zero" immigration policies of the past 30 years are no longer appropriate. On the one hand large numbers of third country nationals have entered the Union in recent years and these migratory pressures are continuing with an accompanying increase in illegal immigration, smuggling and trafficking. On the other hand, as a result of growing shortages of labour at both skilled and unskilled levels, a number of Member States have already begun to actively recruit third country nationals from outside the Union. In this situation a choice must be made between maintaining the view that the Union can continue to resist migratory pressures and accepting that immigration will continue and should be properly regulated, and working together to try to maximise its positive effects on the Union, for the migrants themselves and for the countries of origin. (CEC 2000c: 3)

Given this "new situation," the Commission took the view "that channels for legal immigration to the Union should now be made available for labour migrants" (CEC 2000c: 3); or as put in a more blunt formulation: "the Commission believes zero immigration to be, quite simply, unrealistic" (CEC 2000e: 4). "The main challenge," the Commission (2003h: 10) went on, "will be to attract and recruit migrants suitable for the EU labour force to sustain productivity and economic growth."

The new stance toward labor migration grew out of the decisions taken in Tampere that called for a "more efficient management of migration flows" (CEC 2000b: 9). In order to better "manage," "regulate," and "control" the "increasingly mixed flows of migrants," the Commission has, since then, been a strong advocate of a further development of a "partnership approach" with third countries. As part of this scheme the Union agreed to greatly augment the scope for the issues of migration and asylum in the EU's relations and agreements with third countries (CEC 2000c: 8).

The partnership approach is set to "provide a framework for dealing flexibly with new trends in migration," where migration, rather than being perceived as "simply a one-way flow," now must be construed as a *"pattern of mobility"* (CEC 2000c: 8, 13, italics in original). Hence, if the EU needs to open the door to new labor migrants, it must also ensure that these migrants remain perpetually prone to mobility, that they are encouraged to contribute to the "economic development of their country of origin," and that laws refrain from hampering their opportunities "of moving on or going back as the situation develops in the country of origin and elsewhere in the world." Designed so as to aid sender countries' economic development, partnerships and the flexible and "efficient management of migration flows" are also promoted as means which "in the long term" could help put a curb on the very "incentive to emigrate," and thence facilitate the Union's fight against "illegal immigration" (CEC 2000c: 8, 11, 14; see also CEC 2001c; 2003h: 15).

These objectives were further elaborated at the Seville European Council in 2002. Seville went on to reconfirm that "any future cooperation, association or equivalent agreement which the European Union or the European Community concludes with any country should include a clause on joint management of migration flows and on compulsory re-admission in the event of illegal immigration" (CEC 2002e: 23). In the ensuing Commission Communication (2002e) it was established that the issue of migration and asylum, by necessity, must constitute the centerpiece in all of the EU's development programs, also expressed as "the migration-development nexus" (CEC 2002e: 23). Development assistance to poorer countries is to target more forcefully "the root causes of migration flows"—the so-called push factors—so as to better "manage," "control," and "reduce" global migration flows (CEC 2002e). Another potentially fruitful course of action that was said to need further exploration concerned the connection between labor migration and international protection. Set to be coordinated "in partnership with third countries," the Commission recommended that "[b]etter access to protection in Europe must go hand in hand with a regulated and more transparent framework for a policy on admissions, including for employment purposes" (CEC 2003i: 7; see also CEC 2000c: 15).

Tapping the Extra-European Labor Reserve

As is indicated above, however, the many alleged benefits inherent in partnerships and a flexible management of migration were not only projected onto the future. On the contrary, and reflecting the objectives set out in the Lisbon Strategy, such a flexible management must, above all, be construed as a response to a set of acute predicaments facing the Union's economic competitiveness, demography, and labor market. Prefaced with references to already established and developing recruitment schemes at the member state level (CEC 2003k: Ch. 6; see also CEC 2004f), the Commission called for a coordination of national responses within "an overall framework at EU level" (CEC 2000c: 14). Hence, and since the admission of third-country labor migrants remained a national sphere of authority, the Open Method of Coordination (OMC) was set to complement and support the EU's so far limited legislative instruments (see Caviedes 2004). This was done so as to bring forth common objectives, guidelines, and standards as well as best practices and targets that are sensitive to different national needs (CEC 2001c). In due course, the Commission envisaged, such an OMC-driven process will help establish a common framework for third-country labor migration in the EU. While such coordination of recruitment policies for "economic migrants" had to "address the needs of the market place particularly for the very highly skilled, or for lesser or unskilled workers and seasonal labour," it was also designed to "enable the EU to respond quickly and efficiently to labour market requirements at national, regional and local level, recognising the complex and rapidly changing nature of these requirements" (CEC 2000c: 15). Here, for instance, the Commission took a positive view of the bilateral agreements on seasonal and temporary work that southern European members had signed with various third countries (CEC 2004f). These were commended not only for helping to alleviate labor shortages but even more so for strengthening cooperation with third countries on the fight against illegal immigration. It is also important to note that the Commission did not take issue with the fact that some of these bilateral agreements were not awarding seasonal third country laborers the same working conditions and salary levels as nationals (CEC 2004f: 7).

As already intimated, from now on the Commission advocates an EU policy vis-à-vis new third-country labor migration that is guided by a flexible approach. For a start, "temporary workers who intend to return to their countries of origin" are said to be best admitted on the basis of "temporary" work permits. Subsequently, temporary permits might be extended and, "after a number of years to be determined," workers who "meet certain criteria" may be awarded permanent work permits (CEC

2000c: 17–8). As suggested by the Commission (CEC 2004f: 19), moreover, "the idea of recruiting workers and developing training programmes in countries of origin in skills which are needed by the EU could be explored." Since such programs had already been established by some member states, the Commission opened for the possibility of Community-financed pilot projects in this area.

Having arrived here, and seeing once more how all roads, so to speak, were leading to the flexible labor market, we can now appreciate more fully the intimate and complementary relationship between policies on extra-EU migration and policies on intra-EU integration. If the intra-EU labor reserve of long-term resident TCNs needed to be induced to relocate in step with the labor market's flexibility requirements, the same can be said to apply to select groups from within the extra-EU labor reserve. The fact that the Commission (2000c: 15, emphasis added) requested that recruitment schemes for extra-EU labor migrants address "the need for greater mobility *between* Member States for incoming migrants" is just another case in point underscoring the complementary character of the two policy schemes in question.

A Flexible Integration

But the management of new labor migration was not only promoted under the banner of flexibility and mutually beneficial partnerships between senders and receivers. It also intimated that newcomers should be greeted with measures of integration and with the associated boons of civic citizenship, anti-discrimination policies, and social inclusion. From here on, integration is also construed as a competitive device, as when the Commission urges the member states to "greatly contribute to the integration process," since this "will be particularly important in attracting migrants to highly skilled jobs for which there is world-wide competition" (CEC 2000c: 19).

But if integration, as in this particular instance, could be held up as enhancing the Union's competitive edge, its perceptibly discordant relationship with many of the objectives inherent in the "flexible management" of new labor migration also elicited some hesitation on the part of the Commission as to how extensive integration measures really ought to be. Put differently, if the new labor migrants derive their utility precisely through their flexible status—always open to return and to continual mobility—this was clearly at variance with the Commission's (CEC 2000c: 20) conception of integration as inevitably amounting to "a long-term process." Given this policy conflict, it is little wonder that the Commission, on other occasions, proves equally eager to temper, even retract, its affirmative stance on the integration of new labor migrants. As part of a wavering attempt to paper over the contradiction between *integration* and *flexibility*, the Commission thus suggests that it might be advisable to adopt an "incremental" approach to integration—an approach "[d]ifferentiating rights according to length of stay" (CEC 2000c: 15, 17). However, since the Commission already had established that "length of stay" was to be managed through the issuing of various temporary and renewable work permits and determined solely by the rapidly changing and hence indeterminable market needs, this proposal could not but amount to little more than a tautology. Arguably, it essentially sought to square the integration-flexibility circle by subordinating the issue of integration to the requirements of flexibility. This contradictory endeavor was reflected too in the Commission's subsequent recasting of integration as "reintegration" in the EU's proposal to design a "reintegration framework" "to assist returning migrants to re-settle in their countries of origin" (CEC 2000c: 8, 2001c: 10).

Public Relations Post-"Zero Immigration"

Another, and perhaps even greater, predicament facing the Commission revolved around its undertaking to secure widespread public acceptance of the (official) revocation of the EU's long-established tradition of "'zero' immigration policies" (CEC 2000c: 3). To be sure, "zero immigration" never constituted an actual line of policy in the literal sense of the word; today it is rather used as a generic term, denoting thirty years of restrictive migration policies (in Western Europe) aimed at limiting the (legal) entry of labor migrants from poorer parts of the world. In this sense the Commission's call to end zero immigration must not be allowed to conjure up a picture of the past thirty years as characterized by a true intention to hermetically seal off the borders for certain categories of labor migrants—and where the passivity, even tacit consent, of many governments to industry's exploitation of undocumented labor amounts to just one case refuting such an intention (see e.g. Castles 2004). Neither should it be taken to signify the first step toward a future policy of porous borders and "open door" labor migration. Listening to the Commission, it was, nonetheless, a public reaction partly built on just such an interpretation, which it now set out to forestall. The Commission appeared to be apprehensive that the "host populations" would respond negatively to the abrogation of "zero immigration," possibly interpreting it as portending less restriction and an uncontrolled inflow of immigrants. In its detailed Opinion on the Commission's new approach to migration, the EU's consultative body the European Economic and Social Committee (2001: 111) voiced similar concerns: "It will not be easy to persuade public opinion to take a favourable view of the more open immigration policy now being proposed, but far-reaching work to this end is now urgently required."

In light of the Commission's exceedingly restrictive stance on migration in the 1980s and 1990s, however, such uneasiness is far from surprising. Indeed, for more than two decades (as discussed in Chapter 3) the Commission rarely missed an opportunity to emphasize that a restrictive immigration policy, or "zero immigration," was the only "realistic" way forward. For one thing, this was the foundation on which the Commission formulated its approach to ethnic minority integration; that is, without tight controls (read zero immigration) on new entries, the reasoning went, integration of minorities with migrant background already residing in the Union was considered unfeasible. Moreover, the pledge to uphold (the illusion of) zero immigration also served as one of the core ingredients in the Commission's articulation and promotion of a "European citizenship" during the 1990s. Here, as we discussed in Chapter 3, the underlying assumption was that the EU citizenry, in order to lend support to further integration, needed to be assured that migration and asylum, together with other matters brought forth as assertively related to public safety, were effectively checked at the external borders.

In order to obviate a possible public disapproval of the EU's rather abrupt shift from its promise to perpetuate the policy of zero immigration to its current call for an increase of third country labor migration, the Commission soon came up with a series of public relations measures to be adopted by a range of elite actors. "A shift to a proactive immigration policy," the Commission (2000c: 22, 15) asserted, will "require strong political leadership to help shape public opinion," as well as "a clear commitment to the promotion of pluralistic societies and a condemnation of racism and xenophobia." More specifically, politicians were being urged to highlight the positive effects of migration and to "avoid language which could incite racism or aggravate tensions between communities." In addition, the media was held up by the Commission as having "considerable responsibility in this respect," that is, "in its role as an educator of public opinion" (CEC 2000c: 22).

Still in Control

Apart from these new guidelines, the Commission was also very eager to ensure a presumed "host population" that the admission of new labor migrants by no means implied a laxer *control* of migration flows as such. On the contrary—and as has been repeated ad infinitum ever since—the new migration policy was to be "accompanied by a strengthening of efforts to combat illegal immigration and especially smuggling and trafficking" (CEC 2000c: 22, see also 2001f, 2003m). In its *Study on the links between legal and illegal immigration* (2004), the Commission elaborates on a series of measures that are deemed necessary in order to realize this objective. Here, the main concern revolves around the establishment of more effectual cooperation schemes with third countries on policing, border control, and return of illegal migrants (CEC 2004g). To enable third and neighboring countries to improve their management of migration flows in general, and to reinforce their fight against illegal migration in particular, the Commission is calling for an increase in the EU's technical and financial support within the framework of its various external policies and cooperation programs (CEC 2004g). With the twin purposes of managing the new labor migration to the EU more efficiently on the one hand, and of combating what the Commission enumerates as the "serious threats" of "illegal immigration, organised crime, trafficking of various kinds, terrorism and communicable diseases" on the other, the EU also went ahead and launched the "New Neighborhood Policy," designed to enhance cooperation with countries along the EU's eastern borders and in the Mediterranean basin (CEC 2004d: 23, see also 2003l).

But while the public was to be on the one hand reassured about the EU's commitment to an ever more intense fight against illegal migration and on the other hand educated about the benefits of migration and diversity, the Commission also put forward a third set of conditions to be considered. Here, and in sharp contrast with the critical importance attributed to the task of teaching the public to be appreciative of migration and diversity, the Commission (2000c: 16) sees it necessary also to pay heed to such "factors" as "public acceptance of additional migrant workers in the country concerned, resources available for reception and integration," as well as "the possibilities for social and cultural adaptation etc." Although the Commission refrained from any further elaboration on these "factors," their very incorporation into the Union's overall labor migration scheme is nonetheless quite indicative of an increasingly contradictory migration policy picture. As such, the EU-level approaches to labor migration that developed at this time tallied in important respects with those at national levels. Arguably, the Commission's approach also reflected a tactical move, attempting to appease the discrepant positions on migration between, as well as within, the member states. In this sense, the Commission's reference to "public acceptance of additional migrant workers in the country concerned" is a misnomer and should rather read, "governmental acceptance of additional migrant workers." True, most governments in the post-Amsterdam period came to share the Commission's view that an increase in extra-EU labor migrants had become necessary, but to assume that they were able, let alone prepared, to shoulder the responsibility to "shape public opinion" in an anti-racist and pro-migration direction was a completely different matter. As had been made painfully clear at this moment in time, the relationship between the traditional parties of government and the extreme right was no longer limited to one where the former assimilated many of the proposals and sentiments of the latter; rather, in many member states it had now entered a phase of open cooperation and coalition building.

But instead of addressing this distressing development, the Commission persevered in displacing and projecting the problem of racism and anti-immigrant sentiments onto the "public" and the so-called "host populations." Nor, one needs to add, did it point to those sections of this precise "public"—the plethora of organizations and popular movements—which for years on end had worked against racism and the criminalization of immigration and asylum. In light of these circumstances, the Commission's focus on the European citizens' assumed resentment against immigration could also be interpreted as a convenient way to avoid any discussion or self-examination of its own role and complicity in legitimizing and kindling the past decades' growing hostility toward migrants and asylum seekers (see Morris 2002: 23–4; Huysmans 2006).

Towards a "Common European Asylum System"

New Measures Not Enough to Curb the EU's Old Asylum Crisis

In the post-Amsterdam period, asylum policy was to become subjected to an intensive supranational activity. As a result of Amsterdam's new Treaty provisions and the Tampere agenda, a package of EU directives and regulations was adopted in the area. During this first phase (1999–2004) of the creation of a "Common European Asylum System," a primary objective was to establish a set of common "minimum standards" in a number of areas; for example, minimum standards on "temporary protection" (Council EU 2001a);[2] "reception of asylum seekers" (Council EU 2003b);[3] "the qualification and status of third country nationals or stateless persons as refugees" (Council EU 2004a); and "minimum standards on procedures for granting or withdrawing refugee status" (Council EU 2004b). Prior to these measures, a Council Decision had established the European Refugee Fund (ERF) (Council EU 2000a). In terms of its budget, the ERF makes up the largest program within the EU's asylum and migration policy. Set to operate in accordance with the "principle of solidarity," the fund is to take particular pains to facilitate the so-called burden-sharing between EU countries of the costs of refugee reception. Since its inception in 2000, however, the trend has been toward a "substantially increased" allotment of funds ministering to the return and repatriation of refugees (CEC 2003i: 19; see also CEC 2002e: 38).

On account of Amsterdam's new provisions, moreover, all facets of visa policy have been incorporated into the EU's legal framework (Council EU 2001c).[4] As part of this, the number of countries whose citizens are required to have a visa in order to enter the Union has been further expanded, covering practically all those countries that the EU recurrently reprimands for human rights abuses. Since prospective asylum seekers, as a rule, are denied visas to EU countries, this conversion means that a key legal retrenchment on the possibility to seek asylum, which was subjected to loud criticism when it was developed through intergovernmental cooperation in the 1990s, now has been endowed with supranational sanction. As for the Commission's rationale, it is "illegal immigration" that "represents one of the basic criteria for the determination of those third countries whose nationals are subject to the visa requirement" (CEC 2003m: 4).

In line with the EU's visa policy, an EU Directive on Carrier Sanctions was adopted in 2001 (Council EU 2001b). With the objective of "curbing migratory flows and combating illegal immigration," this directive imposes financial penalties on carriers that transport TCNs who are refused entry into the Union, as well as obliging carriers to send back TCNs. As scores of scholars and organizations have pointed out, this directive not only fails to comply with the Geneva Convention's principle of non-refoulement; it also transmits the responsibility to decide whether or not a person is in need of protection to an unaccountable travel industry (ECRE 2004: 16).

The Eurodac information system, which became fully operational across the EU in 2003, makes up another component of the building of a "Common European Asylum System" (see Council EU 2002b)[5]. Eurodac was established in order to ensure the effective implementation of the Dublin Convention, now replaced by a Council Regulation establishing Dublin II (Council EU 2003c).[6] The Dublin Convention (as described in Chapter 3) stipulates that asylum seekers are allowed to file for asylum in only one member state, whose decision then has legal force in the Union as whole, thus preventing a rejected applicant from taking her case to another member state. Eurodac's main official function is to collect and store fingerprints of all people over the age of 14 who have applied for asylum or been detained while "illegally" entering or residing in a member state.[7]

Despite the vigorous activity and the number of new supranational provisions and measures, the Commission was nonetheless far from satisfied with the trend of events in the area of asylum policy. In its assessment of the Tampere Program, which was presented in the summer of 2004 (at the expiration of Tampere's "five-year timetable"), the Commission stated that, although it was "clear that the successes that have been achieved are considerable," it was equally clear that "the original ambition" had been "limited by institutional constraints, and sometimes also by a lack of sufficient political consensus" (CEC 2004e: 5, see also 2003i: 3; Monar 2003: 119). Equally troublesome, the Commission went on, was the fact that the process embarked upon since Amsterdam had done very little to overcome the alleged crisis that had plagued asylum policy in the EU since at least the early 1990s. On the contrary, the new millennium had just seen a further worsening of this crisis. There was thus a "growing malaise in public opinion" toward the present state of asylum policy. Moreover, "[a]buse of asylum procedures is on the rise, as are hybrid migratory flows, often maintained by trafficking practices involving both people with a legitimate need for international protection and migrants using asylum procedures to gain access to the Member States to improve their economic situation" (CEC 2003i: 3). Brussels viewed the asylum crisis as "a real threat to the institution of asylum and more generally for Europe's humanitarian tradition," and as such it "demand[ed] a structural response" (CEC 2003i: 3). Such a response was not to stop short of measures targeted at the *internal* operation of the EU's developing asylum system. On the contrary, and in line with the measures embarked upon in the EU's new labor migration policy, the core of this structural response needed to be transposed to the so-called "external dimension" of the EU's asylum and immigration policy.

Externalizing the Asylum Crisis

In reality, the nucleus of an externalized asylum policy was introduced already in the early 1990s; the first Schengen Agreement from 1985 could be seen as an even earlier precursor (Boswell 2003). Moreover, externalization through "the exportation of migration control" was a salient component in the accession agreements that formed the basis of the Eastern enlargement (Boswell 2003: 621–2; Lavenex 1999; Grabbe 2002; Jileva 2002). It was not until the Tampere European Council in 1999, however, that a firmer official sanction was bestowed on the increasingly external orientation (Boswell 2003; van der Klauuw 2002). Later, at the European Council in Laeken in 2001, the Council called for the incorporation of the issue of migration and asylum in the EU's "foreign policy." The momentum found further sustenance at the Seville European Council in 2002, where the external dimension was afforded a set of concrete objectives within what was now also referred to as the EU's "global policy" on migration (CEC 2002e: 26). The issue of migration, it was declared, should from then on make up an obligatory and salient feature in all of the EU's external relations (CEC 2002e: 4). Emphasis was placed more firmly on the establishment of "asylum and immigration projects in third countries," a course of action which needed to "be fundamentally incitative by encouraging those countries that accept new disciplines" (CEC 2002e: 4).

As part of this, the Commission also came to confer an ever-growing importance upon the issues of repatriation, expulsion, return, and readmission. Here, the Commission seems unable to emphasize enough that "[a] policy on returns or effective removal from the territory is an absolute necessity for the credibility of the common asylum system and the common procedure" (CEC 2000d: 10). Indeed, "[t]he signal effect of a failed return policy on illegal residents cannot be underestimated" (CEC 2003m: 8). The Commission also became keen to use readmission as a public relations tool; that is, as a promise to a presumed European citizenry hankering for reassurance about the authorities' resolve and relentless crack down on bogus asylum seekers:

> An effective EU Return Policy will increase public faith in the need to uphold the EU humanitarian tradition of offering asylum to those in need of international protection. A quick return, in safety and dignity, immediately following rejection of the application for asylum and the appeal ... will furthermore greatly deter migrants from abusing the asylum channels for non-protection-related reasons. (CEC 2003j: 20)

In its *Green Paper on a Community Return Policy on Illegal Residents*, the Commission also points to the merits of "the forced return of illegal residents," arguing that this can "help to ensure public acceptance for more openness towards new legal immigrants against the background of more open admission policies particularly for labour migrants" (CEC 2002f: 8).

As part of this the Council of Ministers decided (in the spring of 2004) to render the return of "illegal" migrants and rejected asylum seekers more effective by establishing a set of rules and regulations for the promotion of "joint flights for removals from the territory of two or more Member States, of third-country nationals who are subjects of individual removal orders" (Council EU 2004e). Removal by air of migrants and refugees to countries of origin or other countries is something individual member states have made use of for a long time; and in recent years this enterprise has benefited from an increasing intergovernmental cooperation. During the first three years of the new millennium, Germany, for instance, air-deported over 10,000 migrants to, inter alia, Turkey, Sri Lanka, and countries in the Middle East; Britain deported people by air to, inter alia, Kosovo and Afghanistan and Roma to the Czech Republic; and France has since the 1980s carried out airborne deportations to countries in Africa, and, in cooperation with Spain, France has also air-deported Roma to Romania—just to mention a few among many other cases (see further Statewatch 2003; Fekete 2005). Due to this procedure's shaky status vis-à-vis international law and to the fact that it has resulted in many deaths and well-documented cases of human rights violations—physical brutality, torture, forced sedation, racist and degrading treatment, etc.—it has been the subject of much harsh criticism from scores of human rights organizations, researchers and journalists.[8] Partly as a response to this criticism some airlines no longer allow their regular flights to be used for deportations, something that has increased the utilization of chartered flights (Statewatch 2003; Verkaik 2007).

In its decision, needless to say, the Council turns a blind eye to the countless discouraging experiences revealed from much well-founded criticism. Instead, through an "improved operational cooperation among Member States," the decision aims to provide for more cost-efficient and "rational repatriation operations" (Council EU 2004e: 28). Most importantly perhaps, and in order to follow through on Brussels' pledge to the European citizens, "[i]t urge[s] an increase in the use of joint flights and in the rate of returns from the European Union" (CEC 2004h). Nonetheless, by taking pains to emphasize that deportations should involve as little coercive measures as possible, EU decision makers are signaling an awareness of the existent criticism against forced deportations. In so doing, however, the Council decision unintentionally admits that an efficient return policy, as by definition, does contain a significant element of violence. As the Council (2004e: 32–3, 35) goes on to specify in its decision:

> It should be made clear that any disruptive behaviour will not be tolerated and will not lead to the aborting of the removal operation; ... seatbelts shall be kept fastened throughout the entire duration of the flight; ... coercion may be used on individuals who refuse or resist removal. ... any coercive measures should not compromise or threaten the ability of the returnee to breathe normally. In the event that coercive force is used, it shall be ensured that the chest of the returnee remains in upright position and that nothing affects his or her chest in order to maintain normal respiratory function; the immobilisation of resisting returnees may be achieved by means of restraints that will not endanger their dignity and physical integrity; ... The use of sedatives to facilitate the removal is forbidden without prejudice to emergency measures to ensure flight security; ... the returnees shall be free of

handcuffs or any other restraint when handed over to the local authorities; ...

With reference to, inter alia, the European Convention for the Protection of Human Rights (Protocol No. 4, Article 4) and its stipulation prohibiting the "Collective expulsion of aliens" (Council of Europe 2003: 25), numerous human rights organizations and other interested parties have condemned the Council of Ministers' decision on "joint flights for removals" (see e.g. Statewatch 2003). Also voices from within the European Parliament have condemned the decision, referring to deportations by air as a "deplorable practice" (Statewatch 2004a).

In conjunction with this, a series of measures were launched seeking to establish a firm link between development assistance policy and the striking of readmission agreements with third countries. Given that the Cotonou Agreement,[9] or the EU's "Partnership Agreement" with seventy-seven African, Caribbean, and Pacific (ACP) countries (Council EU 2000d), already had been equipped with a readmission clause, the Commission mentioned this agreement as a potential blueprint for forthcoming ones (CEC 2002e: 24; see Lavenex 2002). At the time, the respective agreements between the EU and countries such as Egypt, Georgia, Lebanon, Armenia, Azerbaijan, and Uzbekistan also contained a readmission clause; and in November 2002, the EU adopted a "Return plan for Afghanistan" (CEC 2003j: 21). Subsequently, the Commission was authorized to negotiate (on a country-by-country basis) readmission agreements and other migration- and asylum-related cooperation agreements between the EU and a growing number of countries, the great majority of them (like those already enumerated) with poor human rights records (see CEC 2002e: 25, 2003m: 12–4). In addition, and with the principal objective to further develop the readmission instrument, the EU launched the AENEAS Program in the spring of 2004. This cooperation and development policy program also aims to address the root causes of migration, promote legal labor migration channels, improve third countries' asylum systems, and combat illegal migration and organized crime (European Parliament, Council EU 2004).

Refugee Protection in the Region of Origin

Since the launch of the Tampere Program, the external dimension of EU migration policy has also placed much emphasis on provisions to amplify "refugee protection in the region of origin" (CEC 2003i). Protection in the region of origin also sits at the heart of the UNHCR's agenda, and for years several member states have been promoting it as a more expedient way of managing the world's refugee crisis. Within the policy debate, however, there are different ways of approaching the issue; that is, an EU regional protection policy may be developed into a tool of mere refugee containment, thus perpetuating the ongoing transfer of the refugee burden from richer to poorer countries; or it could be based on a commitment to real protection and human rights, and vested with adequate resources (see Boswell 2003).

In inquiring into the relative strengths of these two approaches, we can turn to Loescher and Milner's (2003) apt scrutiny of the concept and empirical reality of "refugee protection in regions of origin." As they assert (referring to the time period roughly coinciding with the Tampere Program) the reality of protection in the region of origin is a distressing one indeed, and there is little prospect of improvement in the near future. Actually, the trend in recent years has been toward a worsening of conditions in the regions of refugee origin. The ever more underfunded and understaffed UNHCR, for instance, has become "increasingly unable to carry out protection, assistance and activities in pursuit of durable solutions for refugees in regions of origin" (Loescher and Milner 2003: 605). Partially building their case on field research in several such regions, Loescher and Milner (2003: 615) also contend that the EU's governments simply lack "effective policies to address the often deplorable situations for refugees and asylum seekers in regional host countries." Under these circumstances, therefore, it would be not only ineffectual but also unscrupulous for the EU to insist that poorer countries, many of which are already unstable and depleted of resources, should host and offer "protection" to an even larger proportion of the world's refugees (Loescher and Milner 2003: 604; see also ECRE and U.S. Committee for Refugees 2003).

It seems safe to say, then, that even if the Commission should stand firm on a program of regional protection worth its name, it would face an uphill task. This not least since neither adequate funding nor member-state backing were within the Commission's reach at the time. This point was also driven home in the European Council on Refugees and Exiles' (ECRE) (2004: 5) comprehensive assessment of the implementation of the Tampere programme.

Enter New Labour's "New Vision"

Right before the Spring European Council in 2003, regional protection was bumped up to the top of the EU agenda by way of a British proposal, which became the subject of a vast debate. Clearly, this was also what the British government had in mind when it presented its "New Vision for

Refugees," declaring that "[t]here may now be a rare opportunity for the U.K. to truly set the global agenda on this issue" (U.K. Government 2003: 2). The British proposal, which partly sprang from previous Danish interventions and was inspired by Australia's "Pacific solution" (Noll 2003), called for sweeping reform of "the global system" for asylum. In line with other major players, the Blair government grounded its intervention in a depiction of a "failing" current asylum system. Due to this situation, the "Vision Paper"[10] went on to contend, the present asylum system "undermines public confidence" because it is held to be tremendously demanding to expel rejected asylum seekers (U.K. Government 2003: 1–2). In this context the "Vision Paper" also claimed that the asylum system was being abused by terrorists, and that, consequently, a deterrent had to be found to prevent this problem, which recently had "topped the headlines" (2003: 6, 16).

In order to come to terms with the propounded deficiencies, and to follow through on Prime Minister Blair's pledge to radically reduce the number of asylum seekers entering Britain (Noll 2003: 304), the U.K. government put forward a package of far-reaching measures. As proposed, refugee protection in regions of origin was to be enhanced through the establishment of Regional Protection Areas (RPAs), located outside the EU, and operated by the UNHCR (U.K. Government 2003: 2). The RPAs should provide for basic needs so as to prevent refugees from absconding (and turning "illegal") in search of better living conditions. Most of all, however, the RPAs should guard against offering too generous provisions, since this "will act as a magnet to those in need in the surrounding area and cause resentment," "envy or mistrust" (2003: 13, 2). Once the RPAs had been set up, all asylum seekers (with a few exceptions) arriving into Britain and, preferably, the whole of the EU and possibly "other Western States" should be deported to them (2003: 2). Moreover, an agreement should be made initially establishing "the list of nationalities and ethnic origins" that any given RPA would house (2003: 13). As for the processing of asylum claims, the "Vision Paper" approached this as something that "[i]deally ... would not be necessary because the asylum seekers will be able to go home quickly and it is more efficient to provide for all rather than determine claims" (2003: 13). Among the many proposals—of which just a selection can be accounted for here—the "Vision Paper" also affirmed an "international recognition of the need to intervene to reduce flows of genuine refugees and enable refugees to return home." Measures here would range from "non-coercive" to "coercive" action, including military intervention in sovereign states (2003: 3, 11).

As few could have failed to notice, the changes proposed in the British "Vision Paper" "signal[ed] the most radical break with the international refugee regime as we know it" (Noll 2003: 309). In a painstaking analysis of the U.K. proposal, Gregor Noll (2003: 309–10) argues that "[i]t is no exaggeration to state that it could very well mean the end of the 1951 Refugee Convention." It "reflects an ongoing paradigm shift" in asylum policy, one that purports to ameliorate the refugee crisis "by locating the refugee beyond the domain of justice" (Noll 2003: 338; see also Loescher and Milner 2003). This point was also emphatically made by scores of human rights organizations in their sharp condemnations of the British "camp proposal" (see e.g. Amnesty International 2003; Human Rights Watch 2003). The reactions of other EU governments to the British proposal ranged from enthusiastic espousal to outspoken (but abating) disapproval. Whereas Sweden and Finland, for instance, took up the latter stance, Denmark, Holland, and Italy stood out as the keenest backers; but Spain, Belgium, Austria, and (soon) Germany too were among the supporters (Noll 2003).

At the invitation of the European Council, the Commission responded to the U.K. proposal in the summer of 2003 (CEC 2003j). With reference to both the U.K. proposal and EU initiatives being prepared at the time, the Commission began its response by opening up to a "new approach" to asylum policy. While the work to harmonize the "in-country [asylum] process in the EU" was to continue, the new approach was to "move beyond the realm of such processes" and focus even more forcefully on "the phenomenon of mixed flows and the external dimension of these flows." As if required by the situation, the Commission went on to repeat that this was not going to render in-country harmonization "obsolete," since "spontaneous arrivals" of asylum seekers in the EU would continue to occur. However, "the new approach would reinforce the credibility, integrity and efficiency of the standards underpinning the systems for spontaneous arrivals, by offering a number of well defined alternatives" (CEC 2003j: 3).

Despite being in basic agreement with the "Vision Paper's" depiction of the present asylum system as "failing," the Commission was not moved to promote the U.K. proposal as a blueprint for such "alternatives." Instead, the Commission concluded that "before taking any further position" on the matter, key legal questions, involving the proposal's possible conflicts with refugee and human rights conventions, first had to be sorted out (2003j: 6–7).

The Fewer Who Come...

Following the presentation of the U.K. proposal and the subsequent Commission and UNHCR responses, the efforts to target protection, processing and integration of refugees in regions of origin came to overshadow most other activities within EU asylum policy. Included here were, of course, measures to augment the readmission and expulsion instruments, as well as the fight against illegal migration. In conjunction with this, as we discuss below, several other member state governments paraded proposals for external camps, thereby contributing to a normalization of the issue in EU policy discourse. The European Commission though, did not embrace the idea of deportations of asylum seekers from the EU to camps in third countries. At the same time, Brussels did not come close to an all out rejection of London's offer. Rather, by launching (toward the end of Tampere's running time) the concept of "more orderly and managed entry in the EU of persons in need of international protection" the Commission seemed intent on adopting the gist of the original U.K. proposal by way of circumventing some of the proposal's most repugnant and symbolically loaded elements. That is to say, "managed entry" could be construed as set to pave the way for an instrument that would render deportations superfluous since, by this means, future access to EU territory would primarily be open to those refugees selected for, what was now referred to as, various "situation-specific" and "flexible" "resettlement schemes." At all events, this is one plausible way of interpreting the Commission's somewhat ambiguous Communication on the matter (CEC 2004f).

What the Commission is out to resolve is the enduring predicament whereby the great majority of the asylum seekers who enter the EU—most often "illegally"—fails to meet the criteria for international protection. Predictably, this way of framing the problem fails to acknowledge that the approval rate of asylum applications is declining and asylum seekers are forced to make use of irregular channels largely because of the EU's ever more restrictive and securitized asylum and migration policies. As a consequence of the overabundance of immigration controls in and around the EU, the European Council on Refugees and Exiles estimated in 2004 that roughly 90 percent of asylum seekers are forced to utilize irregular (or "illegal") channels in order to gain entrance to the EU (ECRE 2004: 17). But instead of confronting this serious problem, the Commission goes on to present "managed arrivals" through selective resettlement schemes not only as a way to reduce the costs involved in the processing of unfounded applications and the subsequent returns, but also as a means to fight racism:

> [T]he managed arrival of persons in need of international protection would also constitute an efficient tool in *combating sentiments of racism and xenophobia*, as the public support for those positively screened outside the EU and then resettled in the EU is likely to be increased. This is significantly different to the current situation where a majority of the persons applying for asylum are not found to require any form of

international protection. The lack of clarity in terms of public perception of this group threatens the credibility of the institution of asylum. (CEC 2004f: 6, emphasis in original)

Other accentuated advantages ascribed to "legal, orderly and managed entry" concern planning, integration and security:

> The setting up of tailor made integration programmes for specific categories of refugees would also be much more easily devised, if a country knew in advance who was arriving on its territory to stay. Resettling and allowing physical access to the territory of the EU of persons whose identity and history has been screened in advance would also be preferable from a security perspective. (CEC 2004f: 7)

In this connection the pivotal question is also raised concerning the standards to be employed when determining "whether or not a person is suitable for resettlement under a possible EU scheme" (CEC 2004f: 10). From the Commission's perspective, two questions are said to merit special deliberation here: "Do they qualify for international protection?"; and "Are they part of the target group deemed suitable for selection?" (CEC 2004f: 10). By explicitly referring selection criteria to questions regarding security screening and suitability, and to wordings such as "specific categories of refugees," the Commission raised apprehensions within the human rights community. Statewatch saw the Commission Communication as foreboding an EU practice of "cherry picking" refugees. In other words, "what, exactly, does the Commission mean by 'specific categories of refugees'? Ethnic groups, specific nationalities, men, women, children; or perhaps workers with certain skill-sets?" (Statewatch 2004b: 5). Some may well dismiss such words as mere speculative hyperbole. However, in a political climate where proposals for camps were being tabled in rapid succession, and where many governments (and also the European Commission) appeared to be trying to outdo each other in coming up with the most expedient way of managing the "asylum problem," thus progressively pushing the boundaries of what are conceived as "feasible" measures, Statewatch's warning was best taken seriously. As was mentioned earlier, moreover, the Commission had, albeit hitherto in vague terms, begun to introduce the issue of asylum into the discussion of the EU's growing demand for third-country labor migrants. As for the time being, however, the Commission took the question of "selection criteria" to be "a matter for negotiation in any future proposal":

> The question of how to deal fairly with the dissatisfaction of those not selected for resettlement and the rationale for proposing one durable solution to one particular group of people but not to another when

both groups are in a similar situation will also have to be carefully managed. (CEC 2004f: 10)

But whereas "managed entry" through "flexible" resettlement is held up as a means to reduce costs, to retain public confidence in the institution of asylum, to give expression to Europe's humanitarian tradition and to combat racism in the EU, a future EU resettlement scheme would *not* be designed to have any significant impact on the global refugee crisis as a whole. This, simply because of the small number of refugees projected to be selected for future resettlement in the EU (CEC 2004f: 9). So while the internal impact of "managed entry" through resettlement is said to be considerable, the external impact on access to protection is limited to a "strategic" or, perhaps better, symbolic type of "add[ed] value," whereby the EU "express[es] solidarity with and share[s] the burden of countries in the regions of origin faced with protracted refugee situations" (2004f: 9).

The limited external role (and impact on the current refugee calamity) assigned to managed entry via resettlement is, of course, bound up with the fact that, from now on, it is protection in the region of origin that is said to constitute the real and long-term solution to the global refugee crisis. We have already dealt with why the EU's cherished goal of ensuring "effective protection" in the region of origin remains unattainable in the foreseeable future. In many respects, interestingly enough, this assessment is in full agreement with the Commission's (2004f: 16) own:

> There is a long way to go before most of the current refugee hosting countries in the regions of origin could be considered to meet such a standard where they are able and willing to offer effective protection.... None of the durable solutions can be arrived at overnight—they are all products of long term planning.

Nevertheless, as we discuss in more detail in the next chapter, the Commission has decided to go ahead and promote what it has termed "EU Regional Protection Programs." We interpret this as a contradiction because of the Commission's discernible readiness to make refugee protection in certain regions of origin operational *before* the decidedly distant and difficult goal of meeting protection and human rights standards has been fully realized. In its first Communication on the matter, the Commission (2004f) points out that before countries in regions of origin can be considered "robust providers of effective protection" and "proper countries of first asylum," certain "measurable and achievable" "benchmarks" and "indicators" of effective protection first have to be in place. As outlined by the Commission (2004f: 16), there should, for instance, be a "possibility ... to request refugee status" and "to live a safe and dignified life taking into consideration the relevant socio-economic conditions prevailing in the host country." The rather vague and pragmatic formulations in which these benchmarks are couched, however, leave much to be desired. Moreover, given the experience of EU return policy and the designation of "safe third countries," there is good reason to wonder how strictly these "benchmarks" for effective protection will be applied. As Statewatch (2004b: 4–5) notes, the fact that the EU considered Afghanistan safe enough for the return of refugees in 2002 lends further support to such scepticism.

Subsequent to the publication of the Commission's communication (2004f) on EU resettlement schemes and EU regional protection programs (EU-RPP), EU asylum policy became the subject of an ever more intense debate and policy activity. As we will come back to in the ensuing chapter, following an agreement with Libya in August of 2004, the Italian government went ahead and announced that it planned to establish refugee camps in Libya for the purpose of preventing "illegal immigrants" from reaching Italian shores. Around the same time Germany also presented a proposal to set up EU asylum centers outside the Union.[11] With the stated aim of preventing people from jeopardizing their lives on their way to Europe, the German minister of the interior cited Libya, Tunisia, and other countries in North Africa as possible sites for such camps.

Two years after the original U.K. proposal, external EU or EU-sponsored camps for refugees emerged as a viable option. This was further underscored at the informal JHA Council meeting in the Netherlands in October 2004. Here, as part of the EU-RPP initiative, the Commission proposed five pilot projects to help establish asylum centres in Libya, Tunisia, Algeria, Morocco, and Mauritania. Besides housing refugees in Africa en route to Europe, it was also suggested that refugees apprehended in the international waters of the Mediterranean be deported to and housed in these centers. As we discuss at length in the next chapter, finally, it should be mentioned already here that shortly thereafter the EU's new multi-annual migration program, the Hague Program, which succeeded the Tampere Program, went on to confirm that EU Regional Protection Programs was to be vigorously pursued in future years.

Conclusion

The task of analyzing the EU's post-Amsterdam policies on migrant integration *together* with policies on labor migration, illegal migration, and asylum has largely proven to be a matter of grappling with a considerable accumulation of contradictions. We began by examining the EU integration policies' pronounced commitments to "civic citizenship" and extended free movement rights for TCNs on the one hand, and their marked adjustment to the needs of the EU's flexible labor market and the Lisbon agenda's neoliberal communitarian citizenship model on the other. As also elucidated, a similar approach pervades the Commission's policy line on labor migration from third countries. Here, however, the heavy emphasis on flexible and temporary work permits for new labor migrants contradicts the premise of EU integration policy, which holds that migrants' integration always amounts to a long-term process. On the whole, the primacy of market requirements that permeates EU policy on new labor migration leaves very little room for the type of civic citizenship and rights dimension that, despite their inconsistencies, are still endorsed in policies addressing the situation of the EU's "legal" and permanently settled TCNs.

But we also saw that EU integration policy is not only adapted to the Lisbon Agenda's market requirements and labor market flexibility. The aspiration that migrants and minorities should embrace "European values" is also accentuated, as are these groups' responsibilities and obligations in the integration process. The conceptions that underpin this approach to integration are also manifest in the Commission's contradictory endeavor to prepare host populations for the rescission of the policy of "zero" labor migration from third countries. Here, we showed, the Commission's exhortations for increased tolerance of cultural diversity and a greater understanding of the economic benefits of additional labor migrants are made to coexist with the same Commission's deference for an assumed popular skepticism about the prospects for migrants' "social and cultural adaptation," as well as for host populations' possible rejection of new labor migration from third countries. Arguably, such contradictory approaches largely draw upon the political climate in the member states, upon governments' desire to continue to assure citizens protection from the many alleged ills of immigration, and upon what we have chosen to term the "neo-assimilationist" integration and citizenship policies and conceptions that became in vogue in many member states around the turn of the millennium. It partly represents the Commission's adaptation to governments which are intent on inviting in more migrant labour in order to sustain competitive economies, but which have simultaneously fomented anti-immigrant sentiment and played on ethno-cultural identity and citizen politics in order to stay competitive with the extreme right at the polls.

Adding to the contradictory picture, we also pointed to EU policy initiatives that are at odds with such developments and sentiments, above all anti-discrimination and anti-racism policies. Possibly, these may be conceived of as budding elements of a more inclusive future EU citizenship policy, able to address not only the attitudal expressions of discrimination and racism but also, and more importantly, to challenge the barriers and disadvantages that migrants and minorities are facing as a result of widespread institutionally embedded discrimination. However, from a wider perspective, we also need to probe the prospects for an effective EU anti-discrimination policy that, while allowing for an assertively proactive stance on the civil rights dimension of citizenship, is unable, due to its neoliberal underpinnings, to make any firm commitment to the social rights dimension of citizenship and thus speak to the often inextricable connection between racism and ethnic discrimination, on the one side, and social inequality and class disadvantage, on the other.

However, the EU's increasingly externalized policies on asylum, illegal migration, expulsion and border control raise another and perhaps even more pressing question. That is, we have to wonder what the real prospects for anti-discrimination are in a Europe that (once again) is haunted by the "spectre of the camp."[12] It is here, then, at the intersection of benign anti-discrimination objectives and the reprehensible treatment of asylum seekers and "illegals" that we are brought face to face with some of the most pungent contradictions inherent in today's European integration. We have seen how the already diluted right of asylum in the post-Amsterdam EU appears to be on the verge of being debased to the level of a merely formal commitment, set to be outsourced, through the politics of stick and carrot, to poorly resourced countries in the regions of refugee origin. This development forms an integral part of the gradual downgrading of the EU's commitment to resolving the global refugee crisis to the mere globalization of its border controls, and to its "fight" against illegal migration, international crime, and terrorism. The fabrication of a menacing and securitized "problem" of illegal immigration—set in train in the 1980's Single Market Europe—and the subsequent actions that supposedly had to be taken to address it have thus constituted key enabling factors in the gradual undermining of the asylum institute in the EU. In this way, moreover, the EU is exploiting, as a pariah and scapegoat, the very same group—the "illegals"—that simultaneously serve as indispensable cogs in the Lisbon Strategy's much desired flexible economy and labor market.

This undertaking, as was also shown, is carried out for the stated purpose of enhancing Europe's security as well as in the name of the European humanitarian tradition—even in the name of anti-racism. But as we evinced in Chapter 3, it is also—and even more so in the wake of Amsterdam and Tampere—carried out in the alleged interest of the "European citizens," for the benefit of their freedom, welfare and security. As such,

EU migration policy—including its internally directed integration policy toward people who need to be inculcated with "European values"—makes up a key element in, as well as a powerful expression of, an EU-European politics of identity and belonging (see Huysmans 2006). In many crucial respects, therefore, the EU's post-Amsterdam politics of migration is synonymous with its politics of EU citizenship. In reconnecting with the thesis spelled out in our opening chapters, we can now appreciate to the full why the enterprise of describing, analyzing and understanding EU citizenship by necessity must pay close attention to EU migration policy.

Migration policy rose to the top of the EU agenda following the Amsterdam and Tampere agreements. As the next chapter accounts for, the EU's subsequent migration policy program, the Hague Program, will testify to migration policy's further consolidation as one of European integration's most important and pressing issues; this time equipped with an even more powerful political-economic incentive in the form of the relaunched Lisbon agenda.

Notes

1. According to the directive, third-country nationals who have resided legally in a member state for five years qualify for long-term resident status.
2. While Britain decided to opt in to this directive, it does not apply to Ireland and Denmark (Council EU 2001a: 13).
3. Britain has opted in to this directive; Ireland and Denmark do not participate (Council EU 2003b: 19).
4. Britain and Ireland maintain their own visa policies.
5. The Eurodac regulation does not apply to Denmark (Council EU 2002c: 2).
6. The regulation applies to Britain and Ireland but not to Denmark (Council EU 2003c: 2).
7. For a critical examination of Eurodac, see Guild (2006).
8. For a painstaking account of the extensive use of forced deportations of migrants and refugees in the EU and its member states from the 1990s to the present, see e.g. de Stoop (1997), Fekete (2005), and Birnberg Peirce & Partners, "Medical Justice and the National Coalition of Anti-Deportation Campaigns" (2008). Besides forced sedation and a row of other "aids" utilized when forcibly deporting people by air—such as muzzles, straitjackets, hand- and footcuffs and the widespread use of physical abuse—de Stoop also evinces the lucrative market that forced deportations gave rise to in the 1990s.
9. The Cotonou Agreement, which was signed in June 2000, replaced the Lomé Convention.
10. We borrow this term from Noll (2003).
11. Austria, Estonia, Latvia, and Lithuania, for their part, pointed to Ukraine as a possible site for EU refugee camps.
12. We borrow this expression from Noll (2003: 339).

CHAPTER 6

"At the Heart of Citizens' Interests"
EU Migration Policy in the Hague Program

Introduction

At the Brussels European Council in the autumn of 2004 the EU leaders approved the Hague Program for "strengthening freedom, security and justice in the European Union" (Council EU 2004g: 11). Set to run until 2010—when it will be replaced by the Stockholm Program (adopted in December 2009) (Council EU 2009b)—the Hague Program instituted a new five-year agenda for the development of EU migration policy, thus aiming to continue the work that was initiated and carried out within the framework of the Tampere Program (1999–2004). The launching of the Hague Program further accentuated migration's status as a high-profile EU issue. From the outset, and even more forcibly than Tampere, Hague also pointed to the importance of acknowledging and indeed acting on the ever-increasing salience of migration by integrating a migration dimension in a set of other EU policy pursuits—in everything from economic growth and social cohesion to the Union's external relations and fight against terrorism.

Over and above the location of migration in such a broad context, Hague designates *citizenship* as its principal watchword and leitmotif. While this obviously is in line with Tampere, there is no mistaking Hague's greater determination to succeed in having EU migration policy serve as a concrete manifestation of EU citizenship in the public mind. According to the Commission (2005b: 3–4), the Hague Program is not only there to make do on some of "the fundamental objectives of the Union" in general; foremost it is set to deal with issues and problems that are "at the heart of citizens' interests." As such, the Commission (2005b: 4) goes on, Hague "seeks to respond to the expectations of our citizens." The increasing attention paid to citizenship in EU migration policy is further underscored by the fact that it is the item "Fundamental rights and citizenship"—not asylum, illegal migration, or labor migration—that sits atop the list of the Hague Program's "ten priorities for the next five years" (2005–09), as spelled out by the Commission in 2005 (CEC 2005b). Noteworthy too is that the "fight against terrorism" ranks second on Hague's priority list. Even more so than Tampere, Hague stresses the urgent need to integrate the fight against terrorism in the EU's migration policy. At the launching of the Hague Program the Council of Ministers also made sure to articulate this as a duty towards the EU's citizens: "Europe's citizens rightly expect the European Union … to take a more effective, joint approach to cross-border problems such as illegal immigration and trafficking in and smuggling of human beings, as well as to terrorism and organised crime" (Council EU 2004g: 4). According to Balzacq and Carrera (2006: 5, 18), this arbitrary interpretation of citizens' expectations reflects the "security-led approach which dominates the [Hague] Programme" (see further Bigo 2006).

The drive to develop the external dimension of EU migration policy is another of Hague's most outstanding undertakings. The external dimension figures prominently in practically all of Hague's prioritized areas. As in the Tampere Program, this manifests most conspicuously in asylum policy. Since harmonization, according to both the Council and the Commission, already has progressed quite far as concerns the internal asylum system in the Union, more energy will now be devoted to the externalization of EU asylum policy that was initiated toward the end of the Tampere process. At its inception in 2004, Hague declared that "EU Regional Protection Programs" should be established in refugee producing regions by way of partnership agreements between the EU and various third countries. But Hague also attends to the internal dimension of asylum policy and is determined to have a "Common European Asylum System" up and running before the end of 2010 (Council EU 2004g: 17–8); this constitutes one of the few deadlines laid down by the Hague Program. Hague's other prioritized fields of action include "the fight against illegal immigration," external border management, the coordination of increased labor migration to the EU from third countries and integration and anti-discrimination policy.

We should also keep in mind that the start of the revision of EU migration policy in the Hague Program coincided with the revision of EU economic policy in the relaunched Lisbon Strategy and Agenda. In addition to the changes that we examined in the previous chapter, the relaunched

Lisbon Agenda was also furnished with a much more accentuated and explicit migration dimension. In fact, the EU's growth, employment, and competitiveness are now deemed wholly dependent on the future direction of EU migration policy, where the Union is said to have no other alternative but to massively increase labor migration from third countries. On this view, the EU's growth and employment problems cannot be properly tackled unless the EU's demographic crisis gets resolved. But if the EU is to succeed in attracting the large number of labor migrants that is said to be needed in order to sustain the Union's economic prosperity—migrant labor that North American and Asian economies already are competing for—this will also require a well-functioning and attractive migrant integration policy. Owing to this, Lisbon has also conferred a more prominent role to migrant integration policy.

In close conjunction with this, migration has also been elevated on the EU's Social Policy Agenda (SPA) that was adopted in 2006 and which is set to operate within approximately the same time frame as the Hague Program and the relaunched Lisbon Strategy. Under the motto "strengthening Citizens' Confidence," the new SPA is "designed to enable citizens to gain confidence in their own ability to effectively manage change, viz.: increased competition in a global context, technological development and population ageing" (CEC 2005k). In conformity with the EU's "modernizing" social model in general, the SPA is subordinated to Lisbon's overarching objectives concerning growth, competitiveness, and employment. "The new Social Agenda," the Commission states, "goes hand in hand with the revised Lisbon Strategy"; "it is designed as an essential part of the EU's revamped "Lisbon" strategy for growth and jobs" (CEC 2005c: 3, 9). Besides the need to "modernize" the "European Social Model" in accordance with the demands of stiffened global competition, to increase labor market flexibility and make the labor force more employable and productive, SPA goes on to stress that these objectives only can be accomplished if the EU is capable of fashioning a migration policy remedying the demographic crisis.

It is against this crucial background of the neoliberal political economy's continued dominance at the EU level, combined with the increasing importance that the EU attributes to the relation between growth and migration, that the Hague Program needs to be studied. Below, we now go on to discuss the program's most important components and policy initiatives. As in the previous chapter, we start out by examining integration and anti-discrimination policy; then we move on to discuss the areas of labor migration, migration policy externalization, asylum policy, and EU policy to combat "illegal migration."

The Hague Program's Integration and Anti-discrimination Policy

The EU's New Integration Principles

In the original Hague Program the EU's future integration policy is only dealt with somewhat briefly. The most important intervention was made up by the decision to adopt a number of "common basic principles" serving as a foundation for "a coherent European framework on integration" (Council EU 2004g: 19–20). At the Brussels European Council these principles were only described in a few short points. But soon thereafter, on the initiate of the Dutch presidency, the Council of Ministers approved a catalogue of eleven such integration principles, under the heading "Common basic principles for immigrant integration policy in the European Union." Even though the principles were not given any binding legal status, they nonetheless marked a significant step, making up the first real framework agreement on integration ever at the EU level (Monar 2005: 135; Urth 2005: 176–7). In the autumn of 2005, in a communication entitled *A Common Agenda for Integration,* the Commission endorsed the principles and put forth various methods of implementation and suggestions for division of responsibility between national and supranational levels and actors (CEC 2005d).[1]

To begin with, we should note that Hague's approach to integration mainly is in conformity with the one laid down in Tampere. Both the Council and the Commission emphasize "adaptation by immigrants" and integration as "a dynamic, long-term, and continuous two-way process of mutual accommodation" between "immigrants" and "national citizens" (Council EU 2004f: 13; CEC 2005d). As was the case in Tampere, Hague also refrains from providing an explicit clarification as to what really characterizes an "immigrant" and a "national citizen" respectively, and what sets these two, ubiquitously referred to, categories of people apart. At a second glance, though, what induces this mode of categorization is quite easily ascertained, since the two categories implicitly coincide with the prevalent ethno-cultural division between a supposedly homogenous "European" collective (harmoniously harboring the EU's respective national cultures), on the one side, and an almost equally homogenous migrant collective, on the other. In this implicit sense Hague has been more upfront in its intimations than its predecessor. The justificatory basis for this division, however, is still left unexplained; and neither does Hague take any pains to specify the tangible characteristics of the cultural values that are said to distinguish the migrant collective in question. Instead, such specification is almost exclusively conducted in negative terms, with the accent on those "European values" that (preferably Muslim) migrants possibly might *not* embrace.

By comparison with Tampere's policy discourse, then, Hague more readily expresses misgivings concerning "[t]he cultures and religions that immigrants bring with them," seeing these as not always being in agreement with the "European and national values" that EU integration policy rests upon—such as "liberty, democracy, respect for human rights and fundamental freedoms, and the rule of law," as well as "the rights and equality of women" (Council EU 2004f: 13–14, 16; CEC 2005d: 19). In 2006 the then Commissioner in charge of Justice, Freedom, and Security (migration policy sorting under this Directorate-General), Franco Frattini, made the following statement regarding the integration of Muslims in the EU: "We can guarantee respect of traditions of the Muslim community only if these are not in contrast with our core rules, even if they are unwritten" (quoted in Kubosova 2006a). Integration policy in the EU thus has "a responsibility to ensure that cultural and religious practices do not prevent individual migrants from exercising other fundamental rights." This is seen as "particularly important as it pertains to the rights and equality of women, the rights and interests of children, and the freedom to practice or not to practice a particular religion" (Council EU 2004f: 16).

Hague also establishes that migrants should adapt to and "acquire" the "culture of the host society" and be obliged to obtain "[b]asic knowledge of the host society's language, history, and institutions." According to the Council and the Commission such knowledge "is indispensable to integration" (Council EU 2004f: 15; CEC 2005d: 7). Despite the strong emphasis invested in this integration principle, pointers as to what it would entail in terms of actual content are conspicuously absent. Given the fact that there in no society exists a consensus concerning what should count as *the* "basic knowledge" of a country's history and culture—save for those where such a consensus is coerced—this absence is certainly not to be wondered at. Knowledge about history, if we begin there, is, namely, something that cannot be discussed in isolation of interpretation, unless we reduce history to a row of dates and names; and as indicated by the importance the EU attaches to the matter, it is not the reductive approach that Hague's integration policy has in view. As countless contemporary history debates in EU countries illustrate—about the Holocaust, colonialism, Communism, Fascism, refugee policy in the 1930s, the historical treatment of various minorities, to mention but a few—society's concept of history is rather something that is continuously subjected to contestation over interpretation, within academia, politics, and culture. Not only that; EU countries' doings and stances in the past often also constitute sensitive chapters in the respective national histories, something that not least becomes evident in governments' recurrent attempts to cover up new knowledge about historical wrongs committed in the name of the nation.

In the same way we must approach the Hague Program's principle calling on migrants to "acquire" the host country's culture. That is, we must ask who possesses the mandate to settle, once and for all, what makes up a country's culture and cultural values? Here too we witness daily debates raging over which cultural values that should guide and form the basis for a country's conduct within domestic as well as foreign policy. Should gay couples have the right to adopt children? Is it justifiable to export weapons to countries that violate human rights? Should criminal policy be based on rehabilitation or punishment? Which values should guide policy dealing with gender relations and sexuality? Is it defensible to use torture in the fight against terrorism? Should school curricula have a religious foundation or not? Ought parents have the right to use corporal punishment to discipline their children (a "right" upheld in 14 EU countries)? Is forced deportation of rejected asylum seekers in agreement with humanitarian values? And what about abortion and stem cell research? Since the answers to the questions as to what any given society's culture and cultural values *are*, and, respectively, what they *should* be, are as many and varied as the motley crowd who struggles for the preferential right of interpretation, the list of cultural debates can be made as long as the one of debates concerning knowledge about a society's history.

It is against this backdrop that it becomes necessary to ponder why it is precisely migrants who are enjoined to learn *one* historical account and adapt to *one* culture when so many, and often diametrically opposed, views on these matters are allowed to flourish within the rest of the population. Why, one may ask, are not the same demands placed on the population as a whole? In view of the fact that it is taken to be so utterly decisive for integration that migrants know the history and honor the culture of the host society might it not have been advisable for the authorities to first ensure that there truly exists a uniform conception of history and culture among the non-migrant population? Only by so doing could the confusion be avoided for those migrants who are admonished to learn the history and adapt to the cultural values, just to discover soon after that the host society is host to scores of conflicting conceptions of history and cultural values.

Obviously we are not pointing to a realistic scenario here, since such a project of cultural regimentation would not be feasible short of the abrogation of the entire domain of laws and values governing and protecting freedom of expression and all that extends from that liberty—laws and values, we should add, that the EU requires migrants to respect. Instead, the point we are getting at is that EU integration policy seems intent on making such a regimentation project realistic when it comes to certain migrant groups; that is, it seems ready to impose restrictions on migrants' rights to freely form an opinion of the host society's history and register of cultural values. In effect, this also points to a readiness to exclude certain migrants from the enjoyment of precisely those rights of freedom of expression, opinion, and thought that EU integration policy is said to promote and defend, and which are also said to be at the heart of the EU's "European community of values." In some important respects, this pursuit can be construed as a supranational imitation of an age-old nationalist stratagem, whereby, as Balibar (2004: 37) has it, national governments bet that "national citizens can be persuaded that their rights do in fact exist if they see that the rights of foreigners are inferior, precarious, or conditioned on repeated manifestations of allegiance (often baptized "signs of integration")."

Viewed in this light, the turn taken by EU integration policy under Hague must be seen as quite remarkable. It signals that certain migrants are not to be treated as prospective EU citizens, but rather as prospective qualifiers for EU subjecthood. What adds to this impression is the fact that the policy discourse under study says relatively little about the law, as in emphasizing newly arrived migrants' obligation to obey the laws in their respective host societies. Rather, what is highlighted are "values," "traditions," and "norms," vaguely defined as to their concrete meaning and practical manifestation yet with the sting often undisguisedly directed at Muslim migrants and minorities. As the EU's Justice and Home Affairs Commissioner was quoted as saying, above, the EU "can guarantee respect of traditions of the Muslim community" but "only if these are not in contrast with our core rules, even if they are unwritten." To oblige people to follow "unwritten" rules not only invites arbitrariness in the treatment of people, thus jeopardizing the legal rights of the individual, but it also flies in the face of transparency and consistency in formulating policy. While EU integration policy may direct itself to "migrants" and "third-country nationals" (TCNs), it is patently clear that these categories are not meant to be all-inclusive. Hence, they do not apply to, say, migrants in Sweden with Italian passports or to third-country nationals in Ireland with Canadian passports. Yet, this is never explicated in a coherent and transparent fashion but rather left to rest on tacit assumptions whereby merely certain migrants and TCNs are deemed to be in need of integration; that is to say, those seen as being most likely to pose a threat to European values.

A Growing Transnational Convergence Toward Neo-Assimilationism

The current development of EU integration policy must be seen as contingent on the increasingly assimilation-oriented approach to integration adopted by many member states (see Monar 2005: 135). The Hague Program thus confirms what we have referred to as the neo-assimilationist course in EU integration policy, which was introduced during the Tampere Program. Yet Hague does not confer any new supranational competence to the EU in this area. "The development and implementation of integration policy," the Council (2004f: 11) upholds, is "the primary responsibility of individual Member States rather than of the Union as a whole" (see also CEC 2005d). True, the Commission has succeeded in securing the member states' support for the establishment of the European Fund for the Integration of third-country nationals, for the period 2007–2013 (Council Decision 2007/435/EC), which is set to offer financial assistance to member states' integration efforts. While the fund provides the Commission with a new financial instrument, it can hardly be said to amount to a transfer of competence from the national to the supranational level. Instead, the fund is best construed as forming part of the EU's general and unbinding integration framework of common basic principles, strategies, and policy coordination.

The prolonged and meager supranational mandate has been interpreted by many as a clear indication that "the Member States intend to continue to leave this sensitive area largely to domestic policy-making" (Monar 2005: 135). While there is a good deal in that judgement, much of it may depend less on the issue's sensitivity within domestic politics of individual member states, as is commonly claimed, and more on whether or not integration policy will remain a sensitive intergovernmental issue in the EU. Drawing from past experience, policy areas, such as, for instance, asylum and monetary policy, seem to remain sensitive and thus impossible to subject to supranational harmonization not because of their allegedly inherent inseparability from national sovereignty and identity but more so simply because of difference of opinion between governments. Hence, once intergovernmental consensus starts to emerge—as was the case with monetary policy in the early 1990s and asylum policy in the late 1990s—the sensitivity surrounding the particular policy area in question also seems to recede. National monetary policy could thus go from being depicted as a nonnegotiable piece of national sovereignty—the national currency being one of its crown jewels—to being treated as an outmoded obstacle to economic progress ready for chucking into the supranational currency melting pot.

To be sure, there are still significant discrepancies between the member states' respective integration policies. Nonetheless, what has characterized the last few years is a growing convergence among several EU governments toward a neo-assimilationist approach. This is not least seen in the introduction of mandatory integration and citizenship programs and tests in a growing number of EU countries (e.g. Austria, Belgium, Denmark, France, Germany, Poland, Spain, the Netherlands, the U.K.), whereby both prospective and new migrants, but also some of the long-term residents of migrant background, are required to prove their loyalty to certain arbitrarily selected cultural values and their proficiency in, for instance, the official language and national customs in order to obtain a residence permit, social benefits or citizenship (see e.g. Carrera 2006; Council of Europe 2008; Davy 2005; Entzinger 2006; Fekete 2009; Groenendijk 2004). The convergence is also visible in the fact that these tests never are directed at migrants as such but only zoom in on those with non-Western backgrounds and particularly at those from Muslim countries (see further Fekete 2009). In the Dutch case, for instance, migrants who are citizens of other EU member states, Switzerland, the U.S., Canada, Japan, Australia, and New Zealand are exempted from the test, as are those skilled workers with an annual income exceeding a certain amount (Carrera 2006: 101). Listening, moreover, to the rhetoric in which politicians often couch integration tests when marketing them to the public, one is quickly made blatantly aware of these tests' chief objective: that is, to make Muslims know their place (see Fekete 2009). As the chairman of the German government party Christian Social Union of Bavaria (CSU), Edmund Stoiber, told one of the German tabloids when speaking in favor of a German citizenship test: "It has to be clear that in our country the monopoly of power belongs to the state and not the Turkish man" (quoted in *EurActiv* 2006). "When the Koran is put above the German constitution, I can only say, 'Good night, Germany'," said the general secretary of Germany's main government party, the Christian Democratic Union (CDU) (quoted in Landler 2007). The CDU general secretary, Ronald Pofalla, has also stated that "[w]hoever represents Germany, whether a native German or an immigrant, has to identify with the history and culture of our society." "If he does not want to do so," Pofalla went on, "then that national jersey should be removed" (quoted in Younge 2007). Recently, this type of rhetoric has also found an outlet in Brussels' public statements on integration, such as in the then Justice, Freedom, and Security Commissioner (also vice-president of the European Commission) Franco Frattini's spiteful remark: "We are not governed by sharia, after all" (quoted in Kubosova 2006a).

Another step toward convergence of integration policy in the EU was taken in the spring of 2006 when the six largest member states—the so-called G6 countries (Group of Six): France, Germany, Italy, Poland, Spain, and the U.K.—launched a joint initiative to explore the possibilities to make it obligatory for migrants to sign an "integration contract" whereby migrants, upon successful completion of tests, pledge themselves to honor certain European cultural values. At the meeting, which was mainly dedicated to the issues of terrorism and illegal migration, the G6 countries also agreed that such a contract ideally should apply to the EU as a whole. Home secretary of the U.K., Charles Clarke, supported the initiative on the grounds that it is necessary to make sure that "new immigrants live up to the values of our society," suggesting that those who failed to meet the contract's obligations may well be subjected to expulsion (*EurActiv* 2006). It should be noted that France, Germany, Italy, the Netherlands, and Poland separately already have taken measures that enable them to expel persons who voice opinions that can be interpreted as unpatriotic, anti-Western, and pro-violence (Fekete 2006a).

Besides the ethno-cultural and ethno-nationalist biases, however, current national integration programs and tests are also heavily imbued with socioeconomic biases, with the burden to integrate for the most part falling the hardest on those migrants and minorities most dependent on access to social welfare provisions—provisions that they may be disqualified from or lose should they fail their integration obligations (Carrera 2006). This is demonstrated by the fact that more well-to-do migrant groups often are exempted from integration programs and tests, e.g. the highly skilled, those under international contracts, students, researchers and those with personal fortunes (Carrera 2006; Council of Europe 2008). As the intergovernmental organization the Council of Europe (2008) (not to be confused for an EU institution) notes critically, "it seems that mainly poor immigrants without financial resources and in search of economic improvement are targeted by the rigid obligation to integrate." Similarly, Carrera (2006: 102) argues that "[e]conomic status and the level of financial dependency on the receiving State's welfare system seem to be among the main factors determining whether 'the non-national' is or not subject to integration programmes and courses" (see also Guild 2005). This increasingly prevalent approach to migrant integration is about to make already socially disadvantaged and ethno culturally excluded migrants' "failure" to comply with arbitrarily defined national cultural values a justifiable reason for curtailing their social rights even further. What we have, then, is yet another manifestation of the Third Way–inspired neoliberal communitarian citizenship model, as outlined in Chapter 4. But as we qualified in Chapter 5, when discussing how this citizenship model plays out in the specific context of migrant integration, the model's basic mantra of "no rights without responsibilities" is adjusted to something sounding more like "no rights without submission."

Time will show whether or not the growing transnational integration policy convergence will continue and become robust enough to enable binding supranational policy. It is worth repeating that significant national differences remain, differences that speak against such supranationalization in the near future. On the other hand, nothing should be ruled out in advance. This not least since integration policy also has become increasingly articulated in terms of security, thus deriving more and more of its impetus from the so-called war on terror (Carrera 2006), which often operates by means of quite drastic and swiftly enforced measures. For instance, the ink had barely dried on the newspapers announcing (in August 2006) that the U.K. government claimed to have uncovered plans to launch terror attacks against transatlantic flights before the European Commission presented a new counter-terrorism package in which an effort to "train Muslim preachers in European values" constituted one of the centrepieces (*Deutsche Welle* 2006).

Important to note too is that there are signs that the culturally neo-assimilationist and socially exclusive integration approach adopted by many member states already has begun to seep into supranational policy and legislation. Several scholars have pointed to the integration stipulations made in the EU's migration policy directives on long-term resident status for TCNs (see Chapter 5) and the right to family reunification (Council EU 2003d). "The philosophy underlying these Directives," Sergio Carrera (2006: 107, italics in original) argues

> seems to strengthen the evidenced trend in a majority of Member States towards an increasingly restrictive and mandatory integration policy for immigrants. Both Directives negatively link access to the set of rights they confer (inclusion) to compliance by immigrants with a series of restrictive conditions left in the hands of the member states (exclusion). Integration becomes the obligatory juridical condition (*conditionality of integration*) for having access to the set of rights and freedoms that these laws confer and to a more secure juridical status. Member States are given wide discretion to compel immigrants to comply with mandatory integration conditions stipulated by national law in order to have access to the rights they provide.

Thomas Gross (2005: 153; see also Urth 2005; Groenendijk 2004) argues similarly that these EU directives "are the consequence of a new political approach regarding integration not as a process following the entry into the host country, but as a precondition for the granting of immigration rights." This approach, Gross (2005: 153) shows, "is in sharp contrast to the evolution of free movement rights of Union citizens as they are not required to prove appropriate language proficiency or other prerequisites to integration."

Another factor that might speak in favor of a sustained integration policy convergence is bound up with the fact that integration policy has emerged as one of the most important vectors for both national and EU-European identity politics. This identity politics builds on an ever more unconcealed ethno-national and Eurocentric outlook that already has impacted citizenship regimes in an exclusive direction across the EU (see Carrera 2006; Schierup, Hansen and Castles 2006). The point of view—which not too long ago was one exclusively cherished by the extreme right—that it is appropriate to suspect, in advance, certain migrant and minority groups of disloyalty to national and European values has thus gained prevalence in many EU capitals (se further Fekete 2006b), as well as in Brussels.

The Hague Program's pronounced European cultural values dimension constitutes one of the most important alterations made within EU integration policy in comparison with the previous Tampere Program. However, this is not tantamount to a fundamental break in the trend. What stands out as the most notable is rather the policy discourse's (1) much more forcible, even hostile tone of voice; (2) the strong support for messages and measures that until recently were considered both controversial and counterproductive among many within the EU's political leadership; and (3) the Commission's readiness to jump on the neo-assimilationist bandwagon. The latter was further underscored at the Lisbon High-level Conference on Legal Immigration in 2007, when the then Commissioner, Franco Frattini (2007: 5), took the floor to pinpoint Europe's greatest menace:

> The dark side of the "old" migration strategy includes the fact of integration problems, often taking the form of the deliberate denial of Europe's founding values and principles. Until a few years ago, our chosen multicultural approach allowed some cultural and religious groups to pursue an aggressive strategy against our values. The targets of this ill-conceived "attack" were individual rights, equality of gender, respect for women and monogamy. We have to combat this dangerous attitude, which can destroy the fabric of our societies, and we have to work hard to build up and pursue a positive integration approach.

If this ill-concealed depiction of European culture as verging on the edge of being destroyed by an aggressive Muslim "enemy within" signals a turn to a more exclusive EU integration policy—more in tune with national neo-assimilationist enterprises—it also signals a turn to a more exclusive approach to EU citizenship, something we will elaborate more on ahead.

Integration and Paid Work—Two Sides of the Same Lisbon Strategy

Aside from what has been indicated above, the Hague Program's integration policy does not differ much from the one drawn up in Tampere. As already mentioned, Hague gives great emphasis to the relaunched Lisbon Strategy's more streamlined focus on growth and employment. In the "common basic principles" for integration it is stressed that "[e]mployment is a key part of the integration process and is central to the participation of immigrants, to the contributions immigrants make to the host society, and to making such contributions visible" (CEC 2005d: 6). Investment in migrants' entrepreneurship, small business pursuits and paid work through an improved integration in the labor market are consequently keywords also in the Hague Program. As the Commission (2005d: 3) writes in its proposal for *A Common Agenda for Integration:* "the effective and responsible integration of immigrants in the labour market constitutes an important contribution to reaching the Lisbon targets." As such, "[t]he new Integrated Guidelines for Jobs and Growth call on Member States to take action to increase the employment of immigrants," "stressing the gender perspective to fully utilise the potential of immigrant women in the labour market" (CEC 2005d: 3). Since the EU is not granted any supranational mandate to legislate within this field of integration policy either, the Commission puts much emphasis on the need to further develop transnational cooperation, partnerships and networks at local and regional levels in order to exchange information and best practices.

Pulling the Brakes on EU Anti-discrimination Policy?

As to the area of EU anti-discrimination policy, which according to Hague forms part of the Union's overarching integration policy, this was only treated very briefly in the original outline of the Hague Program. The Council confined itself to a short passage calling on the Commission "to give special attention to the fight against anti-Semitism, racism and xenophobia" (Council EU 2004g: 16). Neither did the Council pledge to introduce new laws in the area or to strengthen already existing ones. This provided, a certain amount of frustration could be spotted in the Commission's proposal for a framework strategy against discrimination, which was presented in 2005. "It is clear," the Commission (2005e: 2) contends, "that the implementation and enforcement of anti-discrimination legislation on an individual level is not enough to tackle the multifaceted and deep-rooted patterns of inequality experienced by some groups." Owing to this, the EU must "reinforce its efforts to promote equal opportunities for all, in order to tackle the structural barriers faced by migrants, ethnic minorities … and other vulnerable groups" (CEC 2005e: 2). The Commission (2005e: 6) maintains that discrimination cannot exclusively be solved by means of simple legislation, but that "[p]ositive measures may be necessary to compensate for long-standing inequalities suffered by groups of people who, historically, have not had access to equal opportunities."

Despite these strong formulations about the shortcomings of "legislation on an individual level," the presence of "structural barriers" and, not least, the possible need for "positive measures," the Commission decides against translating these into calls for new measures in its new framework strategy against discrimination. Instead, the Commission chooses to present a list of "priority areas," which include: (1) "targeted training and capacity-building actions for specialised equality bodies, judges, lawyers, NGOs and the social partners"; (2) "Networking and exchanges of experience between relevant stakeholders"; and (3) "Awareness-raising and dissemination of information" (CEC 2005e: 5). One of the reasons why the Commission's rather forthright policy rhetoric peters out into these cautiously worded priorities is probably to be found in the fact that a good deal of work to implement Tampere's anti-discrimination policy still remains to be completed; and that it is this backlog that prevents the Commission (at least in 2005) from launching any new, more comprehensive reform program. The Commission's frustration over many member states' laggard attitude toward implementation of Tampere's directives is quite evident in the new framework strategy. As the Commission (2005e: 4) states:

> The lack of effective and properly resourced Equality Bodies, able to give independent assistance to victims, in some Member States is particularly worrying. Also of concern is the lack of attention paid to disseminating information about new anti-discrimination rights. It is extremely difficult for victims of discrimination to enforce their rights without information and specialised help.

This may partly explain why Tampere's quite bold approach to anti-discrimination policy does not spill over into the Hague Program. Many of Tampere's decisions and intentions have simply not been realized yet; or as the Commission (2005e: 4–5) itself observes: "It is also clear that, in addition to legislative transposition, further measures will continue to be required for some time in order to ensure that anti-discrimination legislation is effectively implemented and enforced across the EU." (see also Adnett and Hardy 2005: 146)

Aside from the question of national implementation, EU anti-discrimination policy must also be analyzed in the context of its potential conflict with other areas of integration policy. Quite obviously there is a latent tension between EU anti-discrimination policy's acknowledgement of a widespread problem with racism in the member states, on the one hand, and many of the ingredients in the neo-assimilationist integration policy adopted in many member states, on the other. There is reason to believe that this tension already has a finger in some member states' reluctance to fully implement Tampere's anti-discrimination directives. But since the Commission—as is evident from Hague's integration principles—in many respects has sided with the neo-assimilationist message, this tension does not only run between the Commission and the member states. Instead, it increasingly leaves its mark also on the Commission's own contradictory approach to these matters.

In line with the overall approach of EU integration policy, we should also mention that Hague seeks to establish a firmer link, as compared to Tampere, between anti-discrimination policy and the Lisbon Strategy's growth and employment objectives. As the Commission (2005e: 2) affirms, "it will be difficult for the EU to achieve the ambitious targets that it has set itself for economic and employment growth if some people are excluded from jobs and higher achievement on the basis of gender, disability, race, age or other grounds." The great importance of coming to terms with discrimination in the labor market, the Commission (2005e: 2) continues, is further underscored "by the demographic challenges facing the EU, which will see its working age population decline by over 20 million during the next 25 years."

The Hague Program and the EU's Growing Demand for Third-Country Labor Migrants

A New EU Framework for "Circular" Labor Migration

With the Hague Program the issue of labor migration has been elevated even further on the EU agenda, and increased labor migration to the EU is seen as decisive for the achievement of the Lisbon Strategy's goals (Council EU 2004g: 19). Shortly after the adoption of the Hague Program this was emphatically confirmed in the Commission's *Green Paper on an EU Approach to Managing Economic Migration:*

> In fact, even if the Lisbon employment targets are met by 2010, overall employment levels will fall due to demographic change. Between 2010 and 2030, at current immigration flows, the decline in the EU-25's working age population will entail a fall in the number of employed people of some 20 million. Such developments will have a huge impact on overall economic growth, the functioning of the internal market and the competitiveness of EU enterprises. In this context ..., more sustained immigration flows could increasingly be required to meet the needs of the EU labour market and ensure Europe's prosperity. (CEC 2005f: 3–4)

"Immigration is an important part of the solution," the Commissioner responsible for External Relations and European Neighborhood Policy, Benita Ferrero-Waldner (CEC 2006d), verifies: "It will help us make the transition to a new economic situation, and maintain a certain level of growth."

Yet the launching of Hague did not signal any major supranational advances in the area. Nonetheless, since its adoption Brussels has been hard at work to persuade the member states about the merits of an EU framework that would encompass not only broad common guidelines for the future labor migration to the Union, but possibly also a limited set of legislative EU measures. This process was formally launched with the publication, in 2005, of the Commission's abovementioned *Green Paper*. Here the Commission made plain its aspiration to reach an agreement with the governments about the establishment of a set of "harmonised common rules and criteria at EU level for admitting economic migrants" (CEC 2005f: 4). Such harmonization would enable a transnational coordination of the intake of labor migrants and thus optimize the utilization of their labor in the EU as a whole. In order to adapt to different national and business sector demands, however, any such prospective EU rules should contain "a high degree of flexibility" (CEC 2005f: 5–6). Specific EU rules could thus be worked out to match, for instance, the needs of the service sector and their demand for seasonal and contracted labor.

In the *Green Paper* the Commission also made a case for looking into the possibilities of facilitating the recruitment of third-country nationals (TCNs) who already are permanent residents in one member state to another member state for the purpose of meeting a labor shortage there. Such an EU scheme would possibly not only rationalize recruitment, but it would also be favorable from an integration perspective, since "[t]he EU could then count on a 'stock' of manpower that has already started to integrate" (CEC 2005f: 7). In addition to this the Commission raised a number of related questions that it wanted answered before a common EU framework could be established. To these belonged, inter alia, the question of whether third-country labor migrants only should be admitted "conditional on a concrete job vacancy," or whether, in parallel, there also should be developed "more flexible systems such as green cards, etc, aimed at attracting workers to fill the short and long term needs of the labour market" (CEC 2005f: 7–8).

Roughly a year later the Commission followed up the *Green Paper* with its Communication on a *Policy Plan on Legal Migration* (CEC 2005l), laying out a "road-map" for the Hague Program's labor migration objectives as well as specifying all the legislation and other measures that would be proposed by Brussels up until the conclusion of Hague in 2010. Most importantly, the *Policy Plan* constitutes a forceful plea for a wholesale adaptation of EU labor migration policy to the objectives of the relaunched Lisbon Strategy. Framed "as part of Lisbon Strategy's comprehensive package of measures aimed at increasing the competitiveness of the EU economy," labor migration is held up as "crucial to satisfying current and future labour market needs and thus ensure economic sustainability and growth," which includes positively impacting the EU's dire demographic outlook (CEC 2005l: 5). As for the legislative proposals, the *Policy Plan* foreshadowed four specific directives and one general framework directive to be proposed by the Commission over a three-year period (2007–2009). Whereas the proposal for a framework directive was said to aim at instituting a single application procedure for a combined work-residence permit in a member state for TCNs, the four specific directives would seek to simplify the admission process and conditions for highly skilled labor, seasonal labor, remunerated trainees, and intra-corporate transferees. As is evident, the Commission is intent on paving the way for a common EU policy on the admission of both high skilled and low-skilled/unskilled labor migrants, although the latter, so far, is limited to seasonal labor.

At the time of writing, only two of the five forthcoming directives have been translated into actual directive proposals. This applies to the *Proposal for a Council Directive on the conditions of entry and residence of third-country nationals for the purposes of highly qualified employment* (CEC 2007d), to which the abovementioned framework directive also was attached. Presented with much fanfare in the autumn of 2007, this directive proposal, also dubbed the "blue card" proposal,

> aims, in particular, to improve the EU's ability to attract ... highly qualified workers so as to increase the contribution of legal immigration to enhancing the competitiveness of the EU economy by completing the set of other measures the EU is putting in place to achieve the goals of the Lisbon Strategy. It specifically aims ... to facilitate and harmonise the admission of this category of workers and by promoting their efficient allocation and re-allocation on the EU labour market. (CEC 2007d: 2)

The general context for the blue card, according to the Commission (2007d: 3), is best described in terms of a "need scenario" with regard to high-skilled labor in the EU. Viewed "in a context of very high international competition" for such migrant labor, this need scenario is said to pose a particular challenge to the EU; this because the Union, in comparison to other major players in the global migration market (e.g. the U.S., Canada, and Australia), has failed "to be considered attractive by highly qualified professionals" (CEC 2007d: 3; 2007e: 1). In order to come to terms with this impasse, the Commission thinks it is high time to start phasing out one of the EU's major comparative disadvantages vis-à-vis its competitors, which lies in high-skilled migrants having to wrestle with twenty-seven different national systems for admission as well as facing several layers of red tape when trying to move jobs within the EU (CEC 2007d: 3). "Europe," the Commission (2007e: 3) insists, "can only succeed in attracting 'the best and brightest' if it speaks with one voice."

At the same time, however, the Commission also qualified that the blue card by no means was intended to be "a blank cheque" to all highly qualified workers (quoted in Goldirova 2007a). As such, Commissioner Frattini underlined, "the blue card is not a permanent card like the American green card" (quoted in Goldirova 2007b). That is to say, the card "does not create a right of admission" (CEC 2007e: 2). Instead it is intended to be "demand driven," invariably requiring that highly qualified third-country migrants show proof of a "job contract" or "binding job-offer" before a blue card is issued (CEC 2007d: 9). By this means, member states "maintain control on which type—and how many—highly qualified workers will enter their labour markets" (CEC 2007e: 2; see also CEC 2007d: 7); a sine qua non, it seems safe to say, in order for the Commission's blue card proposal to be at all feasible. This is further underscored by the fact that the Commission's proposal steers clear of any mention of permanent residence, let alone the prospects thereof, for the would-be blue card holders. Instead it emphasizes that the work permit conferred by the card is to be limited to a maximum of two years stay in a member state, whereupon the blue card migrant will be granted the opportunity to move to another member state provided that "certain conditions" are met, including the mandatory requirement of a valid work contract (CEC 2007d: 6).

Much of this emphasis on temporary work permits finds recourse in assertions of the benefits of "circular migration"—one of the Hague Program's most prominent concepts and buzz words—which, inter alia, is set to limit the blue card's potential "brain drain" effects by facilitating the circulation of highly qualified third-country labor migrants to and fro the EU and their countries of origin. In so doing—Brussels' hopeful message projects—the blue card's circular migration scheme will serve as a means by which poor countries can garner developmental benefits from migration; this is how "[t]he proposal also complies with EU's development policy" (CEC 2007d: 4).

As already intimated, the blue card proposal and its concept of circular migration need to be construed as a compromise. This compromise straddles the Lisbon Agenda's neoliberal quest for an increase in the supply of labor and a more flexible labor market, on the one side, and, on the other, governments' reluctance to setting off on a visibly more open admission policy, with all that this implies in terms of reneging on electoral anti-immigration commitments to the contrary and, not least, in terms of many governments' fear of losing face before the extreme right. In order to make the blue card proposal viable, then, one could argue that the Commission is halfway meeting the demands of the relatively nationally unencumbered neoliberal forces' call for an increased supply of migrant labor, while at the same time respecting governments' desire to continue to appear as being dead set on keeping a firm hand on the labor migration spigot. Hence the emphasis on the blue card's migration scheme as "demand-driven" as well as in no way implying a "a right of admission." As also intimated above, however, there is one crucial element in the blue card scheme that most probably did not require any compromising, and that concerns "circular migration" and, with it, the emphasis on temporary work and residence for new migrants. We will develop further on this specific issue in the discussion ahead.

Third Country Labor Migration as a Means of Development

The Commission also makes a strong point of stressing the necessity of firmly establishing labor migration in partnerships and cooperative frameworks with the sender countries. The work to integrate labor migration policy into the EU's external relations and development and aid policy has therefore moved even higher on the EU agenda, something that becomes evident in the Commission's voluminous Communication *Migration and Development*. Here, the Commission announces its determination to reduce the cost of labor migrants' remittances to their countries of origin. In ready money these remittances are estimated to outdo the EU's entire spending on foreign aid, and Brussels believes that working to reduce the costs of remittance transfers could have a real added development value (CEC 2005g). As noted above, the problems connected with so-called brain drain are also addressed, Brussels proposing that the member states adopt "codes of conduct" in order to limit the recruitment of such labor—e.g., from the healthcare sector—that may have a damaging effect on poor countries' development (CEC 2005g: 8–9). The prospects of such codes of conduct, or "ethical recruitment standards," has so far failed to allay the fears harbored by many governments and NGOs, particularly in Africa, concerning the EU's new plans to increase labor migration from third countries. Several African health ministers, for instance, were quick to speak out against Brussels' blue card proposal, claiming that it could have adverse effects on poor countries, particularly as concerns an already deteriorating health sector (Kubosova 2007).

As in Tampere, finally, the Hague Program is also very eager to promote what it labels as a "flexible" handling of labor migration from poor third countries. Under the caption "circular migration," as discussed above, the Commission accentuates the advantages with "temporary migration," seeing it as contributing to the development of the sending countries (CEC 2005g: 7; see also CEC 2006c). This rests on the belief that the incomes and skills that migrants acquire during their temporary work in the EU will work for the benefit of development in the countries of origin once these migrants return. This means that the issue of return has become all the more important, and the Commission calls on the member states to cooperate in designing programs for labor migrants' return to and "reintegration" in their countries of origin (CEC 2005g: 7; 2005f: 11–2). As seen above, however, in other contexts the Commission is just as keen to emphasize the importance of investing in the *long-term* effort to integrate third-country labor migrants in accordance with Hague's integration principles. Still, though, the Commission refrains from discussing this tension between "circularity," "return," "reintegration," and thus temporary labor migration on the one hand and long-term, neo-assimilationist integration planning on the other.

Least Common Denominators for the Least Possible Commitment to Rights?

At the same time as the Commission does its utmost to frame third-country labor migration as a matter of decisive importance for the future well-being of the EU, it is worth repeating that Hague so far only has begun to address the introduction of (minor) supranational provisions in this area. "Given that access of third country nationals to the labor market is a highly complex issue," the Commission (2005f: 5) explains, "Community policy in this field can only be put in place progressively, in order to facilitate a gradual and smooth move from national to Community rules." As of today, there are few signs indicating that this "complexity" is about to come undone any time soon—complexity here being a euphemism for a lack of sufficient member state support for supranationalization. The only thing that all parties seem able to agree on—at least up until the current economic crisis—is that the EU area has a great future demand for labor migrants. But due to the many differences between member states' economies, labor markets, industrial structures, and welfare systems, their respective demand for new labor migration is also highly diverse—both in terms of the sheer number of migrants needed and the type of skills required (see further Schierup, Hansen and Castles 2006).

A common EU policy is also rendered difficult by the significant differences between EU countries in how labor migration is being dealt with in their respective domestic *politics*. It is here, in the world of political struggles, that the "complexity" of the matter becomes most evident. In countries with strong labor unions, for instance, governments tend to be more prone (than in those with weak unions) to listen to demands for upholding regulations aimed at preventing that new labor migration leads to social dumping and a relaxation of labor laws. Other important factors that work to hamper common EU policy stem from national differences as regard the political influence of the extreme right, as well as regards the inclination on part of governments and traditional parties to exploit the issue of labor migration in order to appease or appeal to the extreme right's constituency. It needs to be remembered, too, that as a consequence of the so-called transition rules on labor migration (free movement) from the new EU members to the old ones, which are still in place in many old member states, we cannot even speak of a common position on labor migration *within* the Union itself—such consensus coming undone over the first Eastern enlargement in 2004.

Amid the many national differences, however, it is also possible to discern an emergent set of least common denominators among a growing number of EU governments. Apart from the consensus as to the future need for increased labor migration, such concord coalesces around a marked reluctance to incorporate new labor migrants into national welfare and social insurance systems. This became apparent in the debate on and design of the transition rules for the new EU members (in 2004 and 2007); and especially so since these rules were designed to prevent *EU citizens* from the new members from gaining access to social provisions when working in the old member states. Although each set of transition rules was designed in accordance with national specific preferences they all nonetheless shared this common reluctance. Governments in the EU have thus become much more hesitant to commit themselves to social rights provisions for new labor migrants. In turn this means that the bond between work, on the one hand, and social (but also political) rights and, in the end, citizenship has been weakened. To migrate with one's labor, in other words, has ceased to be synonymous with the simultaneous commencement of a migration into a regime of social rights of citizenship, so to speak, which became the case in Western Europe during the postwar period's great labor migration boom—this also in those countries that officially defined their labor migrants as "guest workers" (see Schierup, Hansen and Castles 2006).

When the Commission now undertakes to establish a common EU framework for third-country labor migration, it is easy to spot the compatibility between these least common denominators of member state reluctance toward migrants' social incorporation, on the one side, and the concepts and arrangements around which the Commission suggests an EU framework be developed, namely: circularity, flexibility, return, temporary migration, seasonal labor, and labor migrants' reintegration in their countries of origin. Even though specifically designed for professionals and highly qualified labor, also the Commission's blue card proposal bears testimony to this development. What characterizes these arrangements, which all member states, individually, already have adopted to a greater or less extent, is that they entail few social commitments on the part of the host state and thus leave little room for any substantial rights for the migrants (since such rights for the most part are tailored exclusively for permanent residents).

Whether such arrangements will be harmonized and launched on an EU scale remains to be seen. As discussed above, there are several obstacles to this taking place anytime soon, and in its first report on the member states' implementation of the Hague Program, published in 2006, the Commission noted that EU policy concerning labor migration from third countries was "still in its infancy" and that member state action had been almost nonexistent, in some cases even counterproductive (CEC 2006b: 13). Similarly, in the Commission's second report on the implementation of Hague, published in 2007, no new progress was reported (CEC 2007b). For Brussels to succeed in procuring future member state support for supranational harmonization it is not a daring guess to assume the continuation of the least-common-denominator politics described above.[2]

Hague's External Dimension, Asylum Policy, and "Fight Against Illegal Migration"

Rerouting EU Asylum Policy

Asylum and "illegal migration" are those areas that receive the most attention in the original Hague Program (as presented in November 2004). This is partly due to these being the only ones where Hague laid down deadlines for supranational policy development and lawmaking. With Hague the second phase of the creation of a Common European Asylum System (CEAS) was launched, and as the Hague Program spells out the aim is to have "a common asylum procedure and a uniform status for those who are granted asylum or subsidiary protection" up and running by the end of 2010 (Council EU 2004g: 17). Owing to quite a bit of work having been invested in evaluating the asylum policy instruments enacted during Tampere and the first phase of CEAS, however, the second phase has been slow in materializing; as matters stand now it seems unlikely that the 2010 deadline will be met (Vucheva 2009). It would take until the summer of 2007 before the Commission decided the time ripe for the consultation process to begin on charting the course for the second phase of CEAS. This process was formally launched with the presentation of the Commission's *Green Paper on the future Common European Asylum System* (CEC 2007c). As far as the internal dimension of EU asylum policy is concerned, the *Green Paper* does not contain much in terms of new features. It reiterates the Commission's commitment to establish "a common asylum procedure and a uniform status valid throughout the EU" by 2010. If not novel as such it is worth mention that the Commission wants to invest much more work in ensuring that asylum seekers who are granted protection quickly are made available to the labor market; this in order to both meet EU labor market demands and to improve migrant integration (CEC 2007c: 8). But other than that the work to develop the *internal dimension* of EU asylum policy does not contain much more in terms of new initiatives, as compared to Tampere.

But if the activity as regards the internal dimension has been rather dormant, the *external dimension* of EU asylum policy has been even more prioritized than was the case in Tampere. However, Hague does not introduce many new substantial policy initiatives. The leading feature of Hague is rather its more marked displacement of focus from the internal to the external dimension. Hague is intent on developing on and, where possible, putting into practice Tampere's objectives for the external dimension (Monar 2005: 133). Under the heading "the external dimension of asylum and migration" the Hague Programme declares:

> EU policy should aim at assisting third countries ... in their efforts to improve their capacity for migration management and refugee protection, prevent and combat illegal immigration, inform on legal channels for migration, resolve refugee situations by providing better access to durable solutions, build border-control capacity, enhance document security and tackle the problem of return. (Council EU 2004g: 20)

On this basis, the Council runs over Hague's areas of main concern. High on the priority list is refugee protection in regions of origin, together with an extension of the EU's migration cooperation and partnerships with third countries. As part of this the Council instructed the Commission "to develop EU-Regional Protection Programmes in partnership with the third countries concerned" (Council EU 2004g: 21). A Commission proposal for such a program is set to be based on the experiences from a number of "pilot programs," located in the Ukraine, Moldavia, Belarus, and Tanzania. As of the summer of 2007 these pilot programs were still just beginning to take shape. Since the practical operationalization of the concept of EU-Regional Protection Programs (EU-RPP) is to be founded on an evaluation of the pilot programs (CEC 2007c: 12)—which is still pending as of the summer 2009—it may take quite some time before the Commission tables a comprehensive proposal on EU-RPP.

Apart from the description of EU-RPP that we provided in the previous chapter it is thus difficult at the present point in time to say so much more about these programs' prospective design and scope. What we can say with some certainty though, drawing from the Commission's Communication *On Regional Protection Programmes* (CEC 2005h) (presented in the autumn of 2005), is that the prognosis for robust financial resources for future EU-RPP remains poor. This fact has in no way dampened the Commission's eagerness to launch the programs. What is more, the Commission does not try to conceal that there is a PR purpose behind the choice of regions for the pilot programs: "In order to obtain the necessary political support at EU level for action taken however, and gain confidence of the third countries involved, it is important to select a region which will allow for rapid and measurable results" (CEC 2005h: 5). Besides those countries that have been selected for the pilot programs, the Commission states that future EU-RPP first and foremost need to be established in North Africa, the Afghanistan region, and on the Horn of Africa. North Africa, the Commission (2005h: 7) points out, "is also clearly a preoccupation of Member States and is already the focus of much Community sponsored action."

In addition to what was said in Chapter 5 about the EU's and member states' intensified migration and security cooperation with North African regimes it deserves mention that Italy—with EU assistance—since the conclusion of Tampere in 2004 already deports refugees and migrants (who have come to Italy from North Africa, or who are on their way to the EU from North Africa) to camps in Libya (Human Rights Watch 2005). This conduct is enabled by a cooperation agreement between Italy and Libya that was signed in the summer of 2004, with strong support from, among others, the German government (*International Herald Tribune* 2006). Since the agreement—brought about, according to the Italian government, in order to better fight illegal immigration—necessitated Italian military assistance to Libya, it also necessitated that the EU lifted its arms embargo on Libya. This proved quite an uncomplicated task for Rome to accomplish and already in the autumn of 2004 the Council of Ministers decided to lift the embargo (Council EU 2004h; *Daily Telegraph* 2004). The Council did voice some degree of worry as to the human rights situation in Libya; but this did not prevent the Council from also requesting the Commission to carry out "a technical mission to Libya ... to examine arrangements for combating illegal immigration" (Council EU 2004h).³ Besides Libya's tattered human rights reputation, the country has not signed any international refugee conventions and neither does it have any cooperation agreement with the UNHCR (Human Rights Watch 2005).

The Italian-Libyan agreement has met with loud criticism from human rights organizations (see e.g. Human Rights Watch 2005; Statewatch 2005), and some voices claimed early on that it was not far-fetched to see the agreement as a precursor to future EU initiative in the migration area. "The deal between Italy and Col Muammar Gaddafi's regime," wrote *The Daily Telegraph* (2004), "is widely seen as a pilot project for a European Union policy of processing asylum seekers before they reach EU soil." Whether this will be the case, of course, remains to be seen; and even if many member states, among them the U.K., Germany, and Austria, do support an external "camp solution" to the EU's alleged refugee and illegal migration problem, there is also quite some skepticism toward it. It should be emphasized, though, that the Commission subsequently has been eager to promote closer cooperation between the EU and Libya on migration matters. In the spring of 2008, it proposed that talks should begin on concluding the very first framework agreement between the EU and Libya, highlighting the key role to be played by Libya in averting illegal immigration to the EU, as well as in securing the EU's future oil supply (*EurActiv* 2008; see also CEC 2005i: 9).

Development Assistance, Security, and Return

In close connection with the deliberations on EU-RPP the Hague Program also calls on the Commission to work in behalf of strengthening the migration dimension of the EU's development assistance policy. Within a year after Hague's adoption the EU's heads of state and government agreed that it was high time to work out an overarching strategy on "migration and external relations." In a document entitled *A Strategy for the External Dimension of JHA* (Justice and Home Affairs), the Council (2005: 1) outlines this as follows:

> In order to meet the expectations of its citizens the European Union must respond to the security threats of terrorism and organised crime, and to the challenge of managing migration flows. If the EU is to be effective in doing so it needs to work with countries outside the EU.... The EU should therefore make JHA a central priority in its external relations and ensure a co-ordinated and coherent approach.

The Commission followed up on this in its Communication *Priority actions for responding to the challenges of migration*, which, according to Commission President Barroso, presents "a list of priority actions for improving global migration, with a special focus on the African region" (CEC 2005i: 2). As with Tampere, Hague is fast to point out that the external dimension must consider "both the security and development aspects of migration" (CEC 2005i: 2). Upon closer scrutiny however—again, in conformity with Tampere—it is clearly the former, security aspect that is in the forefront when it comes to the concrete policy picture. Among the prioritized measures addressed in the Commission communication just mentioned, it is the fight against illegal immigration, the strengthening of border controls, and return of unlawfully residing migrants that loom into the foreground. The Commission anticipates the implementation of a number of new instruments to render the fight against "illegal migration" more effective, particularly in the Mediterranean (CEC 2005i: 4–5).

The Commission also clarifies that the economic aid for the reinforcement of migration and border controls that the EU grants to various countries (e.g. in Eastern Europe, Southern Caucasus and Central Asia) should be further developed as part of the Country and Regional European Neighborhood Policy programs (CEC 2005i: 7–8). This will apply in particular to countries in North Africa, where large EU efforts already have been made and where even greater ones are in the pipeline. Central planks of these efforts are the return of "illegal migrants" and the conclusion of additional readmission agreements between the EU and third countries (CEC 2005i: 8).

The key importance assigned to this enterprise was further manifested in the Commission's subsequent directive proposal on return of "illegally staying third-country nationals," which aimed to establish common EU rules for "return, removal, use of coercive measures, temporary custody and re-entry" (CEC 2005j: 3, 2). In this context the Council of Ministers subsequently made a call "for a further increase in the use of joint flights" (see Chapter 5) for the removal of "illegally" residing TCNs; this "as a means of demonstrating the commitment of the EU in relation to joint return actions making more effective use of resources, thus increasing the rate of returns from the Member States" (Council EU 2006: 34).

The Commission's directive proposal on return, or the "return directive," would soon stall due to a lack of agreement between the member states. Much of the controversy centered on how long an unlawfully staying migrant should be allowed to be detained while awaiting deportation, a matter which also has been closely monitored by many human rights organizations. In the summer of 2008 however, after almost three years of quarrels, the Council and the European Parliament finally adopted the return directive. As it turned out it was those advocating the imposition of extensive detention measures who got the best of it. The EU-wide rules[4] on return contained in the directive stipulate, inter alia, that an individual subject to deportation, in certain cases, can be kept in custody for up to eighteen months.

The directive agreement would immediately set off a storm of criticism; but this time around the most forceful condemnations would come from voices outside the EU. The UN High Commissioner for Human Rights, Louise Arbour, attacked the directive on the grounds that it obstructed "the fundamental principles of the protection of individuals' rights who are in a very vulnerable situation" (quoted in *EUobserver* 2008a). Amnesty International's secretary general, Irene Khan, did not mince her words either, deeming it necessary "to remind European governments that just because some persons do not have documents, it does not mean they do not have rights." Amnesty also slammed the "excessive period of detention of up to 1.5 years" as setting "an extremely bad example to other regions in the world" (quoted in *EUobserver* 2008). The most pungent criticism, however, was unleashed from governments in Latin America, with one of its trade blocs, the Andean Community (consisting of Ecuador, Peru, Colombia, and Bolivia), going so far as to threaten to suspend trade talks with the EU over what the block's then president, also Ecuador's president, Rafael Correa, referred to as the "hate directive" (quoted in Phillips 2008a). The continent's other trade bloc, Mercosur (Argentina, Brazil, Paraguay, Uruguay, and Venezuela) also expressed strong misgivings, stating in a resolution that its members "reject any attempt to criminalise the irregular migration and the adoption of restrictive immigration policies," to which was added that Europe should remember that South America had greeted with "generosity and solidarity millions of European migrants in previous centuries" (quoted in Phillips 2008b).

New Refugee Crises and the EU's Increased Focus on Africa

With the Hague Program the EU has stepped up its efforts to gain control over migration movements in the Mediterranean region, particularly as these play out in North Africa. This is partly explained by heightened security concerns related to the so-called war on terror, but it is also directly linked to this being one of the regions in the world where the global migration crisis manifests itself most dramatically and visibly. For years now, the images of crammed and capsized refugee boats and reports of drowned Africans floating ashore on the beaches of Spain or Italy have become everyday fare in the news media. Despite the EU having invested heavily in border controls and surveillance systems in the Mediterranean, the number of refugees and migrants trying to make the passage as well as the death toll and other tragedies show no signs of receding. On the contrary, the number of fatal casualties has been on a steady increase, which is partly due to the EU's militarized border controls forcing refugees to opt for ever more perilous waterways (see e.g. Fekete 2004; Kopp 2007; Lutterbeck 2006). The International Centre for Migration Policy Development (ICMPD) estimates that at least 10,000 people have died in the Mediterranean Sea between 1993 and 2003 (ICMPD 2004: 8). Other approximations put the figure much higher, and all analysts agree that the number of unrecorded cases is very high.

The migration crisis' dire consequences are also playing out on the mainland around the Mediterranean. Recent years' many tragedies in and around the Spanish North African "enclaves," Melilla and Ceuta (which are situated on the Moroccan Mediterranean coast), bear stark witness to this. Since Melilla and Ceuta are fully incorporated into metropolitan Spain, they are also fully integrated into the EU (see Gold 2000; Hansen 2002). From the time when Spain became an EU member, Ceuta and Melilla have increasingly been made to serve as key hubs in Spain's and the European Union's escalating fight against so-called illegal immigration. In the 1990s the enclaves, and thus the EU's borders in Africa, were gradually transformed into outright fortifications, walled in by miles and miles of parallel fences, hedged off by barbed wire entanglements, and equipped with electronic sensors and thermocameras (Hansen 2002).

To these fortifications thousands of people go yearly in the hope of crossing into the EU to find work or seek asylum. Often they live under deplorable conditions in makeshift shanties on the Moroccan side (Smith 2005). In September and October 2005, developments took a new and serious turn when several hundred of the shanty dwellers attempted to break through by storming the fences surrounding Ceuta. The Spanish-Moroccan guard responded by opening fire, possible killing as many as five people, while many were seriously wounded in the stampede. A week later a similar breakthrough attempt took place at the EU border to Melilla, with the Spanish-Moroccan guard acknowledging that it had shot and killed at least six people (Mead 2005). In the ensuing Spanish debate, attention was mostly focused on the need to reinforce the borders around the enclaves and on means to increase the deportation of "illegals" from the areas in and around Ceuta and Melilla. The new socialist government in Madrid promptly announced that it intended to seek assistance from the army in the fight against illegal immigration (Mead 2005). The European Commission's reaction was in line with Madrid's and consisted, initially, of dispatching a group of border control experts to the area and of an offer to the Moroccan government of €40 million for border control reinforcement. Subsequently, the Commission also called on the Moroccan government to sign a readmission agreement with the EU (ECRE 2005).

The tragedies (and massacres) at Ceuta and Melilla in 2005[5] caused quite a bit of debate and contributed to bring about the large conference on migration and development that was held in Rabat in the summer of 2006. An even greater incentive to the Ministerial Euro-African Conference on Migration and Development consisted of the greatly increased entry of migrants to the EU from Africa in 2005 and 2006. Being two of the main destination countries for these migrants, Spain and Malta demanded time and again during 2006 that the EU as a whole take its financial and political responsibility for the mounting migration crisis in the Mediterranean. Here the Spanish government contended, much like the Commission, that the long-term solution cannot only rest with security policy measures, but that it first and foremost is to be found in measures reducing the disparities between the North and the South (Mead 2005). In conformity with the Hague Program, then, the conference in Rabat, where ministers from fifty-eight countries participated, adopted both the security and development dimensions of migration on its agenda. But as is the case in the Hague Program it was the security approach to migration that got the best of it also in Rabat. As Gregor Noll (2006: 1) has it:

> A significant part of the plan of action agreed at Rabat focuses on repressive measures: one item is a comprehensive reinforcement of border control by air, naval and police forces (African included); another concerns "readmission agreements" between target, transit and source countries, so as to facilitate return of undocumented Africans; a third deals with enhanced registration of African migrants.

That it was the security approach that emerged victorious in Rabat was also clearly reflected in many of the participant ministers' statements. As Malta's foreign minister noted with satisfaction, referring to the agreement reached in Rabat: "Fighting international criminal organisations, repatriation of illegal immigrants and stopping the flow of illegal migration are indeed very important factors in addressing illegal immigration holistically" (quoted in Balzan 2006).

This is not to imply that the Conference was void of a development and aid dimension. As elaborated in the previous chapter, it is rather to underscore that the aid allotted to Africa does not even begin to come near fulfilling its stated purpose, namely to work for a gradual reduction of the huge gap in living standards between the EU and Africa. As we also noted, EU countries simply lack both the political will and the viable economic instruments to assume such a far-reaching project, a project that, needless to say, hardly could be initiated short of a sweeping transformation of the current political-economic world order (see Jordan and Düvell 2003). As long as the enormous disparities between Africa and the

EU remain, and as long as the EU's economy continues to demand the services of irregular migrant labor, there is nothing to indicate a sharp drop in undocumented migration from Africa anytime soon. In addition, the EU's total spending on foreign aid today falls well short of the remittance payments made by migrants to their countries of origin. For several countries these remittances make up a major source of national revenue, a fact that indicates that the governments in the South may have little interest in preventing their citizens from migrating to the EU. Despite the increased EU aid to Africa that was effectuated at the Rabat conference, this increase only had marginal impact on the big gap between migrants' remittances and the EU's aid (Noll 2006).

One of the first measures that came out of the Rabat conference resulted in the setting up of a common EU coast guard that was tasked to patrol the waters between the African mainland and the Canary Islands. According to the then EU Commissioner in charge of migration affairs, Franco Frattini, this operation was "truly a historic moment in the history of EU immigration policies and a very tangible expression of EU solidarity amongst member states" (quoted in Kubosova 2006b). The EU's coast guard sorts under the European External Borders Agency (FRONTEX), which was established by a Council Regulation in 2005 (Council EU 2004i). Despite Frattini's assurance about the coast guard's "humanitarian character," it did not take long until it was accused of causing the death of forty-six boat refugees. As the news agency *EUobserver* reported in August of 2006, several eyewitnesses surviving the catastrophe claimed that the authorities at sea had forced their boat to turn around as it was approaching the Canaries and that forty-six of those aboard therefore had died due to shortage of food and water (Kubosova 2006b).

Notwithstanding the optimism created by the Rabat conference and the swiftly launched measures to stave off the "illegals," the arrival of African migrants in the Canaries soon broke new records, causing a heated atmosphere within the EU leadership. Commission President Barroso responded to the crisis by sending out an appeal to all governments, calling for increased solidarity with those member states hardest hit by the migration crisis. Barroso also called for a prompt agreement on a curtailment of the national veto on migration policy in order to facilitate common EU measures to come to terms with the crisis at the Union's southern borders.

Instead of solidarity, however, Barroso's initiative was met with disagreement and division at the meeting of the EU's JHA Ministers, hosted by the Finnish presidency in September of 2006. Here, some governments argued that Spain basically had itself to blame for the crisis around the Canaries. Spain's decision in 2005 to regularize and thus grant permanent residence to most but not all of its roughly one million undocumented migrants, these governments claimed, had simply sent the wrong signals and worked to encourage continued "illegal" migration from Africa. "It's no solution," the Austrian Home Secretary declared, "to legalize people, as was done by Spain, because it gives some kind of pull factor to the people in Africa, as we unfortunately saw in the last months." Germany, France, and the Netherlands issued similar criticism, the latter stating that "the traffickers, the smugglers, see very well what is happening: they won't miss an opportunity to send illegal immigrants" (quoted in Mahony 2006a). The Commission also spoke unfavorably about the Spanish regularization; and later on, in the summer of 2008, it went on to announce its formal disapproval of "mass regularizations" of irregular migrants as such, arguing that it is counterproductive to the "fight against illegal immigration" (CEC 2008b). The Commission thus shared the view that the migration crisis around the Canaries to some extent had to be seen as self-inflicted by the Spanish government (Mahony 2006b).

Not long after the JHA meeting in Finland the European Commission met with the African Union (AU) in Addis Ababa (in October of 2006). This was an unprecedented event, marking the Commission's first major meeting ever held outside the EU, thus highlighting Brussels' ambition at staking out a more independent role in migration policy (see CEC 2006e). At the meeting, the Commission presented a package of proposals which, in a nutshell, can be said to capture the gist of the migration policy that the Commission and the Hague Program want the EU to pursue toward Africa and the rest of the developing world in the years to come. The Commission made it plain to its African partner that the EU has a great demand for migrant labor in many sectors of the economy and that it is willing to increase labor migration from unemployment-ridden countries in Africa. But the Commission was equally clear in pointing out that the EU will be the one calling the shots as to who will be admitted for employment and when and where the migrant labor will be needed to fill positions (Brostrand 2006). This was evident from the Commission's concrete proposals and their emphasis on temporary work permits and seasonal labor, which, as shown above, are in line with the EU's principal position on third-country labor migration. Among other things, Brussels let it be known that an unspecified number of unemployed Africans may, in the near future, be granted temporary work permits in the EU to carry out seasonal work in agriculture, fill positions in the medical service and to work as maids in European households. The package of proposals also included a section stating that African labor migrants would be obliged to learn one of the EU's official languages and that they familiarize with the laws and culture of the host countries (Brostrand 2006). The Commission also called for a further strengthening of the militarized guarding of the frontier in the Mediterranean and the Atlantic, as well as for closer security cooperation with African countries in order to better combat illegal immigration.

Conclusion

This chapter covers the development up until early 2009 (roughly speaking). Leaving off with Hague set to be in operation for at least another year we are not about to engage in any predictions or speculations as to the program's more exact outcomes. This does not, however, prevent us from saying something substantial about Hague's tendency; and as for this tendency the policy package formulated by Commission in Addis Ababa can be said to be both elucidatory and representative. As such, the package links up the four broad areas on which the EU's and the Hague Program's migration policy rests; i.e. (1) labor migration, (2) illegal migration, (3) asylum, and (4) migrant integration. And it does so notwithstanding the fact that it is specifically directed at Africa.

Here we find, firstly, a pronounced call for an EU policy to manage an increased *labor migration from third countries* in the South. This policy basically spells seasonal labor and temporary work permits in agriculture and the service sector, as well as in other sectors where the EU is in want of labor. Some EU members have since long been busy recruiting expensively educated medical personnel from resource depleted and AIDS-ridden countries in precisely Africa, and this with very harmful consequences since many African countries suffer from an acute shortage of medical staff (see e.g. Aiken et al. 2004; Connell et al. 2007). Secondly, we see a big push for *EU policy to fight "illegal" migration* from the South, which, of course, also has implications for *EU asylum policy*. This push basically spells reinforced militarized guarding of the EU's land and sea frontiers, combined with closer security cooperation with various regimes that systematically violate human rights. Some of these same regimes, we should add, are also eyed as potential future providers of the "refugee protection" that the EU wants to outsource and shirk responsibility for. Third, and finally, the package presented in Addis Ababa also contains a portion of the Hague Program's *migrant integration policy*, which spells obligations on part of labor migrants to learn the language and adapt to the laws and culture of the host country—this for people who are only said to be needed for seasonal and other forms of temporary work.

By and large, the Commission's African policy package also illustrates how Brussels and the Hague Program perceive the intended dynamic, as a whole, between the fields of labor migration, "illegal" migration, asylum policy, and migrant integration. The EU is eager to import labor from poorer parts of the world to service economic growth and competitiveness. At the same time, the EU reserves full liberty of choice in deciding who and how many labor migrants to admit so as to effectively calibrate migration to those sectors presently suffering from labor shortages. In order to assume such control of the "flows" of labor migrants, Brussels considers it an absolute necessity to step up the fight against "illegal" immigration and "bogus" asylum seeking. By this means, the EU is to guard itself against the importation of unemployment and poverty from the poor world, as well as against the socioeconomic "burden" of processing and housing asylum seekers, many of whom (due to being too old or not old enough, trauma, various legal obstacles, etc.) will be prevented from being at the labor market's immediate disposal.

Given that labor demands in many sectors may fluctuate quite rapidly, the EU also wants to guard itself against a situation where relatively newly arrived labor migrants all of a sudden are out of work, with all that this involves in terms of social and economic costs. Indeed, as a result of the current economic crisis and the rising unemployment in the EU, this logic—often fraught with xenophobic sentiments—is already kicking in, with several EU governments devising policies to have labor migrants leave their countries (see e.g. McInerney 2009; *The New York Times* 2009). It is by recommending the issuing of temporary work permits for third-country labor migrants, as well as preparing for an active return policy if jobs should dry up, that the Commission wants to obtain instruments to avert such a situation from occurring. In this way many member states' already hard-pressed welfare systems may well be spared from shouldering the social responsibility that permanent residence would entail. Despite the continued hollowing out of national citizenship rights, permanent residence (whether obtained through employment, refugee protection, for family reasons, etc.) still provides migrants and refugees with a set of basic civil, social, and political rights, and thus also goes to make up the gateway to full formal citizenship. As Castles and Davidson (2000: 94–5) underscore, "[t]he pivotal right [for migrants] is clearly that of permanent residence, for once a person is entitled to remain in a country, he or she cannot be completely ignored."

To this equation, finally, is added an integration policy component, obliging migrants to learn the language of the host country and to adapt to its cultural values, something that, as we discussed above, serves to appease an allegedly anti-immigration public opinion that has yet to become aware of the indispensability of increased labor migration for the EU's economic growth.

Taken together, the EU's increasing policy focus on Africa—which is growing as we write this—also becomes emblematic of how Brussels, in a practical sense, believes itself capable of generating a productive dynamic between the security-oriented migration policy and Hague's intensified "fight against illegal migration," on the one side, and the neoliberally oriented Lisbon Strategy's "fight for growth and jobs," on the other.

To be sure, our account only amounts to a rough outline; and as such it fails to do justice to the fact that, for one, EU migration policy still is permeated with a number of political conflicts (regarding both means and ends) *between* as well as *within* the supranational and national domains. And, to add the obvious, it seems unlikely that the current economic crisis will work to mitigate these conflicts of interest. It may also be somewhat misleading to try and capture a complex line of development in such rather intentional terms that we employ in our rendering above. Hence, our rough outline rather aims to capture the more general logic and dynamic that increasingly have come to leave their mark on the EU's migration policy. In other words, we have tried to outline how those actors, interests, and institutional forces that most influence the development of EU migration policy construe of the policy's overarching objectives, logic, and dynamic. As we have accounted for throughout, there are undoubtedly many other forces and voices—as in the row of NGOs, within the EU parliament, but also within national parliaments, governments and the Commission—who hold more or less divergent views on the matter. Many of these criticize the fight against illegal immigration for being both inhumane and counterproductive, claiming instead that the solution is to be found in the EU taking the initiative to a global policy for the reduction of North-South inequalities worth its name. Obviously, however, these are voices from an opposition, and as such they further confirm our thesis that it is possible to discern a *dominant policy line* within EU migration policy, a fact that—as we have tried to cash in on in our rough outline above—also enables us to say something fundamental about the probable logic of the general development of EU migration policy in the years to come.

This should not be taken to mean that the Hague Program will "succeed" in the sense of the objectives of the dominant forces being fulfilled—dominant forces, we may add, that far from always are in monolithic agreement with each other. More important from an analytical perspective, however, is that Hague refrains from tackling the contradictions that have been present in EU migration policy ever since the commencement of European integration in the 1950s and 60s, contradictions that in recent decades not only have grown in number but that also have grown ever more serious in their consequences. Suffice it to mention the thousands upon thousands of migrants and refugees who have died in the Mediterranean in recent years. At a general level, these intensified contradictions are highlighted by the fact that those principally in charge of shaping EU migration policy not only advocate a further securitization of migration policy, an increase of cheap and temporary labor migrants, a further trimming of welfare systems and labor market regulations, as well as toughened integration policies to put Muslims in their place. They also claim to advocate an asylum policy based on humanitarian values, robust refugee protection in regions of origin, migrants' social inclusion, integration built on intercultural dialogue, and vigorous measures to fight racism and discrimination. In the next and concluding chapter these and other decisive contradictions and question will be further discussed and analyzed, specifically accounting for how they are to be understood in the context of EU citizenship.

Notes

1. For the complete list of the common basic principles for migrant integration policy in the European Union, see Council EU (2004f) and CEC (2005d).
2. We could add that the blue card directive proposal was adopted in the spring of 2009, albeit in a watered-down version more attuned to the restrictive preferences of the member states (see Pop 2009; Council EU 2009a).
3. The Commission did conduct such a "technical mission" to Libya in 2005. For a further discussion of this, see Statewatch (2005).
4. The directive does not apply to the U.K. and Ireland, these countries having decided against an "opting-in" to this particular area of EU law.
5. In 2006 three more African migrants died while trying to force their way through the border fencing at Melilla; and in the summer of 2008 a series of new attempts by migrants to break through the border to the EU at Melilla were being staged (*International Herald Tribune* 2008).

CONCLUSION

The Politics of European Citizenship
Power Asymmetries, Contradictions, and Trajectories

There is always a temptation to round out an analysis of this nature by focusing on the uncertain future of citizenship politics in the EU—speculating on how this future will unfold alongside the turbulence that currently engulfs the integration project as a whole. Our concluding remarks will try to steer clear of this temptation as much as possible; not because we feel that it exaggerates the EU's instability, but rather because such a narrow focus tends to gloss over the question of when, if ever, citizenship politics in the EU have actually been characterized by a stable, predictable trajectory. As our analysis in the previous pages has highlighted, this has become all the more apparent in recent years where brief moments of euphoria surrounding, for example, the unveiling of a new treaty or the announcement of new round of enlargement, have come to serve as the exception rather than the rule of an EU project consistently plagued by protracted intervals of turbulence and legitimacy crises, which, in their wake, put the future sustainability of the Union in doubt.

At the same time, we do not choose to "go the safe route" and merely summarize the book's findings in their entirety—much of this work has already been done through the fairly substantial summaries of the respective chapters. Our purpose is instead to synthesize what we feel to be the most significant and original aspect of our critical-historical analysis in the preceding chapters: namely, the unravelling of various power asymmetries that underpin citizenship politics in the EU. Once this has been systematically summarized, we return to the Introduction's discussion of post-referenda dynamics by discussing the implications of the EU's currently unfolding legitimacy crisis for the politics and policy of EU citizenship. Putting all of this into perspective, we then conclude with a discussion of what constitutes the "ideal citizen" in the policy discourses of social and political forces at the heart of the EU project.

The Power Asymmetries of EU Citizenship

In Chapter 1 we argue that the existing literature, whether focused narrowly on normative prescription or institutional problem solving, faces severe limitations in explaining the social purpose of EU citizenship: *who benefits* from it and *what kind* of polity it seeks to promote (Holman 2004; van Apeldoorn 2002). In order to grasp the social purpose of EU citizenship as our alternative problématique, we draw inspiration from critical political economy literature on EU integration and governance, which conceptualizes the EU as a hybrid capitalist form of statehood, whose content and form are shaped by competing hegemonic projects emanating from capitalist social relations. As an alternative theoretical approach to citizenship, we adapt this framework to analyze the ways in which the asymmetrical relations of power and contradictions engendered by these struggles historically shape and transform the politics of citizenship in the EU. Our utilization of this framework in empirical analysis reveals what we consider to be key interrelated and asymmetrical relations of power underpinning citizenship politics in the EU since the early 1950s.

Perhaps the most obvious of these relations of power comes in the form of the widening asymmetries between citizenship politics in the supranational and national political arenas. As Otto Holman (2004) has convincingly argued, the historical rise of embedded neoliberal hegemony has led to an asymmetrical pattern of regulation in the EU, one characterized by the dominance of negative integration and a lack of meaningful social policy in the supranational political arena. Crucially, however, Holman goes on to demonstrate how this asymmetrical form of regulation does not only result in a disjuncture between supranational positive and negative integration, but also signifies that "re-regulation at the EU-level in terms of Single Market and monetary integration causes deregulation at the national level in social terms" (Holman 2004: 716).

In this vein, we can pinpoint how the pattern of asymmetrical regulation has manifested itself in the realm of citizenship, whereby the supranational dominance of neoliberal market making has meant that the extension of rights to the supranational level has been limited to those that compliment and enhance already existing negative integration (the free movement of people to compliment the free movement of goods, services, and capital), with social citizenship rights serving to facilitate desired forms of labor mobility. At the same time, the asymmetrical character of EU regulation—privileging deregulation, privatization and fiscal austerity—results not only in the absence of supranationally provisioned social rights, but also leads to a dismantling of the national social rights that were built up in EU member states in the embedded liberal postwar order. Furthermore, it is crucial to note that the introduction of the EU's socially thin formal citizenship model in the Maastricht Treaty did not only fail to compensate for the hollowing out of national social citizenship provisions, but also in many ways marked a step backward from the "de facto transnational citizenship regime" of the postwar period, which made concerted efforts to strengthen the supranational dimension of social policy. As we have noted in previous chapters, the introduction of the restrictive, so-called transition arrangements by the old members on the free movement for the new member state citizens in 2004 and 2007 marked a new setback for this transnational citizenship regime. The transition arrangements were thus primarily prompted by the old member states' reluctance to grant labor migrants from the new member states the social rights belonging to the EU's regime of free movement and citizenship.

In viewing these dynamics through the lens of our critical history, it is therefore clear that asymmetrical citizenship has by no means been a constant nor inevitable feature of the EU project. Instead we have three more or less precise "moments" of EU citizenship that allow us to trace the gradual shift toward institutional asymmetry. As documented in Chapter 2, under the postwar embedded liberal order (ca. 1950–1975), the EU's de facto transnational citizenship regime found relative symmetry with national Marshallian citizenship regimes, pressuring for provisions that would extend nationally constituted social rights to EU internal migrants in order to provide incentives for cross-national mobility to meet the demands for labor in light of skyrocketing growth rates (particularly in West Germany). This was buttressed by a concerted effort by the European Commission to extend the role and scope of supranational social and welfare policy on behalf of intra-Community labor migrants throughout the 1960s and 70s. As was shown in Chapter 2, moreover, this effort, albeit futile, was to be gradually broadened in the 1970s to also incorporate the plight of third-country migrants.

The *explanatory* foundations of the symmetry between the supranational and national political arenas in this period are to be located, as Chapter 2 goes on to suggest, in the examination of the social relations underpinning the postwar order, particularly in the capital-labor relation where the latter found itself in a relatively strengthened position. On the one hand, the postwar economic boom provided the impetus to business to lobby for the development of a regulatory infrastructure to promote intra-European labor mobility necessary to fuel growth in industrial centers. Yet, on the other hand, the incentive structures offered to internal migrant workers through inclusion into the extensive social rights provisions of the Keynesian welfare national state (KWNS) (Jessop 2002) of host member states had the effect, perhaps unintended, of strengthening labor's power in the supranational arena; a fact evidenced in trade union cooperation with the Commission in areas of social policy. Even though this period would witness the development of the now commonplace dualism between internal and external migrants, the Commission especially during the 1970s set its sights on eliminating this dualism through the extension of rights to "legally" and "illegally" resident TCNs. The supranational efforts in areas of social and migration policy in the postwar order thus offered a sort of buffer limiting the extent to which liberalization at the supranational level would impact asymmetrically on national social citizenship regimes, an arrangement reflective of underlying efforts to curb the power of capital vis-à-vis workers on the one hand, and to put external migrant workers on relative par with EU citizens on the other.

It was not until the extended relaunch of the integration project (ca. 1985–2000), in response to the crises of Western European capitalism and the deadlock of Euro-pessimism (ca. 1975–1985), that these congruencies would gradually give way to growing asymmetries. In place of a concerted effort to foster supranational social rights as found in the de facto citizenship regime of the postwar order, the Commission instead began to emphasize more explicitly the ethno-cultural underpinnings of EU citizenship, and replaced its concern with the social situation of TCNs with a campaign to secure the EU's borders against the perceived external threats of "illegal" migration. As Chapter 3 makes clear, the socially thin character of the market citizenship model that emerged in the extended relaunch served as a facilitator, rather than a buffer against the commanding thrust toward supranational liberalization. This had obvious implications for Marshallian national citizenship regimes as the rescaling and restructuring that these liberalization measures entailed sought to bring national welfare states more in line with the supposed exigencies of the Single Market and the approaching monetary union.

Again, our critical-historical framework has sought to explain the deepening asymmetries between the supranational and national arenas— bound up in the broader shift from the embedded liberal order of the postwar period to the embedded neoliberal order of the extended relaunch—alongside transformations in underlying social power relations in the EU. It is no mere coincidence that the European Commission's demotion of the social rights agenda went hand in hand with a decline in labor's influential position in supranational policy making and the simultaneous ascent of the European Roundtable of Industrialists (ERT) as *the* predominant social force shaping the policy framework of the extended relaunch. The ascendance of the ERT can be regarded as the eventual outcome of the European responses to the structural crisis of the 1970s (see Chapter 2; van Apeldoorn 2002). In specific terms, the globalization (and Europeanization) of capital mobility subsequent to the 1970s crisis served to bolster the structural power of capital (Gill and Law 1989), giving it a crucial "exit option" that served to discipline the actions of governments and labor. The new "footloose" orientation of Europe's capitalist class—coupled with rampant stagflation and unemployment in continental Europe—therefore severely compromised the bargaining power of labor. This was especially the case for external migrant labor, as seen in diminished incentives to promote their integration, or assimilation, into regimes of social rights.

Chapter 4 explains how the new Lisbon Strategy era (2000–2010) represented a continuity, rather than radical break, with the embedded neoliberal order of the relaunch. Accompanying the ethno-cultural dimensions of EU citizenship was an emergent neoliberal communitarian citizenship model that placed new emphasis on promoting citizen "responsibilities," especially the responsibility to make themselves "employable" in light of the thrust toward neoliberal labor market restructuring. Meanwhile, as outlined systematically in Chapters 5 and 6, the EU's migration policy under the Tampere and Hague programs would place—alongside the increasingly belligerent security discourse on fighting "illegal" migration—a focus on neo-assimilationist measures to purportedly integrate TCNs and ethnic minorities into common cultural value systems, articulated in a Eurocentric and nationalist idiom, while effectively sidestepping commitments to social rights.

These findings obviously stand in direct contradistinction to claims made by Lisbon supporters that the "modernization" of the European Social Model would address the existing and intensifying asymmetries between supranational and national citizenship regimes by finally extending meaningful social rights into the supranational realm. Paradoxically, however, the Lisbon Agenda appears indeed to be eliminating the asymmetry between national and supranational citizenship, but in ways completely opposite to how it is commonly presented by EU institutions and the power elite. Instead of instituting EU-level social rights in ways that render supranational citizenship more compatible with national citizenship regimes, the neoliberal communitarian and neo-assimilationist underpinnings of citizenship politics under the Lisbon, Tampere, and Hague agendas work to further restructure national social citizenship regimes more compatible with a socially thin EU citizenship.

Inevitably bound up with Lisbon's failure to address institutional asymmetries is the further reinforcement of the asymmetrical social power relations that have been intensifying since the extended relaunch. In this way, the Lisbon Agenda has deepened, rather than solved, the contradictions emerging out of the extended relaunch. This we evinced, for instance, in Chapter 4's discussion of the exhaustion of society that stems from the attempts to impose the burden of socioeconomic restructuring on citizens in the form of "responsibilities," and in Chapters 5's and Chapter 6's identification of the tension between the continued drive to securitize EU borders and attempts to boost external migration in order to fulfil the Lisbon Agenda goals. With these contradictions in mind, the central question that remains concerns the long-term sustainability of the neoliberal communitarian, securitarian, and neo-assimilationist nexus of EU citizenship politics. This is a question that was given renewed impetus with the latest major setbacks for the EU project: the Dutch and French rejections of the EU's Constitutional Treaty and the initial Irish rejection of the Lisbon Treaty.

Post-Referenda EU Citizenship

Reconnecting to the Introduction's discussion of the Dutch, French, and Irish referenda, we can now go on to further assess the implications of the latest round of setbacks for citizenship politics in the EU. It is in many respects far too early to come to any definitive conclusions concerning the impact of the referenda rejections. Yet if nothing else, what these events bring to light are the limitations, and indeed failures, of Third Way–inspired neoliberal communitarian and neo-assimilationist EU citizenship in fulfilling the stated goal of legitimizing the integration project to the European public. What we seek to explore further in this section, then, is how, if at all, the EU has sought to reorient citizenship politics in light of this most recent, and still unfolding, legitimacy crisis.

One of the most remarkable and recent transformations related to the social register of EU citizenship—i.e. the traits of a desirable social citizen—has been the death of the Third Way as a hegemonic political slogan (see also Ryner 2008). The Third Way's eulogy was already being written with the arrival of the Barroso Commission, and the burial of the movement itself came with the fall from grace of Tony Blair and Gerhard Schröder, and the emergence of figures such as German chancellor Angela Merkel and French president Nicolas Sarkozy. Indeed, explicit reference to Third Way discourse has all but disappeared from EU policy making, yet its underlying mantra of "no rights without responsibilities"—which informs the EU's own neoliberal communitarian approach to social citizenship—remains largely unchallenged.

To be sure, a large part of the EU's citizenry continually uses its referenda voice to resist the extension of Third Way–influenced integration measures. But beyond this and other largely deconstructive exercises, no alternative counter-hegemonic projects anchored in a de-commodified conception of EU social rights have gained enough political momentum to fundamentally challenge the power asymmetries that currently lie at the heart of the neoliberal communitarian model. So far this holds true even with the world and Europe facing the worst economic crisis since the 1930s. In the wake of EU political paralysis, it appears that this challenge to neoliberalism's crisis of legitimacy is more likely to surface initially in the member state political arena. The rise of the German Left Party (die Linke) may in this regard constitute the first "counter hegemonic post-neoliberal emancipatory project" (Solty 2008: 26) that has the force to push de-commodified social rights back into the prevailing political discourse. At the same time, however, the extreme right has witnessed its own resurgence in the past few years with stunning electoral successes in Italy, the Netherlands, Belgium, Denmark, and Austria, where the country's two far-right parties witnessed an electoral resurgence that nearly eclipsed the vote totals of the ruling Social Democrats.

In comparing the most recent resurgence of the extreme right in Austria to its initial rise to prominence in the 1999 national elections, the most remarkable change can be found in political reactions across the wider EU. While the admittance of the Austrian Freedom Party into the ruling coalition in 2000 caused a major uproar across the region—leading to an EU-coordinated attempt to isolate Austria—the recent electoral successes have been met with hardly a whimper. The change of heart across the EU has not been due to an ideological transformation of Austria's radical right parties—whose racist anti-immigrant rhetoric is as blatant as ever—but rather to the fact that the extreme right parties increasingly have become a normal feature of European political life. This brings us to the other main register of EU citizenship, migration policy, through which the ever-increasing mainstream political focus on the alleged threat posed by "illegal migration," together with the neo-assimilationist turn, have undoubtedly served as important mechanisms for the normalization of extreme right-wing ideology on migration throughout the EU.

For example, no EU government so far has bothered to take issue with the Italian government's current crackdown on irregular migrants and the planning of mass incarceration in camps of these same migrants. Neither have they lifted a finger to oppose the outburst of racist violence and legally decreed ethnic cleansing against Italy's Roma and Sinti populations (Aradau 2009). Said Italy's Home Secretary and member of the extreme right Lega Nord party, Roberto Maroni, after a mob had firebombed and assaulted a Roma settlement in Naples, forcing some eight hundred Roma to flee: "that is what happens when Gypsies steal babies"; to which another minister added: "the people do what the political class isn't able to do" (quoted in Milne 2008). In addition, the Berlusconi government has carried out a program of forced ethnic or racial registration and fingerprinting of Roma, "as well as passing a law which defines the mere presence of Roma in a given area as a state of emergency" (Cahn 2008). While Italy's forced registration scheme drew much nongovernmental condemnation and also put many European Parliamentarians on the alert, the review conducted by the European Commission decided in favor of the scheme, finding it to be in compliance with the EU's human rights and non-discrimination standards (Kubosova 2008). After all, said Franco Frattini, Italy's foreign minister and former EU Commissioner responsible for migration matters, "[t]hese things are done by many other countries in Europe without causing any scandal." (quoted in Aradau 2009: 3)

The EU's "European Pact on Immigration and Asylum" (adopted in October of 2008) that was spearheaded by the French EU presidency and President Nicolas Sarkozy represents yet another recent manifestation of this normalization of certain aspects of extreme right-wing ideology on migration (see e.g. Thomas 2009). Again thought to be highly controversial just a decade ago, the pact looks to shrink EU asylum policy responsibilities even further while intensifying the crackdown on "illegal" migration by instituting swift expulsion policies, increased border surveillance, and doing away with mass regularizations of irregular migrants. The pact, furthermore, seeks to bring about more obliging migrant integration measures and an increase of high-skilled migration through the development of an EU system for temporary work permits known as the "blue card" scheme (as discussed in Chapter 6) (Barber 2008). As Carrera and Guild (2008: 1–2) underscore, the French presidency deliberately pushed for the European Council's adoption of the EU immigration pact with the aim of setting the tone and agenda for the next multi-annual migration and security policy program, i.e. the Stockholm Program (2010–2015) (see Council EU 2009b). The fact that the Sarkozy pact has been met with little opposition is a telling indicator of the prevailing dominance of the Tampere and Hague Programs' general approach to migration policy in the EU, which, like the Lisbon Agenda's social policy counterpart, has not yet been met with any substantial counter-hegemonic challenge.

This should not, however, detract us from questioning the long-term sustainability of the EU's current migration policy in light of its deepening contradictions. How long can the fight against illegal migration proceed with an economy that is more and more dependent on undocumented workers? How long can the same political forces that emphasize the need for increased labor migration from outside the EU continue to exacerbate and exploit public hostilities toward certain migrant populations? How long can the EU maintain an integration policy in which migrants' exclusion is sometimes explained with reference to a widespread prevalence of discrimination in the host society—as it is in the integration policy's anti-discrimination branch—and at other times with reference to the migrants' faulty cultural values and disinclination to integrate into the host society? And how long can EU asylum policy continue to invoke humanitarian values, the Geneva Convention, and other international conventions and laws when in practice this asylum policy is increasingly at odds, both formally and rhetorically, with these obligations? The ways in which these contradictions are addressed by competing social forces will play a determinant role in steering the trajectory of EU migration and citizenship policy in the years to come.

The Ideal EU Citizen?

At the heart of institutional and elite discourse is a normative vision of what constitutes the ideal EU citizen, and the role it should play within the hegemonic embedded neoliberal order of the current Lisbon Strategy period. Based on our analysis throughout Section II of the book, we can identify certain characteristics that are associated with this ideal EU citizen. Most importantly, it should be someone who is not reliant on social rights, is completely flexible in the labor market, does not exercise political rights in a way that hinders further EU integration, and is also devoid of national allegiances toward any particular member state. Who within the EU polity possesses these particular characteristics? Oddly enough, this description unintentionally captures most closely the experiences of the estimated eight million undocumented TCNs "illegally" residing throughout the EU. For undocumented TCNs, the lack of political status denies them the ability to access citizenship rights, whilst socioeconomic insecurity more often than not compels them to be entirely flexible in working life, taking on whatever employment opportunities are available in whatever place. It is also this precariousness in social life that stands as a key factor in stunting the development of national loyalties towards any EU member state among these migrants; a state of coerced cosmopolitan subsistence, as it were.

The flip side of this precariousness, however, is that it inhibits the development of a migrant sense of belonging to the EU polity as well. This condition appears in an even starker light once we consider the temporary, "circular," "flexible" and thus precarious status assigned also to the Union's anticipated millions of new "legal" labor migrants. When coupled with the fact that most TCNs in the EU's flexible labor market (whether they are "illegal" or temporary "legal" migrants) lack the ethno-cultural traits commonly associated with EU citizenship, the vision of what constitutes the ideal citizen becomes increasingly blurred. Of course the majority of the EU's "formal" citizens do possess these prescribed ethno-cultural traits, but they too fail to live up to the vision of the ideal citizen because they are, in the words of transnational capital, too pampered by national social citizenship regimes, and, as EU political leaders claim, too misinformed and jaded by nationalism and anti-immigration sentiments to see that a vote against EU integration is a vote against their own best interests. On other occasions though, such as when EU migration policy is being drawn up, the envisioned EU citizen is precisely one whom should gratefully receive Brussels and governments' crackdown on the "illegals," their neo-assimilationist policy prescriptions, anti-Muslim rhetoric, and pledges to enact ever more stringent asylum policies.

Clearly, the ideal citizen in EU policy discourse has not found a concrete worldly citizen equivalent encompassing all its different characteristics. The question that remains is whether or not it is even possible for this conception of the ideal citizen to find a worldly equivalent given the contradictions outlined above. As we noted in our Introduction, there are several, oftentimes contradictory and, not least, situation-specific registers of EU citizenship that European elites choose to draw from, or ignore, when designating an ideal EU citizen. In any case, our empirically oriented critical-historical analysis has sought to highlight the dangers of focusing too closely on the abstract characteristics of the ideal citizen, as this tends to gloss over the power asymmetries and contradictions that lie at the heart of citizenship politics in the EU. In this sense, our book is to be regarded as a rallying cry to reorient the study of EU citizenship in particular and citizenship studies in general toward analyses of historical struggle over rights. In times such as these, when rights are on the retreat, this task appears as all the more urgent.

Afterword to the Paperback Edition

The original hardcover edition of this book went to print in the summer of 2009 amid fundamental uncertainty about the future course of the European integration project. As we were putting the finishing touches on the book, we felt compelled to make some preliminary remarks about the deep-seated crisis that was unfolding before our eyes. In short, we raised fundamental doubts about the viability of the EU project in light of the most severe crisis of global capitalism since the 1930s and the protracted crisis of legitimacy for the EU project, which manifested itself in a series of EU referenda rejections. But even this rather gloomy assessment now looks almost cheerful given the events that have unfolded since then.

By early 2010 the EU had been violently thrust into a sovereign debt crisis that spread from its periphery (the so-called PIGS, Portugal, Ireland, Greece, and Spain) into founding member states such as Italy and Belgium. With half of the contributions coming from Germany and France, the €780 billion thus far contributed to the European Financial Stability Facility has done little to restore confidence. Interest rates on government bonds in crisis-stricken countries continue to rise, exacerbating worries over the sustainability of their debt. Meanwhile rating agencies continue to downgrade Eurozone government credit ratings, citing fears of immanent defaults. Even Germany, the veritable symbol of fiscal discipline, risks losing its AAA rating. These latest developments mark the most grueling test ever for the EU project and may constitute the grimmest challenge for the European continent since the Second World War.

As we prepare this new Afterword for the paperback edition, the initiatives proposed to combat the crisis change almost daily. Given the current political wrangling, it is too early to tell whether the sovereign debt crisis will result in a fiscal union, the introduction of Eurobonds, a "two-speed" union, or even the disintegration of the Euro or the EU project itself. In this climate, we are as unsure about the future as anyone;

including Eurozone bondholders who now dread severe losses on what were once considered "risk-free" investments. What we can do, however, is offer a preliminary assessment of how the most recent developments in the crisis have impacted the politics of European citizenship, particularly in terms of what we refer to as the deepening contradictions in social rights and migration policy.

In the original edition of this book we argued that from its very inception in the early 1990s the EU's formal citizenship model had become characterized by asymmetrical "neoliberal communitarianism." EU citizenship is asymmetrical because it has been limited to rights that compliment and enhance negative integration (neoliberal market making). This results not only in a "socially-thin" model of citizenship at the EU level, but also, in seeking to legitimize the EU's drive towards deregulation, privatization, and austerity, reinforces the dismantling of *national* social rights. This neoliberal aspect of EU citizenship is combined with Third Way communitarianism, based on the mantra of "no rights without responsibilities." In response to hollowed-out national social citizenship regimes and the lack of a meaningful "social Europe," citizens are expected to fend for themselves in the realm of social welfare whilst at the same time remain active participants in political and civil life. But even this emphasis on the civil and political rights amounts to an empty gesture when EU elites dismiss engaged voters in EU referenda as ungrateful, nationalist, and selfish.

Now in the wake of the sovereign debt crisis the EU's formal citizenship model appears to be gravitating towards a more purely neoliberal form. The austerity programs being instituted in heavily indebted member states, orchestrated by the EU, have led to savage cuts in social expenditures, with nothing in the way of EU level social rights to compensate for national retrenchment (at the time of writing the EU had approved its own austerity budget for 2012). Meanwhile any semblance of democracy that characterized EU citizenship has been abandoned. The EU has thrown its full support behind technocratic "caretaker" governments in Italy and Greece that have vowed to push forward with austerity based on supposedly objective "economic" imperatives shielded from political interference (i.e. from democratic decision making). Nowhere was this undermining of the democratic process more blatant than in Greece. When the democratically elected Greek Socialist Party proposed in the autumn of 2011 to subject the harsh conditions of its EU bailout deal to a popular referendum it was immediately rebuked by EU political elites, who insisted that leaving the fate of restructuring in the hands of citizens would shatter "market confidence."

The political responses to the sovereign debt crises have served to intensify the asymmetrical relations of power underpinning citizenship politics in the EU. On the one hand, the undemocratic and socioeconomically disastrous drive towards austerity reinforces the dominance of Europe's transnational capitalist class over ordinary citizens. The social, political, and civil rights of citizens at both the national and EU levels are being subordinated to the supposed exigencies of the "bond market" dominated by a consortium of large banks. On the other hand, as the future of the integration project becomes more uncertain, citizens are pitted against each other. Notions of pan-European solidarity and identity are hastily abandoned and the narrative suddenly switches from *European citizens* to "industrious" Germans who begrudgingly foot the bill for "slapdash" Greeks and Italians.

Of course there are social forces that have resisted these developments. Trade unions and social movements across the EU have actively challenged the idea that austerity represents some sort of objective economic necessity. With unemployment rising sharply across the EU since 2008 in hand with cuts in public expenditures, progressive forces, as seen in the Occupy movement, have highlighted the political dimensions of austerity as it pushes the burden of restructuring onto society's most vulnerable.

But at the same time, the current turbulence has also provided fertile ground for radical right wing ideology that scapegoats certain categories of migrants, ethnic communities, and asylum seekers, in general, and Muslims, in particular. Since we wrote this book, the racist extreme right has made new electoral gains, lending it even further clout and normalcy in the EU's political landscape. This, of course, has gone in tandem with the continued "lepenization" of the mainstream and EU's political establishment. When Angela Merkel, David Cameron, Nicolas Sarkozy, and Jose Maria Aznar all decided to proclaim multiculturalism an utter "failure" in 2010 and 2011—Cameron and Sarkozy blaming it for causing Muslim radicalization and contempt for European values, among other things—representatives for the extreme right rushed to the occasion, pocketing yet another heap of credibility points. The leaders of the French *Front National*, Marine Le Pen, and the British National Party, Nick Griffin, applauded David Cameron's message, the latter greeting it as "a further huge leap for our ideas into the political mainstream." (quoted in *The Guardian*, 30 July 2011). Such satisfaction should be easy to understand. After all, when Sarkozy, as part of his dismissal of multiculturalism, claimed that "we in France do not want people to pray in an ostentatious way in the street" (*AFP*, 10 February 2011), he merely provided the light version of Marine Le Pen's earlier statement where she likened Muslims street praying in France to the Nazi occupation. Accordingly, in September 2011 a new law banning Muslim street praying was put into effect.

What we refer to as the neo-assimilationist migrant integration policy—built in large parts around more or less unconcealed anti-Muslim attitudes and tactics—has thus taken rapid strides since we finished the book. Indeed, even a hold out like the Council of Europe (not to be confused for an EU institution), which we cited for its apt criticism of EU governments' "rigid" integration obligations, has now caved in, offering, in 2011, its full endorsement of EU leaders' abovementioned attack on multiculturalism. As the Council's secretary general, former Norwegian prime minister Thorbjørn Jagland, let it be known, "multiculturalism allows parallel societies to develop ... This must be stopped. It is also clear that some parallel societies have developed radical ideas that are dangerous. Terrorism cannot be accepted." (quoted in *Financial Times*, 17 February 2011).

This provided, it was no surprise that practically all politicians, journalists, and experts initially pointed to Islamic extremists as the self-evident perpetrators of the Utøya massacre and Oslo bombing on the 22 of July 2011. Although the word was out almost immediately that the gunman allegedly was a blond, Norwegian-speaking man, this did not prevent even some of the staunchest reporters and media outlets to jump to the banal Islamophobic conclusion. As the *Financial Times* (23/24 July 2011) reported: "... the gunman was reportedly blond and spoke Norwegian well. But experts see the intent to punish Norway for its involvement in Afghanistan or Libya as the most plausible motivation. ... The attack is likely to spark fresh debate in Norway and its neighbors over increasing immigration from Muslim-majority countries in recent years." Not so; and when Anders Behring Breivik's manifesto subsequently caught public attention it was actually possible to identify a sense of unease, even shame, among Europe's motley crew of Islamophobes. Because as the manifesto had made all too clear, if Breivik had acted alone, he certainly had not invented the sentiments and ideas upon which he acted. Gunnar Herrmann of *Süddeutsche Zeitung* put it well: "Words alone do not kill, but they can help shape a ghastly world view and they can incite awful outrage. Evidently, the political debate provided Breivik with more than enough raw material to patch together his 1500 page long justification for the mass murder. This ought to be a reason to reflect upon the political climate in northern Europe." (28 July 2011) Having formed part of this exact "raw material" may explain Thorbjørn Jagland's U-turn following the Utøya massacre. All of a sudden he made it appear as if his vigorous support of European leaders' frontal attack on multiculturalism had never happened. Explicitly addressing these same EU leaders he now urged them to take a more "cautious" approach to multiculturalism and Islam: "We should be very cautious now, we should not play with fire. Therefore I think the words we are using are very important because it can lead to much more. ... We also need to stop using 'Islamic terrorism,' which indicates that terrorism is about Islam" (quoted in *The Guardian*, 30 July 2011).

Given the demographic "greying" of the EU, and its over a decade long effort to increase its attractiveness for immigration vis-à-vis its global competitors in the U.S., Canada, and elsewhere, one would think there to be all the more reason for EU leaders to engage in such reflection on the current "political climate" in Europe. This is also one of the questions that we decided to finish this book on in 2009: "How long can the same political forces that emphasize the need for increased labor migration from outside the EU continue to exacerbate and exploit public hostilities toward certain migrant populations?" Well, it seems they can go on doing this for a very long time, and this seeming contradiction apparently creates headaches for the EU's Home Affairs Commissioner, Cecilia Malmström. Since taking office in 2010 she has been even more emphatic than her predecessors about the Union's dire need for new labor migrants, stating on several occasions that a massive increase in labor migration is necessary "in order to secure our economic survival." The strong wording expresses a frustration, and when underscoring the need for millions of new labor migrants in an interview with *Financial Times* in 2011 she notes that practically all of the EU ministers responsible for labor market policy that she meets with agree about "the need for immigrant workers." "But," she continues, "when the ministers go and speak in front of their national publics, this message is not to be heard at all" (quoted in *Financial Times*, 15 June 2011). Malmström cannot, of course, mention that this might have something to do with precisely the fact that most EU governments today are quite invested in inciting anti-immigration sentiments, animosity towards Muslims and scorn for multiculturalism, something the Commission too has taken part in. To mention this, would require more serious reflection and self-examination concerning EU governments and the European Commission's roles in creating the current political climate towards migration.

The protracted and deepening crisis is another factor complicating the Commission's position on labor migration to the EU. After all, how does one motivate and justify the import of millions of new labor migrants to countries with unemployment rates between 10 and 25 percent, not to speak of youth unemployment? We must also ask how Brussels will be able to sell this to countries where the prospects of employment have grown so slim that people have started to emigrate in large numbers? Countries such as Latvia and Lithuania already suffered from net-emigration before we wrote this book, but since then they have been joined by Ireland and Spain, while Greece, Portugal, even Italy, are expected to follow suit. As a result of the crisis, Portugal has in the last few years seen tens of thousands of its citizens emigrate to oil-booming Angola alone; and on 18 December 2011 the conservative Portuguese prime minster, Pedro Passos, did the unthinkable by publicly encouraging Portuguese citizens to emigrate, suggesting Angola and Brazil as the most suitable destinations. Over and above that, several EU countries have taken steps to curtail regular labor migration and some have also sought to make unemployed migrants on temporary permits leave their countries. In the summer of 2011 the Spanish government decided to reintroduce the ban on migration from Romania on account of Spain's severe unemployment problem. Soon after the Netherlands indicated that it was entertaining a similar move. At the same time the Commission rushed to the defense of its policy; according to Commissioner Malmström the crisis had altered nothing and the Commission's position on labor migration was thus to stay the course.

Since the onset of the crisis the plight of the many irregular labor migrants in the EU have also grown more severe. In Spain, for instance, many migrants (both regular and irregular) previously employed in construction have been forced to scramble for work in the most poorly paid horticulture and agriculture industry. Since this industry has lowered its costs even further it has also been even more prone to utilize irregular migrant workers. According to the UK charity Anti-Slavery International, the conditions for the irregular migrants working in Spain's agriculture have now deteriorated to the point that they in many places can be likened to outright slavery. There is even a shortage of food, which has forced the Red Cross to provide food for thousands of Spain's irregular migrant workers.

Even though new labor migrants are regarded as decisively important for the EU's future growth, competitiveness and demographic balance they can still expect little in the form of social rights, family reunion, and possibilities to obtain permanent residence. This manifests with great clarity in the various policy proposals coming out of Brussels since this book went to print. Just to mention one case in point we can turn to the Commission's proposal for a directive on seasonal labor migration, which was presented in 2010. The proposal builds on the alleged fact that the EU faces a permanent and expanding "structural need for low-skilled and low-qualified workers" that cannot be satisfied by "EU national workers, primarily owing to the fact that these workers consider seasonal work unattractive." As such, the directive intends to put the idea of circular migration into practice, particularly vis-à-vis African countries. Here the Commission emphasizes, firstly, that the directive proposal "provides for incentives and safeguards to prevent a temporary stay from becoming permanent;" and, secondly, that "Member States shall require that the seasonal worker will have sufficient resources during his/her stay to maintain him/herself without having recourse to the social assistance system of the Member State concerned." As the Commission succinctly explains it in its 2011 "Communication on migration": "Enabling the people with the right skills to be in the right place at the right time, is key to the success of business, research and innovation in Europe." At the same time though, the Commission also underscores that the EU must "ensure that the need for enhanced mobility does not undermine the security of the Union's external borders"; and therefore "[t]he control of the EU's external border must be continuously improved to respond to new migration and security challenges." "Citizens", moreover, "need to feel reassured that external border controls are working properly", and accordingly authorities need to demonstrate that "[p]reventing irregular migration and maintaining public security are compatible with the objective of increased mobility." The EU thus remains firmly convinced that labor migration can increase only if it goes in tandem with the militarized reinforcement of its external borders. This explains why it comes natural for the EU to increase the budget of its external border agency (Frontex)—for the stated purpose of staving off migrants and refugees from North Africa—while the Home Affairs Commissioner during the very same week (in June 2011) tells *Financial Times* (15 June 2011) that "we need hundreds of thousands, millions in the long term," of labor migrants.

Hence, while the EU claims that labor migrants are needed in large numbers, it also claims that their entry must be tightly monitored and that strong measures have to be implemented in order to prevent their temporary or just-in-time stay from becoming permanent. Rather than accounting for labor migrants as the social creatures they are, with all that this implies in terms of social needs, the tendency in today's austerity-stricken EU is more and more one of reducing them (even in the explicit) to human capital and production factors pure and simple, set to optimize the labor market on which they should be made to circulate. With circular migration the European Commission and member state governments have thus found a policy concept which, in one fell swoop, is compatible with both the political climate of anti-immigration—since those coming are not going to be allowed to stay and get an opportunity to join the citizenry—and with neoliberal crisis management—since circular migration will not allow for any social rights, thus keeping welfare expenditures at a minimum. Over and above that, circular migration, at least as pertains to low-skilled work, can also be made to sidestep the issue of high unemployment. As seen above, the European Commission establishes that there is a "structural need for low-skilled and low-qualified workers" that cannot be satisfied by "EU national workers, primarily owing to the fact that these workers consider seasonal work unattractive." In the Commission's view, then, unemployed "EU national workers" are not going to be available to satisfy this need for cheap, flexible, and competitiveness-friendly labor; and in this sense there need not be a contradiction between mass unemployment and mass immigration.

The approach to circular migration further underscores the much more pure neoliberal form that EU citizenship policy has taken since the onset of the crisis. This needs to be understood against the background of a general European, but also global, tendency in which migration policy is more and more detached from the fundamental issue concerning migrants' social conditions: migration policy, in other words, ceases to be embedded in policies of social incorporation. As economic historian Karl Polanyi once tried to teach us, in the modern classic *The Great Transformation* from 1944, the notion of such a socially unembedded human being is a dangerous fiction, since every attempt at its realization, every attempt to actually treat a human being as was she socially naked and only dressed for the market, always risks having catastrophic consequences. "The commodity description of labor," Polanyi (1957: 72) explains, "is entirely fictitious," since "[t]o allow the market mechanism to be sole director of the fate of human beings ... would result in the demolition of society." This is so because "the alleged commodity 'labor power' cannot be shoved about, used indiscriminately, or even left unused, without affecting also the human individual who happens to be the bearer of this peculiar commodity." When, under such a regime, a person's labor commodity is discarded or treated as a disposable, one-use commodity, this would be tantamount to the elimination of this person's entire being (1957: 73).

Given the almost non-existent social content vested in the policy concept of circular migration suggests that we might be better off conceptualizing circular migration less in terms of *migration*, as in *people* moving and settling in an EU country, and more in terms of Karl Polanyi's notion of fictitious commodities; that is, in terms of the "shoving about of labor." We can also begin to discern that the precarious and rightless position that has made "illegal" labor migrants so popular on the EU labor market now in some important respects forms the model for the EU's circular labor migration regime and its projected management of the Union's great demand for new "legal" labor migrants—at least as pertains to low-skilled migrants. As a consequence, the very same people on whom the EU's future economic growth and prosperity, indeed its very "economic survival," are said to depend are offered nothing in return. It seems as if the EU wants the poor world's labor, but not its people, at least not in the form of social beings and prospective rights-bearing residents and citizens.

At yet another level circular migration must be construed as structurally interlinked with a simultaneous effort to capitalize even further on the international division of labor by way of establishing this division more firmly and tangibly in the heart of Europe itself. This course of action will not only risk exacerbating ethno-racial discrimination in the EU, particularly on its already ethnically segmented labor market; with a militarized migration control serving as the new regime's ultimate regulator, it will also risk worsening the migration crisis at the EU's external borders. As regards the latter, during the first seven months of 2011 almost 2000 migrants and refugees were reported to have died in the Mediterranean while trying to reach the EU. Although the Arab Spring certainly has contributed to widening the public exposure of the EU's shady migration cooperation with now overthrown regimes in North Africa—most notably with Gaddafi's Libya, a cooperation that the European Commission decided to deepen as late as in October 2010—such embarrassing revelations of complicity in blatant human rights violations have not prompted any change in EU migration policy towards North Africa.

Conversely though, the Arab Spring has had some significant repercussions for the working of the EU's internal migration policy. When France, in the spring of 2011, decided to impose de facto border controls to prevent the entry of mainly Tunisian refugees arriving from Italy (thanks to Italian authorities' facilitation of this onward movement), this not only tested Franco-Italian relations but also dealt a heavy and, as it turned out, irreversible blow to the Schengen accord. Following Denmark's subsequent decision to reintroduce permanent customs checks, Brussels began an as of yet unfinished process of reforming Schengen, most likely to end up allowing for more curbs on free movement in the EU.

But this is but a few instances in a long catalogue of conflicts that have erupted over internal migration policy in the EU since we concluded this book in 2009. In contrast to the case of Tunisian migrants above, moreover, many of these conflicts do not revolve around the intra-EU movement of external migrants and asylum seekers but are now increasingly triggered by the movement of EU citizens themselves. This tendency was heralded by the old member states' introduction of so-called transition rules in order to restrict the free labor movement and social incorporation of the new EU citizens in anticipation of the EU enlargements in 2004 and 2007 respectively, a development that we discuss in this book. Since then several new rows in the old member states over labor migration from the new ones have taken place. These have revolved around new ways of preventing labor migration from poorer eastern member states to the richer western ones, stemming from growing opposition and hostility to migration and migrants from the eastern members. But it has also been triggered by new and EU sanctioned legal instruments that have enabled employers to lower wages and working conditions for posted workers who, for competitive purposes, are brought from the poorer new member states for work in the old. While this practice has raised well-founded concerns within the labor movement about social dumping, it has also been exploited by the extreme right as a means to pit the domestic labor force against alleged immigrant job-stealers from Eastern Europe.

Adding to the EU's increasingly conflict-laden internal migration scene we, of course, also have to mention the illegal French mass expulsions of Roma EU citizens that caught the headlines in the summer of 2010. This had been common practice in France for some time (but also, to a lesser extent, in other EU countries) with over 10,000 Roma EU citizens being expelled in 2009 alone; in 2010, however, Sarkozy decided to turn these expulsion into an outright PR campaign. Just prior to that, moreover, it was revealed that the Dutch government was preparing to take forth measures to allow for the expulsion of EU citizens who, inter alia, were making "disproportionate claims" on the social benefit system, something that immediately set off an angry Polish reaction. And the list could certainly be made much longer; we have already noted that Spain has reintroduce its labor migration ban on Romanian citizens and that the Netherlands, who last year vetoed Romania and Bulgaria's Schengen entry, is contemplating issuing similar labor migration restrictions.

And this is indeed how the issue is increasingly being articulated today: as *migration* rather than free movement. This became obvious already when the debate on transition rules erupted at the time for the first Eastern enlargement when the promise of "free movement" for the cousins in the east quickly degenerated into a bitter and hostile debate about Eastern European "immigration problems." Whereas EU policy discourse always has associated free movement with positives such as economic growth, a dynamic and open labor market, and with rights and freedom of EU citizens, we know equally well that migration in large part has come to be associated with the opposite: international crime, terrorism, illegal migration, asylum fraud, social welfare cheating, job-stealing, trafficking, cultural conflicts, and other integration problems, to mention but a few.

For the longest time EU governments placed the onus of alleged migration problems exclusively on those coming from outside the EU, mostly the "non-Europeans." Since the Eastern enlargements many of these problems are now increasingly being projected also onto EU citizens themselves. As a consequence, the European migration drama is now being played out between EU member states as well, pitting British against Poles, Dutch against Romanians, and so on, in much the same way as the nationalist articulation of the current sovereign debt crisis (e.g. pitting "diligent" Germans against "lazy" Greeks). This is of course connected to the fact that socioeconomic disparities have widened both within and between member states, something that has paved the way for political forces that stoke the flames of, and in turn feed off of, xenophobia. And such forces are far from reducible to those on the far right. This was confirmed with utmost clarity in the aggressive debate about the transition rules where several old member state governments spoke about forestalling a potential wave of East European immigration that would increase crime and swamp their labor markets and welfare systems. But this was before the current crisis; and if the political momentum for amending socioeconomic disparities, both within and between the member states, was nonexistent already then, today's austerity policy seems intent on turning this nonexistence into a virtue. So, what would happen if much larger numbers of people from socioeconomically disintegrating member states in, let's say, southern or eastern Europe were to start moving north and west? About this we can only speculate. But the indications so far do not bode well and thus it may not take too many before the migration alarm will go off. In this potentially ugly situation, those who persist in claiming that the EU project of market and monetary integration once and for all should have resolved the national question in Europe will finally have to think again.

Already we see some of the most ardent supporters starting to question some of these long cherished beliefs. Even Jürgen Habermas, one of the founding fathers of post-national cosmopolitanism, is now warning that the sovereign debt crisis, and especially the Greek referendum debacle, is leading towards the "disenfranchisement of European citizens" (*Der Spiegel Online*, 24 November 2011). In short, Habermas feels betrayed by what he refers to as the "post-democratic" German and French-led political response to the crisis. The post-democratic EU polity emerging since the crisis, Habermas claims, has empowered the "market" at the expense of democratic decision-making. It has left the European Parliament toothless, the Commission confused, and the European Council, the institutional lynchpin of intergovernmentalism, with powers that run counter to the EU constitution.

Of course it would be easy for us to celebrate Habermas' change of heart as a confirmation of our own views. Yet the apparent similarities between our own criticisms of the EU and Habermas' newfound critical views are only superficial. First of all, as our critical history of EU citizenship makes clear, the problems of legitimacy for the EU stretch back much further than the current crisis, to at least the mid-1980s when Habermas and other post-national cosmopolitans were celebrating the EU as the institutional blueprint for a more progressive world order. Secondly, Habermas' explanation for, and solution to, the current malaise rest on the assumption that the problem is too much intergovernmentalism and not enough supranational integration. Our own analysis in this book tries to get beyond this rather facile dichotomy of intergovernmentalism versus post-national cosmopolitanism. As we argue clearly in chapter two, any attempt to grasp the EU's current turbulence and legitimacy crisis must go beyond the mere form of EU integration, and delve into the content, to understand and explain who benefits from EU integration and its concomitant citizenship model. As this book argues, the main obstacle to a more progressive, alternative Europe is the power asymmetries that underpin and structure the integration project. So while it is somewhat heartening to see Habermas take a more critical view of the most recent developments, his intervention does not go far enough.

In the end, it is difficult not to be apocalyptic about the future of citizenship politics in the EU. If nothing else what this book does is situate the current malaise within a long-term historical context. We hope that in some way our analysis will help to ignite serious debate about what it means to belong to the EU polity as citizens and non-citizens alike. The answers may seem unsettling, but it is precisely the unsettling nature of the EU project that has caused its crisis of legitimacy in the first place. And to reiterate what we said in the preface, any un-, pre-, or post-democratic formation that is hampered by constant crises of legitimacy is much less scary than one that is not. Finally, to unravel the deep-seated contradictions that lie at the heart of the EU project is a necessary precondition for any envisioning of democratic and humane alternatives to the current disorder.

Norrköping and Toronto
January 2012

References

Adnett, N. and S. Hardy. 2005. *The European Social Model: Modernisation or Evolution?* Cheltenham: Edward Elgar.
Aiken, L. H., et al. 2004. "Trends in International Nurse Migration," *Health Affairs* 23(3): 69–77.
Albo, G. 1994. "'Competitive Austerity' and the Impasse of Capitalist Employment Policy," in R. Miliband and L. Panitch (eds), *Socialist Register 1994: Between Globalism and Nationalism.* London: Merlin.
Ali, T. 2000. "The Blair Kitsch Project," *Monthly Review* 51(8): 13–25.
Alibhai-Brown, Y. 2001. "Mr Blunkett has insulted all of us," *The Independent*, 10 December.
Amnesty International. 2003. *"UK/EU/UNHCR: Unlawful and Unworkable—Amnesty International's views on proposals for extra-territorial processing of asylum claims."* AI Index: IOR 61/004/2003, 18 June.
Amnesty International. 2004. "More Justice and Freedom to Balance Security: Amnesty International's Recommendations to the EU." 27 September, http://news.amnesty.org/index/ENGEUR01270920042004 (10 December, 2004).
Anderson, M., et al. 1995. *Policing the European Union.* Oxford: Clarendon Press.
Aradau, C. 2009. "The Roma in Italy: Racism as usual?," *Radical Philosophy* 153: 2–7.
Archibugi, D. 1998. "Principles of Cosmopolitan Democracy," in D. Archibugi, D. Held and M. Köhler (eds), *Reimagining Political Community: Studies in Cosmopolitan Democracy.* London: Stanford University Press: 198–228.
Archibugi, D., and M. Koenig-Archibugi. 2003. "Globalization, Democracy and Cosmopolis: A Biographical Essay," in D. Archibugi and M. Koenig-Archibugi (eds), *Debating Cosmopolitics.* London: Verso.
Ascoli, U. 1985. "Migration of Workers and the Labour Market: Is Italy Becoming a Country of Immigration?" in R. Rogers (ed), *Guests Come to Stay: The Effects of European Labor Migration on Sending and Receiving Countries.* Boulder: Westview Press.
Atkins, R. 2008. "Eurozone Growth Prospects Crumble," *Financial Times*, 25 July.
Baldoni, E. 2003. "The Free Movement of Persons in the European Union: A Legal-historical Overview," State of the Art Report, *PIONEUR Working Paper*, 2.
Balibar, E. 2004. *We, the People of Europe?* Princeton: Princeton University Press.
Balzacq, T. and S. Carrera. 2006. "The Hague Programme: The Long Road to Freedom, Security and Justice," in T. Balzacq and S. Carrera (eds), *Security Versus Freedom? A Challenge for Europe's Future.* Aldershot: Ashgate.

Balzan, A. 2006. "Europe and Africa agree on common plan to tackle migration," *EUobserver*, euobserver.com, 12 July.

Barber, T. 2008. "France's blunt warning of Irish No," *Financial Times*, 9 June, Retrieved 17 September 2008 from FT.com.

Barber, T. 2008. "EU Migration Pact Set to Encourage Skilled Migration and Discourage Illegals," *Financial Times*, 25 September, Retrieved 1 October 2008 from FT.com.

Barber, T. and G. Parker. 2004. "Prodi says European efforts to catch US 'a failure'," *Financial Times*, 25 October.

Barnard, C. and S. Deakin. 1999. "A Year of Living Dangerously? EC social rights, employment policy, and EMU," *Industrial Relations Journal* 30(4): 355–372.

Barroso, J. M. 2005a. "Choosing to grow—a new agenda for growth and jobs," Speech/05/188, 18 March, Warsaw.

Barroso, J. M. 2005b. "The Lisbon Strategy—a key priority of the European Commission," Speech/05/125, 1 March, Brussels.

Barroso, J. M. 2005c. "Growth and Jobs: a new start for the Lisbon strategy," Speech/05/152, 9 March, Strasbourg.

Barroso, J. M. 2005d. "Key challenges for the European Union: Enlargement and Governance," Speech/05/195, 1 April, Madrid.

Barroso, J. M. 2005e. "Working together for jobs and growth: A new start for the Lisbon Strategy," Speech/05/67, 2 February, Brussels.

Beck, U. 2006. *The Cosmopolitan Vision*. Cambridge: Polity Press.

Beck, U. and A. Giddens. 2005. "Nationalism has now become the enemy of Europe's nations," *The Guardian*, 4 October.

Beck, U. and E. Grande. 2007. *Cosmopolitan Europe*. Cambridge: Polity Press.

Beetham, D and C. Lord. 1998. *Legitimacy and the European Union*. London: Longman.

Bellamy, R., Castiglione, D. and J. Shaw (eds). 2006. *Making European Citizens: Civil Inclusion in a Transnational Context*. Basingstoke: Palgrave.

Bellamy, R. and A. Warleigh. 1998. "From an Ethics of Integration to an Ethics of Participation: Citizenship and the Future of the European Union," *Millennium* 27: 447–70.

Bellamy, R. and A. Warleigh (eds). 2001. *Citizenship and Governance in the European Union*. London: Continuum.

Betz, H-G. 2002. "Xenophobia, Identity Politics and Exclusionary Populism in Western Europe," in L. Panitch and C. Leys (eds), *Fighting Identities: Race, Religion and Ethno-Nationalism*. London: The Merlin Press.

Bieler, A. 2006. *The Struggle for a Social Europe: Trade Unions and EMU in Times of Global Restructuring*. Manchester: Manchester University Press.

Bieling, H-J. 2003. "European employment policy between neoliberal rationalism and communitarianism," in H. Overbeek (ed), *The Political Economy of European Employment: European integration and the transnationalization of the (un)employment question*. London: Routledge.

Bigo, D. 2006. "Liberty, whose Liberty? The Hague Programme and the Conception of Freedom," in T. Balzacq and S. Carrera (eds), *Security Versus Freedom? A Challenge for Europe's Future*. Aldershot: Ashgate.

Birnberg Peirce & Partners, Medical Justice and the National Coalition of Anti-

Deportation Campaigns. 2008. *Outsourcing Abuse: The use and misuse of state-sanctioned force during the detention and removal of asylum seekers.* July.
Boqvist, M. 1997. "Nyckeln i Nicosia," *Sydsvenska Dagbladet,* 12 December.
Bornschier, V. and P. Ziltener. 1999. "The revitalization of Western Europe and the politics of the 'social dimension'," in T. P. Boje, B. van Steenbergen and S. Walby (eds), *European Societies: Fusion or Fission?* London: Routledge.
Boswell, C. 2003. "The 'external dimension' of EU immigration and asylum policy," *International Affairs* 79(3): 619–38.
Bottomore, T. 1992. "Citizenship and Social Class, Forty Years On," in T. H. Marshall and T. Bottomore (authors), *Citizenship and Social Class.* London: Pluto Press.
Bourdieu, P. 1998. "A Reasoned Utopia and Economic Fatalism," *New Left Review* 227: 125–130.
Bourdieu, P., Lebaron, F. and G. Mauger. 1998. "The Cause of the Unemployed," *The Nation,* 2 March.
Boyer, R. 1990. *The Regulation School: A Critical Introduction.* New York: Columbia University Press.
Boyer, R. 2004. *The Future of Economic Growth: As New Becomes Old.* Cheltenham: Edward Elgar.
Brostrand, K. 2006. "Afrikanska unionen överväger EU-förslag," *Ekot* (Swedish Radio), 2 October, http://www.sr.se/cgi-bin/ekot/artikel.asp?artikel=957597.
Buck, T. 2005. "Brussels Seeks to Streamline EU's Lisbon Agenda for Economic Reform," *Financial Times,* 18 January.
Budgen, S. 2002. "The French Fiasco," *New Left Review* 17: 31–50.
Busch, N. 1998. "Massaresteringarna vid EU-toppmötet i Amsterdam: ett steg mot det nya Europas övervakningsstruktur," in M. Hörnqvist (ed), *Gränslös kontroll: Schengen, Europol och det europeiska polissamarbetet.* Stockholm: Federativs.
Butt Philip, A. 1994. "European Union Immigration Policy: Phantom, Fantasy or Fact?" *West European Politics* 17(2): 168–91.
Cafruny, A. and M. Ryner. 2007. *Europe at Bay: In the Shadow of US Hegemony.* Boulder: Lynne Rienner Publishers.
Cahn, C. 2008. "EU must act to stop Italy racism crisis," *EUobserver,* euobserver.com, 21 August.
Calhoun, C. 2007. *Nations Matter: Culture, History, and the Cosmopolitan Dream.* London: Routledge.
Callinicos, A. 1999. "Social Theory Put to the Test of Politics: Pierre Bourdieu and Anthony Giddens," *New Left Review* 236: 77–102.
Caporaso, J. 1996. "The European Union and Forms of State: Westphalian, Regulatory or Post-Modern?" *Journal of Common Market Studies* 34(1): 29–52.
Carchedi, G. 2001. *For Another Europe: A Class Analysis of European Economic Integration.* London: Verso.
Carrera, S. 2006. "Integration of Immigrants Versus Social Inclusion: A Typology of Integration Programmes in the EU," in T. Balzacq and S. Carrera (eds), *Security Versus Freedom? A Challenge for Europe's Future.* Aldershot: Ashgate.
Carrera, S. and E. Guild. 2008. "The French Presidency's European Pact on Immigration and Asylum: Intergovernmentalism vs. Europeanisation? Security vs. Rights?," *CEPS Policy Brief,* No. 170, September. Retrieved 10 June 2009 from http://www.libertysecurity.org/article2230.html.

Carter, A. 2001. *The Political Theory of Global Citizenship*. London: Routledge.
Castles, S. 2004. "Why migration policies fail," *Ethnic and Racial Studies* 27(2): 205–27.
Castles, S. and A. Davidson. 2000. *Citizenship and Migration: Globalization and the Politics of Belonging*. London: Routledge.
Castles, S. and G. Kosack 1985. *Immigrant Workers and Class Structure in Western Europe*, 2nd ed. Oxford: Oxford University Press.
Castles, S. and M. J. Miller 2003. *The Age of Migration*, 3rd ed. New York: The Guilford Press.
Caviedes, A. 2004. "The open method of co-ordination in immigration policy: a tool for prying open Fortress Europe?" *Journal of European Public Policy* 11(2): 289–310.
CEC. (Commission of the European Communities) 1973. "Declaration on the European Identity." *Bulletin of the EC*, 12, (Clause 2501).
CEC. 1976 [1974]. "Action programme in favour of migrant workers and their families." COM(74) 2250, 14. 12, *Bulletin of the EC*, Suppl. 3/76.
CEC. 1984. "Towards a European television policy." *European File*, 19, December.
CEC. 1985a. "A People's Europe: Reports from the *ad hoc* Committee." *Bulletin of the EC*, Suppl. 7/85.
CEC. 1985b. *Completing the Internal Market: White Paper from the Commission to the European Council*. COM(85) 310 final, Brussels, 14. 6.
CEC. 1985c. *Guidelines for a Community policy on migration*. COM(85) 48 final, 1. 3.
CEC. 1988. "A people's Europe." *Bulletin of the EC*, Supplement 2/88.
CEC. 1993a. *A Citizen's Europe*. Luxembourg: Office for Official Publications of the EC.
CEC. 1993b. *Report from the Commission on the Citizenship of the Union*. COM(93) 702 final, Brussels, 21 December.
CEC. 1993c. *Green Paper: European social policy*. COM(93) 551, 17 November.
CEC. 1993d. "Growth, competitiveness, employment: The challenges and ways forward into the 21st century, White Paper." *Bulletin of the EC*, Supplement 6/93.
CEC. 1993e. *Report from the Commission on the Citizenship of the Union*. COM(93) 702 final, Brussels, 21 December.
CEC. 1994a. *European Social Policy—A Way Forward for the Union: A White Paper*. COM(94) 333 final, Brussels, 27 July.
CEC. 1994b. *A portrait of our Europe: Information on the Member States and the development of the European Union*. Luxembourg: Office for Official Publications of the EC.
CEC. 1994c. *On immigration and asylum policies*. COM(94) 23 final, Brussels, 23. 2.
CEC. 1994d. *Report on the Education of Migrants' Children in the European Union*. COM(94) 80 final, Brussels, 25. 3.
CEC. 1995a. *European Community action in support of culture*. COM(95) 110 final, Brussels, 29. 03.
CEC. 1995b. *European integration: The origins and growth of the European Union*. Luxembourg: Office for Official Publications of the EC.
CEC. 1995c. *Communication from the Commission on racism, xenophobia and anti-Semitism; and Proposal for a Council Decision designating 1997 as European Year against Racism*. COM(95) 653 final, 95/0355 (CNS), Brussels, 13. 12.
CEC. 1996a. *Promoting a Social Europe—Europe on the move*. Luxembourg: Office for Official Publications of the European Communities.

CEC. 1996b. *1st report on the consideration of cultural aspects in European Community action.* COM(96) 160 final, Brussels, 17. 04.
CEC. 1996c. *Europe ... questions and answers: The European Union—What's in it for me?* Luxembourg: Office for Official Publications of the EC.
CEC. 1997a. *Second report from the Commission on citizenship of the Union.* COM(1997) 230 final, Brussels, 27. 5.
CEC. 1997b. *Citizens' access to culture.* DG X, Culture, Culture Action.
CEC. 1997c. "Amsterdam: A new treaty for Europe," *Supplement – Frontier-free Europe* (No. 7/8).
CEC. 1998a. *EURO 1999.* Luxembourg: Office for Official Publications of the EC.
CEC. 1998b. "The euro in practice: work is advancing!" *Infeuro,* No. 7.
CEC. 2000a. *Social Policy Agenda.* COM(2000) 379 final, Brussels, 28. 6.
CEC. 2000b. *Living in an area of freedom, security and justice: Justice and home affairs in the European Union.* Luxembourg: Office for Official Publications of the EC.
CEC. 2000c. *On a Community Immigration Policy.* COM(2000) 757 final, Brussels, 22. 11.
CEC. 2000d. *Towards a common asylum procedure and uniform status, valid throughout the Union, for persons granted asylum.* COM(2000) 755 final, Brussels, 22. 11.
CEC. 2000de. *Asylum and immigration debate.* Communiqués de presse de l'UE, IP/00/1340, Brussels, 22 November.
CEC. 2001a. *Proposal for a Council Directive concerning the status of third-country nationals who are long-term residents.* COM(2001) 127 final, Brussels, 13. 3.
CEC. 2001b. *The institutions and bodies of the European Union—Who's who in the European Union?—What difference will the Treaty of Nice make?* Luxembourg: Office for Official Publications of the EC.
CEC. 2001c. *On an open method of coordination for the Community immigration policy.* COM(2001) 387 final, Brussels, 11. 7.
CEC. 2001d. *Proposal for a Council framework decision on combating racism and xenophobia.* COM(2001) 664 final, 2001/0270 (CNS), Brussels, 28. 11.
CEC. 2001e. *On the common asylum policy, introducing an open coordination method.* COM(2001) 710 final, Brussels, 28. 11.
CEC. 2001f. *On a Common Policy on Illegal Immigration.* COM(2001) 672 final, Brussels, 15. 11.
CEC. 2002a. *Towards integrated management of the external borders of the Member States of the European Union.* COM(2002) 233 final, Brussels, 7. 5.
CEC. 2002b. *Commission Recommendation for the 2002 Broad Guidelines of the Economic Policies of the Member States and the Community.* ECFIN/210/02-EN, Brussels.
CEC. 2002c. *Communication from the Commission concerning Corporate Social Responsibility.* COM(2002) 347 final, Brussels, 2. 7.
CEC. 2002d. *The Lisbon Strategy—Making Change Happen.* COM(2002) 14 final, Brussels, 15. 1.
CEC. 2002e. *Integrating migration issues in the Union's relations with third countries.* COM(2002) 703 final, Brussels, 3. 12.
CEC. 2002f. *Green Paper on a Community Return Policy on Illegal Residents.* COM(2002) 175 final, Brussels, 10. 4.
CEC. 2003a. *Mid-term review of the Social Policy Agenda.* COM(2003) 312 final, Brussels, 2. 6.

CEC. 2003b. *Commission Recommendation on the Broad Guidelines of the Economic Policies of the Member States and the Community (for the 2003–2005 period)*. COM(2003) 170 final/2, Brussels, 24. 7.

CEC. 2003c. *Modernising Social Protection for and Better Jobs: a comprehensive approach contributing to making work pay*. COM(2003) 842 final, Brussels, 30. 12.

CEC. 2003d. *Strengthening the social dimension of the Lisbon strategy: Streamlining open coordination in the field of social protection*. COM(2003) 261 final, Brussels, 27. 5.

CEC. 2003e. "Establishing a status for long-term residents." http://europa.eu.int/comm/justice_home/fsj/immigration/residents/fsj_immigration_residents_en.htm (10 March, 2003).

CEC. 2003f. "A dynamic integration policy bestowing equal rights and obligations." http://europa.eu.int/comm/justice_home/fsj/immigration/integration/fsj_immigration_integration_en.htm.

CEC. 2003g. "Fighting all forms of discrimination in the European Union." http://europa.eu.int/comm/justice_home/fsj/rights/discrimination/fsj_rights_discrim.en.htm.

CEC. 2003h. *On immigration, integration and employment*. COM(2003) 336 final, Brussels, 3. 6.

CEC. 2003i. *On the common asylum policy and the Agenda for protection*. COM(2003) 152 final, Brussels, 26. 3.

CEC. 2003j. *Towards more accessible, equitable and managed asylum systems*. COM(2003) 315 final, Brussels, 3. 6.

CEC. 2003k. *Employment in Europe 2003*. DG for Employment and Social Affairs, Luxembourg: Office for Official Publications of the EC.

CEC. 2003l. *Wider Europe—Neighbourhood: A New Framework for Relations with our Eastern and Southern Neighbours*. COM(2003) 104 final, Brussels, 11. 3.

CEC. 2003m. *On the Development of a Common Policy on Illegal Immigration, Smuggling and Trafficking of Human Beings, External Borders and the Return of Illegal Residents*. COM (2003) 323 final, Brussels, 3. 6.

CEC. 2004a. *Strengthening the implementation of the European Employment Strategy*. COM (2004) 239 final, 2004/0082 (CNS), Brussels, 7. 4.

CEC. 2004b. *Scoreboard on implementing the Social Policy Agenda*. COM(2004) 137 final, Brussels, 1. 3.

CEC. 2004c. *The social situation in the European Union: 2004 Overview*. Brussels.

CEC. 2004d. *Building our common Future: Policy challenges and Budgetary means of the Enlarged Union 2007–2013*. COM(2004) 101 final/2, Brussels, 26. 2.

CEC. 2004e. *Area of Freedom, Security and Justice: Assessment of the Tampere programme and future orientations*. COM(2004) 401 final, Brussels, 2. 6.

CEC. 2004f. *On the managed entry in the EU of persons in need of international protection and the enhancement of the protection capacity of the regions of origin—"Improving access to durable solutions."* COM(2004) 410 final, Brussels, 4. 6.

CEC. 2004g. *Study on the links between legal and illegal migration*. COM(2004) 412 final, Brussels, 4. 6.

CEC. 2004h. "Area of freedom, security and justice: Asylum and immigration." *Bulletin of the European Union*, Issue 7/8, http://europa.eu/bulletin/en/200407/p103004.htm.

CEC. 2005a. *Working together for growth and jobs: A new start for the Lisbon Strategy*. COM (2005) 24, Brussels, 2. 2.

CEC. 2005b. *The Hague Programme: Ten Priorities for the next five years.* COM(2005) 184 final, Brussels, 10. 5.
CEC. 2005c. *The Social Agenda 2005–2010.* DG for Employment, Social Affairs and Equal Opportunities, Luxembourg: Office for Official Publications of the EC.
CEC. 2005d. *A Common Agenda for Integration: Framework for the Integration of Third-Country Nationals in the European Union.* COM(2005) 389 final, Brussels, 1. 9.
CEC. 2005e. *Non-discrimination and equal opportunities for all—A framework strategy.* COM(2005) 224 final, Brussels, 1. 6.
CEC. 2005f. *Green Paper on an EU Approach to Managing Economic Migration.* COM (2004) 811 final, Brussels, 11. 1.
CEC. 2005g. *Migration and Development: Some concrete orientations.* COM(2005) 390 final, Brussels, 1. 9.
CEC. 2005h. *On Regional Protection Programmes.* COM(2005) 388 final, Brussels, 1. 9.
CEC. 2005i. *Priority actions for responding to the challenges of migration.* COM(2005) 621 final, Brussels, 30. 11.
CEC. 2005j. *Proposal for a directive ... on common standards and procedures in Member States for returning illegally staying third-country nationals.* COM(2005) 391 final, Brussels, 1. 9.
CEC. 2005k. *The Social Policy Agenda (2006–2010).* http://europa.eu/scadplus/leg/en/cha/c10127.htm.
CEC. 2005l. *Policy Plan on Legal Migration.* COM(2005) 669 final, Brussels, 21. 12.
CEC. 2006a. *The Period of Reflection and Plan D.* COM(2006) 212 final, Brussels, 10. 5.
CEC. 2006b. *Report on the implementation of the Hague programme for 2005.* COM(2006) 333 final, Brussels, 28. 6.
CEC. 2006c. "Migration and development: the European Policy." Speech by Commissioner Franco Frattini, Bologna, 26 November, 2005.
CEC. 2006d. "Migration, External Relations and the European Neighbourhood Policy." Speech by EU Commissioner Ferrero-Waldner, Brussels, 21. 1, 2006.
CEC. 2006e. "The European Commission and the Commission of the African Union meet in Addis Ababa." IP/06/1277, Brussels, 28 September.
CEC. 2007a. *The European Interest: Succeeding in the age of globalisation.* COM(2007) 581 final, Brussels, 3. 10.
CEC. 2007b. *Report on the implementation of the Hague programme for 2006.* COM(2007) 373 final, Brussels, 3. 7.
CEC. 2007c. *Green Paper on the future Common European Asylum System.* COM(2007) 301 final, Brussels, 6. 6.
CEC. 2007d. *Proposal for a Council Directive on the conditions of entry and residence of third-country nationals for the purposes of highly qualified employment.* COM(2007) 637 final, Brussels, 23. 10.
CEC. 2007e. "Attractive conditions for the admission and residence of highly qualified immigrants." MEMO/07/423, Brussels, 23 October.
CEC. 2007f. *Third Annual Report on Migration and Integration.* COM(2007) 512, Brussels, 11. 9.
CEC. 2008a. *Commission Staff Working Document.* SEC(2008) 153, Brussels, 13. 2.
CEC. 2008b. *A Common Immigration Policy for Europe: Principles, actions and tools.* COM (2008) 359 final, Brussels, 17. 6.
Chalmers, D. and M. Lodge. 2003. "The Open Method of Co-ordination and the European Welfare State," *CARR Discussion Paper Series,* No. 11, London: Centre

for Analysis of Risk and Regulation, London School of Economics and Political Science.
Coates, K. 1998. "Unemployed Europe and the Struggle for Alternatives," *New Left Review* 227: 131–4.
Cocks, P. 1980. "Towards a Marxist theory of European integration," *International Organization* 34(1): 1–40.
Collins, D. 1975. *Social Policy of the European Economic Community*. New York: John Wiley & Sons.
Commission for Racial Equality. 1994. *Citizens, Minorities and Foreigners: A guide to the EC*. London: CRE.
Conference of the Representatives of the Governments of the Member States. 2004. *Treaty establishing a Constitution for Europe*. CIG 87/1/04, REV 1, Brussels, 13 October.
Connell, J., et al. 2007. "Sub-Saharan Africa: Beyond the health worker migration crisis?" *Social Science & Medicine* 64: 1876–91.
Council EC. (Council of the European Communities) 1968a. "Council Directive 68/360/EEC of 15 October 1968 on the abolition of restrictions on movement and residence within the Community for workers of Member States and their families." *Official Journal of the European Communities* L 252, 19. 10.
Council EC. 1968b. "Regulation (EEC) No 1612/68 of the Council of 15 October 1968 on freedom of movement for workers within the Community." *Official Journal of the European Communities* L 257, 19. 10, (English special edition: Series I Chapter, 1968(II): 475).
Council EC. 1974. "Council Resolution concerning a social action programme." *Official Journal of the European Communities* C 13, 12. 2.
Council EU. (Council of the European Union) 1997a. *Amsterdam European Council: Draft Treaty*. Intergovernmental Conference, Brussels.
Council EU. 1997b. *Amsterdam European Council: Draft Treaty*. Intergovernmental Conference, Brussels, June.
Council EU. 1997c. *Council Regulation (EC) No 1035/97 of 2 June 1997 establishing a European Monitoring Centre on Racism and Xenophobia*. Brussels.
Council EU. 2000a. "Council Decision of 28 September 2000 establishing a European Refugee Fund." *Official Journal of the European Communities* L 252 (2000/596/EC), 6. 10.
Council EU. 2000b. "Council Decision of 27 November 2000 establishing a Community action programme to combat discrimination (2001 to 2006)." *Official Journal of the European Communities* L 303 (2000/750/EC), 21. 12.
Council EU. 2000c. "Council Directive 2000/43/EC of 29 June 2000 implementing the principle of equal treatment between persons irrespective of racial or ethnic origin." *Official Journal of the European Communities* L 180, 19. 7.
Council EU. 2000d. "Partnership agreement between the members of the African, Caribbean and Pacific Group of States of the one part, and the European Community and its Member States, of the other part, signed in Cotonou on 23 June 2000." *Official Journal of the European Communities* L 317, 15. 12.
Council EU. 2000e. "Council Directive 2000/78/EC of 27 November 2000 establishing a general framework for equal treatment in employment an occupation." *Official Journal of the European Communities* L 303, 2. 12.

Council EU. 2001a. "Council Directive 2001/55/EC of 20 July 2001 on minimum standards for giving temporary protection in the event of mass influx of displaced persons and on measures promoting a balance of efforts between Member States in receiving such persons and bearing the consequences thereof." *Official Journal of the European Communities* L 212, 7. 8.

Council EU. 2001b. "Council Directive 2001/51/EC of 28 June 2001 supplementing the provisions of Article 26 of the Convention implementing the Schengen Agreement of 14 June 1985." *Official Journal of the European Communities* L 187, 10. 7.

Council EU. 2001c. "Council Regulation (EC) No 539/2001 of 15 March 2001 listing the third countries whose nationals must be in possession of visas when crossing the external borders and whose nationals are exempt from that requirement." *Official Journal of the European Communities* L 81, 21. 3.

Council EU. 2002a. *Initiative by the Kingdom of Spain for the adoption of a Council Decision introducing a standard form for exchanging information on incidents caused by violent radical groups with terrorist links.* 5712/1/02, Brussels.

Council EU. 2002b. *2455th Council meeting—Justice, Home Affairs and Civil Protection.* C/02/308, 12894/02, Luxembourg, 14/15 October.

Council EU. 2002c. "Council Regulation (EC) no 407/2002 of 28 February 2002 laying down certain rules to implement Regulation (EC) no 2725/2000 concerning the establishment of 'Eurodac' for the comparison of fingerprints for the effective application of the Dublin Convention." *Official Journal of the European Communities* L 62, 5. 3.

Council EU. 2003a. "Council Decision of 22 July 2003 on guidelines for the employment policies of the Member States." *Official Journal of the European Union* L 197 (2003/578/EC).

Council EU. 2003b. "Council Directive 2003/9/EC of 27 January 2003 laying down minimum standards for the reception of asylum seekers." *Official Journal of the European Union* L 31, 6. 2.

Council EU. 2003c. "Council Regulation (EC) No 343/2003 of 18 February 2003 establishing the criteria and mechanisms for determining the Member State responsible for examining an asylum application lodged in one of the Member States by a third-country national." *Official Journal of the European Union* L 50, 25. 2.

Council EU. 2003d. "Council Directive 2003/86/EC of 22 September 2003 on the right to family reunification." *Official Journal of the European Union* L 251, 3. 10.

Council EU. 2004a. *Council Directive on minimum standards for the qualification and status of third country nationals or stateless persons as refugees or as persons who otherwise need international protection and the content of the protection granted.* 2001/0270 (CNS), 8043/04, Asile 23, Brussels, 27. 4.

Council EU. 2004b. *Amended proposal for a Council Directive on minimum standards on procedures in Member States for granting and withdrawing refugee status.* 2000/0238 (CNS), 8771/04, Asile 33, Brussels, 30. 4.

Council EU. 2004c. "Council Directive 2003/109/EC of 25 November 2003 concerning the status of third-country nationals who are long-term residents." *Official Journal of the European Union* L 16, 23. 1.

Council EU. 2004d. "Council Decision of 22 December 2004." *Official Journal of the European Union* L 396 (2004/927/EC), 31. 12.

Council EU. 2004e. "Council Decision of 29 April 2004 on the organisation of joint flights for removals from the territory of two or more Member States, of third-country nationals who are subjects of individual removal orders." *Official Journal of the European Union* L 261 (2004/573/EC), 6. 8.

Council EU. 2004f. *2618th Council Meeting: Justice and Home Affairs.* C/04/321, 14615/04 (Presse 321), Brussels, 19 November.

Council EU. 2004g. *Presidency Conclusions.* Brussels European Council 4–5 November 2004, 14292/1/04, Brussels, 8. December.

Council EU. 2004h. "Libya—Council Conclusions." General Affairs and External Relations Council, 11 October.

Council EU. 2004i. "Council Regulation (EC) No 2007/2004 of 26 October 2004 establishing a European Agency for the Management of Operational Cooperation at the External Borders of the Member States of the European Union." *Official Journal of the European Union* L 349, 25. 11.

Council EU. 2005. *A Strategy for the External Dimension of JHA.* 14366/1/05, Brussels, 24. 11.

Council EU. 2006. "2725th Council Meeting Justice and Home Affairs Luxembourg, 27–28 April 2006." Press Release, C/06/106 (Presse 106), Brussels.

Council EU. 2009a. "Council adopts the 'EU Blue Card'." 10266/09 (Presse 151), Brussels, 25 May.

Council EU. 2009b. "The Stockholm Programme—An open and secure Europe serving and protecting the citizens." 17024/09, Brussels, 2 December.

Council EC, CEC. 1992. *Treaty on European Union.* Luxembourg: Office for Official Publications of the EC.

Council of Europe. 2003. *Convention for the Protection of Human Rights and Fundamental Freedoms as amended by Protocol No. 11.* Registry of the European Court of Human Rights, September.

Council of Europe. 2008. "The relationship between integration and the fight against racism and racial discrimination." Human Rights and Legal Affairs. Retrieved 8 August 2008 from http://www.coe.int/t/e/human_rights/ecri/1-ECRI/4-Relations_with_civil_society/1-Programme_of_action/28-Seminar_national_specialised_bodies_2008/2-Briefing_eng.asp.

Cox, R. W. 1992. "Global Perestroika," in R. Miliband and L. Panitch (eds), *Socialist Register 1992: The New World Order.* London: Merlin Press.

Cox, R.W. 1986. "Social Forces, States and World Order: Beyond International Relations Theory," in R.O. Keohane (ed), *Neorealism and its Critics.* New York: Columbia University Press.

Crouch, C. 1998. "The Social Contract and the Problem of the Firm," in M. Rhodes and Y. Mény (eds), *The future of European Welfare: A New Social Contract?* Houndmills: Macmillan.

Crouch, C. and W. Streeck 1997. "Introduction: The Future of Capitalist Diversity," in C. Crouch and W. Streeck (eds), *Political Economy of Modern Capitalism: Mapping Convergence and Diversity.* London: Sage.

Daily Telegraph. 2004. "Gaddafi joins EU campaign to foil illegal migrants," 28 September.

Dannreuther, C and P. Petit. 2006. "Regulation Theory and the EU," *Competition and Change* 10(2): 180–99.

Davies, M. 2005. "The Public Sphere of Unprotected Workers," *Global Society* 19(2): 131–54.
Davy, U. 2005. "Integration of Immigrants in Germany: A Slowly Evolving Concept," *European Journal of Migration and Law* 7(2): 123–44.
Deacon, B. 2001. "International Organizations, the EU and Global Social Policy," in R. Sykes, B. Palier and P. M. Prior (eds), *Globalization and European Welfare States: Challenges and Change*. Houndmills: Palgrave.
de la Porte, C. and P. Pochet. 2002. "Conclusion," in C. de la Porte and P. Pochet (eds), *Building Social Europe through the Open Method of Co-ordination*. Brussels: P.I.E.-Peter Lang.
Delanty, G. 1995. *Inventing Europe: Idea, Identity, Reality*, Houndmills: Macmillan.
Delanty, G. 2005. "What Does it Mean to be 'European'?" *Innovation* 18(1): 11–22.
Delors, J. 1992. *Our Europe: The Community and National Development*. London: Verso.
Den Boer, M. 1995. "Moving between bogus and bona fide: the policing of inclusion and exclusion in Europe," in R. Miles and D. Thränhardt (eds), *Migration and European Integration: The Dynamics of Inclusion and Exclusion*. London: Pinter.
Den Boer, M. 1999. "An Area of Freedom, Security and Justice: Bogged Down by Compromise," in D. O'Keeffe and P. Twomey (eds) *Legal Issues of the Amsterdam Treaty*. Oxford: Hart Publishing.
Deppe, F. 2005. "Habermas' Manifesto for a European Renaissance: A Critique", in L. Panitch and C. Leys (eds.), *Socialist Register 2005: The Empire Reloaded*. London: Merlin Press.
Deutsche Welle. 2006. "Passenger Profiling Among EU's Proposed Anti-Terror Measures," dw-world.de, 17 August.
Diamantopoulou, A. 2000. *Europe, Globalisation, and Social Policy*, Speech/00/166, 5 May, Brussels.
Diamantopoulou, A. 2003. "European perspectives for Employment and Social Policy within the Lisbon Strategy." *Meeting of the European Banking Federation*, 4 April, Athens.
Dietz, G. and B. Agrela. 2004. "Commentary," in W. Cornelius, et al. (eds), *Controlling Immigration: A Global Perspective*, 2nd ed. Stanford: Stanford University Press.
Dinan, D. 1999. *Ever Closer Union: An Introduction to European Integration*. Houndmills: Macmillan.
Dinan, D. (ed). 2000. *Encyclopedia of the European Union*. Boulder: Lynne Rienner Publishers, Inc.
d'Oliveira, H. U. J. 1994. "Expanding External and Shrinking Internal Borders: Europe's Defence Mechanisms in the Areas of Free Movement, Immigration and Asylum," in D. O'Keeffe and P. M. Twomey (eds), *Legal Issues of the Maastricht Treaty*. London: Wiley Chancery Law.
Downes, T. 2001. "Market Citizenship: Functionalism and Fig-leaves," in R. Bellamy and A. Warleigh (eds), *Citizenship and Governance in the European Union*. London: Continuum.
Drainville, A.C. 2004. *Contesting Globalization: Space and Place in the World Economy*. London: Routledge.
Duménil, G. and D. Lévy. 2004. *Capital Resurgent: Roots of the Neoliberal Revolution*. Cambridge: Harvard University Press.

Eaglesham, J. and G. Parker. 2006. "Struggling with the paradox of a 'neo-liberal' Europe," *Financial Times*, 24 July.
Ebbinghaus, B. and J. Visser, J. 1997. "European Labor and Transnational Solidarity: Challenges, Pathways, and Barriers," in J. Klausen and L. A. Tilly (eds), *European Integration in Social and Historical Perspective: 1850 to the Present*. Lanham: Rowman and Littlefield.
Economic and Social Committee. 2001. "Opinion of the Economic and Social Committee on the 'Communication from the Commission to the Council and the European Parliament on a Community immigration policy'." *Official Journal of the European Communities* No C 260 (2001/C 260/19), 17. 9.
ECRE. (European Council on Refugees and Exiles) 2004. *Broken Promises—Forgotten Principles: An ECRE Evaluation of the Development of EU Minimum Standards for Refugee Protection*. London: ECRE Secretariat.
ECRE 2005. "Justice and Home Affairs Council 12–13 October." AD2/10/2005/EXT/RW, Brussels, 10 October.
ECRE and U.S. Committee for Refugees. 2003. *Responding to the Asylum and Access Challenge: An Agenda for Comprehensive Engagement in Protracted Refugee Situations*. RR1/04/2003/ext/AS, April.
Edmondson, G. 1998. "France: A Quiet Revolution," *Business Week*, 29 June.
Employment Taskforce. 2003. *Jobs, Jobs, Jobs: Creating more employment in Europe*. The Employment Taskforce.
Entzinger, H. 2006. "The parallel decline of multiculturalism and the welfare state in the Netherlands," in K. Banting and W. Kymlicka (eds), *Multiculturalism and The Welfare State: Recognition and redistribution in contemporary democracies*. Oxford: Oxford University Press.
ERT (European Roundtable of Industrialists). 2001. *Actions for Competitiveness through the Knowledge Economy in Europe*. Brussels: ERT.
ERT. 2003. *The European Challenge. Message from the European Round Table of Industrialists to the Spring European Council*. Brussels: ERT.
ERT. 2004. *Message on eve of Council Spring Summit*. 16 Feb.
ERT. 2005. *The Chairmanship of Morris Tabaksblat*. Brussels: ERT.
ETUC (European Trade Union Confederation). 2005. "'Revitalize the Lisbon Strategy' by keeping the balance between the economic, social and environmental pillars and by the reform of the macro-economic policy framework." *Resolution adopted by the ETUC Executive Committee in their meeting in Brussels on 15–16 March*. http://www.etuc.org/a/1006?var_recherche=lisbon+agenda.
EUobserver. 2008. "Global outcry against EU immigration directive," euobserver.com, 19 June.
EurActiv. 2006. "EU ministers ask for 'integration contract' for immigrants," 24 Marsh, www.euractiv.com.
EurActiv. 2008. "EU to deepen relations with Libya, starting with trade deal," 28 February, www.euractiv.com.
European Citizen Action Service. 2006. "What way out of the EU constitutional labyrinth?" Authors: E. Gilmartin and B. Napieralski. February, Brussels.
European Parliament. 1990. *Report drawn up on behalf of the Committee of Inquiry into Racism and Xenophobia*. Session Documents, Doc. A3–195/90, Brussels–Luxembourg, 23. 7.

European Parliament. 1991. *Report of the Committee on Youth, Culture, Education, the Media and Sport.* A3–0201/91.
European Parliament. 1993. *Reflection on Information and Communication Policy of the European Community.* (Report by the group of experts chaired by Mr. Willy De Clercq, Member of the European Parliament) March 1993, R. P./1051/93, Rapporteur: Mr. Jean-Pierre Haber.
European Parliament. 2000. "Social and employment policy—General principles." *European Parliament Fact Sheets,* http://www.europarl.europa.eu/factsheets/4_8_1_en.htm (28 July, 2007).
European Parliament. 2001a. *Report on the Commission Communication to the Council and the European Parliament on a Community immigration policy.* Session document, A5–0305/2001, final, 14. 9.
European Parliament. 2001b. *Report on the proposal for a Council Directive concerning the status of third-country nationals who are long-term residents.* Session document, A5–0436/2001, final, 30. 11.
European Parliament, Council EU. 2004. "Regulation (EC) No 491/2004 of the European Parliament and of the Council of 10 March 2004 establishing a programme for financial and technical assistance to third countries in the areas of migration and asylum (AENEAS)." *Official Journal of the European Union* L 80, 18. 3.
European Union. 2000. "Charter of Fundamental Rights of the European Union." *Official Journal of the European Communities* No C 364, 18. 12.
Faist, T. 2001. "Social Citizenship in the European Union: Nested Membership," *Journal of Common Market Studies* 39(1): 37–58.
Falk, R. 2000. "The Decline of Citizenship in an Era of Globalization," *Citizenship Studies* 4(1): 5–17.
Fekete, L. 2004. "Deaths at Europe's borders," *Race & Class* 45(4): 75–83.
Fekete, L. 2005. *The Deportation Machine: Europe, Asylum and Human Rights.* London: Inst. of Race Relations.
Fekete, L. 2006a. "Europe: 'speech crime' and deportation," *Race & Class* 47(3): 82–92.
Fekete, L. 2006b. "Enlightened fundamentalism? Immigration, feminism and the Right," *Race & Class* 48(2): 1–22.
Fekete, L. 2009. *A Suitable Enemy: Racism, Migration and Islamophobia in Europe.* London: Pluto Press.
Ferrera, M. 2005. *The Boundaries of Welfare: European Integration and the New Spatial Politics of Social Protection.* Oxford: Oxford University Press.
Flanagan, R. J. 1993. "European Wage Equalization Since the Treaty of Rome," in L. Ulman, B. Eichengreen and W. T. Dickens (eds), *Labour and an Integrated Europe.* Washington D.C.: The Brookings Institution.
Flyghed, J. 1998. "Gränslös kontroll – eller kontroll utan gräns?" in M. Hörnqvist (ed), *Gränslös kontroll: Schengen, Europol och det europeiska polissamarbetet.* Stockholm: Federativs.
Frattini, F. 2007. "Enhanced mobility, vigorous integration strategy and zero tolerance on illegal employment," Speech/07/526, High-level Conference on Legal Immigration, Lisbon, 13 September.
Frey, E. and W. Hall. 1999. "Big Gain for Far Right in Austrian Elections," *Financial Times,* 4 October.

Garrett, G. and B. R. Weingast 1993. "Ideas, Interests, and Institutions: Constructing the European Community's Internal Market," in J. Goldstein and R. O. Keohane (eds), *Ideas and Foreign Policy: Beliefs, Institutions, and Political Change*. Ithaca: Cornell University Press.

Geddes, A. 2000a. "Thin Europeanisation: The social rights of migrants in an integrating Europe," in M. Bommes and A. Geddes (eds), *Immigration and Welfare: Challenging the borders of the welfare state*. London: Routledge.

Geddes, A. 2000b. *Immigration and European Integration: Towards Fortress Europe?* Manchester: Manchester University Press.

Geddes, A. 2003. *The Politics of Migration and Immigration in Europe*. London: Sage.

Giddens, A. 1998. *The Third Way: The Renewal of Social Democracy*. Cambridge: Polity Press.

Giddens, A. 2000. *The Third Way and its Critics*. Cambridge: Polity Press.

Gill, S. and D. Law. 1989. "Global Hegemony and the Structural Power of Capital," *International Studies Quarterly* 33(4): 475–499.

Gold, P. 2000. *Europe or Africa? A contemporary study of the Spanish North African enclaves of Ceuta and Melilla*. Liverpool: Liverpool University Press.

Goldirova, R. 2007a. "EU proposes 'blue card' to attract skilled immigrants," *EUobserver*, euobserver.com, 23 October.

Goldirova, R. 2007b. "'Blue card' to attract top talent from outside EU," *EUobserver*, euobserver.com, 27 July.

Goodman, J. 1997. "The European Union: reconstituting democracy beyond the nation-state," in A. McGrew (ed), *The Transformation of Democracy? Globalization and Territorial Democracy*. Cambridge: Polity Press.

Grabbe, H. 2002. "Stabilizing the East While Keeping Out the Easterners: Internal and External Security Logics in Conflict," in S. Lavenex and E. M. Uçarer (eds), *Migration and the Externalities of European Integration*. Lanham: Lexington Books.

Grahl, J. and P. Teague. 1989. "The Cost of Neo-Liberal Europe," *New Left Review* 174: 33–50.

Grahl, J. and P. Teague 1990. *1992—The Big Market: The Future of the European Community*. London: Lawrence and Wishart.

Groenendijk, K. 2004. "Legal Concepts of Integration in EU Migration Law," *European Journal of Migration and Law* 6(2): 111–26.

Gross, T. 2005. "Integration of Immigrants: The Perspective of European Community Law, *European Journal of Migration and Law* 7(2): 145–61.

Guibernau, M. 2001. "Globalisation, Cosmopolitanism and Democracy: An Interview with David Held," *Constellations* 8(4): 427–41.

Guild, E. 1999. "The impetus to harmonise: asylum policy in the European Union," in F. Nicholson and P. Twomey (eds), *Refugee Rights and Realities: Evolving International Concepts and Regimes*. Cambridge: Cambridge University Press.

Guild, E. 2005. "Cultural and Identity Security: Immigrants and the Legal Expression of National Identity," in E. Guild and J. Van Selm (eds), *International Migration and Security: Opportunities and Challenges*. Oxford: Oxford University Press.

Guild, E. 2006. "The Bitter Fruits of an EU Common Asylum Policy," in T. Balzacq and S. Carrera (eds), *Security Versus Freedom? A Challenge for Europe's Future*. Aldershot: Ashgate.

Guiraudon, V. 2000. "The Marshallian Triptych Reordered: The Role of Courts and Bureaucracies in Further Migrants' Social Rights," in M. Bommes and A. Geddes (eds), *Immigration and Welfare: Challenging the Borders of the Welfare State*. London: Routledge.
Görg, C. and J. Hirsch. 1998. "Is international democracy possible?" *Review of International Political Economy* 5(4): 585–615.
Habermas, J. 2006. *The Divided West*. Cambridge: Polity Press.
Habermas, J. 2001a. *The Postnational Constellation: Political Essays*. Cambridge: Polity Press.
Habermas, J. 2001b. "Why Europe Needs a Constitution," *New Left Review* 11: 5–26.
Habermas, J. and J. Derrida. 2003. "February 15, or, What Binds Europeans Together," *Constellations* 10(3): 291–7.
Haddad, Y. Y. 1993. "The 'New Enemy'? Islam and Islamists After the Cold War," in P. Bennis and M. Moushabeck (eds), *Altered States: A Reader in the New World Order*. New York: Olive Branch Press.
Hager. S.B. 2008. "New Europeans for the New European Economy: Citizenship and the Lisbon Agenda," in B. van Apeldoorn, J. Drahokoupil and L. Horn (eds), *Contradictions and Limits of Neoliberal European Governance: From Lisbon to Lisbon*. Basingstoke: Palgrave.
Hager, S.B. 2007. "Hedge Fund Power and the Limits to Regulation in the European Union," *Paper Presented at the Nordic International Studies Association (NISA) Conference*, 24–25 May, Odense: University of Southern Denmark.
Hailbronner, K. 1998. "European immigration and asylum law under the Amsterdam Treaty," *Common Market Law Review* 35: 1047–67.
Hainsworth, P. 2006. "France Says No: The 29 May 2005 Referendum on the European Constitution," *Parliamentary Affairs* 59(1): 98–117.
Hallstein, W. 1972. *Europe in the Making*. London: George Allen & Unwin Ltd.
Hammar, T. 1990. *Democracy and the Nation-State: Aliens, Denizens and Citizens in a World of International Migration*. Aldershot: Avebury.
Hansen, P. 1997. "Education in a Multicultural European Union: Between Intercultural Visions and a Realpolitik of Immigration," *Migration* 32: 5–40.
Hansen, P. 2000a. *Europeans only? Essays on identity politics and the European Union*. Umeå: Umeå University.
Hansen, P. 2002. "European Integration, European Identity and the Colonial Connection," *European Journal of Social Theory* 5(4): 483–98.
Hansen, P. 2008. *EU's migrationspolitik under 50 år: Ett integrerat perspektiv på en motsägelsefull utveckling*. Lund: Studentlitteratur.
Hansen, P. 2009. "Post-national Europe—without cosmopolitan guarantees," *Race & Class* 50(4): 20–37.
Hansen, R. 1998. "A European citizenship or a Europe of citizens? Third country nationals in the EU," *Journal of Ethnic and Migration Studies* 24(4): 751–68.
Hansen, R. and P. Weil (eds). 2001. *Towards a European Nationality: Citizenship, Immigration and Nationality Law in the EU*. Houndmills: Palgrave.
Hantrais, L. 1995. *Social Policy in the European Union*. Houndmills: Macmillan.
Hathaway, J. C. 1993. "Harmonization for Whom? The Devaluation of Refugee Protection in the Era of European Economic Integration," *Cornell International Law Journal* 26(3): 719–35.

Hay, C. 1996. *Re-Stating Social and Political Change*. Buckingham: Open University Press.

Hay, C. and B. Rosamond. 2002. "Globalisation, European Integration and the Discursive Construction of Economic Imperatives," *Journal of European Public Policy* 9(2): 147–67.

Hay, C. and M. Watson. 2003. "Diminishing Expectations: The Strategic Discourse of Globalization in the Political Economy of New Labour," in J. M. Ryner and A. Cafruny (eds), *A Ruined Fortress? Neoliberal Hegemony and Transformation in Europe*. Lanham: Rowman and Littlefield.

Hedemann-Robinson, M. 1999. "The Area of Freedom, Security and Justice with Regard to the UK, Ireland and Denmark: The 'Opt-in Opt-outs' under the Treaty of Amsterdam," in D. O'Keeffe and P. Twomey (eds), *Legal Issues of the Amsterdam Treaty*. Oxford: Hart Publishing.

Hedström, I. 1998. "Vänsterekonom åter i centrum," *Dagens Nyheter*, 5 December.

Held, D. 1991. "Democracy and the Global System," in D. Held (ed), *Political Theory Today*. Cambridge: Polity Press.

Held, D. 2006. *Models of Democracy*. London: Stanford University Press.

Helleiner, E. 1994. *States and the Re-emergence of Global Finance: From Bretton Woods to the 1990s*. Ithaca: Cornell University Press.

Hentges, G. 2002. "Refugee and Asylum Policy Influenced by Europeanisation," in The Evens Foundation (ed), *Europe's New Racism? Causes, Manifestations and Solutions*. New York: Berghahn Books.

High Level Group. 2004. *Report of the High Level Group on the future of social policy in an enlarged European Union*. European Commission, Directorate-General for Employment and Social Affairs.

High Level Group chaired by Wim Kok. 2004. *Facing the Challenge: The Lisbon strategy for growth and employment*. Brussels.

Hines, C. 1997. "Might of the Roundtable," *The Guardian*, 20 August.

Hix, S. 1999. *The Political System of the European Union*. New York: St. Martin's Press.

Hofheinz, P. 2005. Cited in an LCEC press release entitled "A New Beginning," 2 February, Brussels: LCEC.

Holland, S. 1980. *Uncommon Market: Capital, Class and Power in the European Community*. New York: St. Martin's Press.

Holman, O. 2004. "Asymmetrical Regulation and Multidimensional Governance in the European Union," *Review of International Political Economy* 11(4): 714–35.

Holman, O. and K. van der Pijl 1996. "The Capitalist Class in the European Union," in A. Moschonas and G.A. Kourvetaris (eds), *The Impact of European Integration: Political, Sociological and Economic Changes*. London: Praeger.

Hoogenboom, T. 1992. "Symposium: The Status of Non-Community Nationals in Community Law," *European Journal of International Law* 36(1): 36–52.

Hooghe, L. and G. Marks 1999. "The Making of a Polity: The Struggle over European Integration," in H. Kitschelt, et al. (eds), *Continuity and Change in Contemporary Capitalism*. Cambridge: Cambridge University Press.

Hoskyns, C. 1996. *Integrating Gender: Women, Law and Politics in the European Union*. London: Verso.

Human Rights Watch. 2003. "An Unjust 'Vision' for Europe's Refugees." June 17.

Human Rights Watch. 2005. "Country Summary: European Union," January, www.hrw.org.
Huysmans, J. 1995. "Migrants as a security problem: dangers of 'securitizing' societal issues," in R. Miles and D. Thränhardt (eds), *Migration and European Integration: The Dynamics of Inclusion and Exclusion*. London: Pinter.
Huysmans, J. 2006. *The Politics of Insecurity: Fear, migration and asylum in the EU*. London: Routledge.
International Herald Tribune. 2006. "EU struggling to agree on immigration policy," 26 May.
International Herald Tribune. 2008. "Spain says Africans tried to rush border during Spain-Italy soccer game," 23 June.
Ireland, P.R. 1996. "Asking for the Moon: The Political Participation of Immigrants in The European Union," in G. A. Kourvetaris and A. Moschonas (eds), *The Impact of European Integration: Political, Sociological, and Economic Changes*. Westport: Praeger.
Irish Times. 2004. "Barroso Intent on Shifting EU to the right," 7 February.
Jessop, B. 1990. *State Theory: Putting the Capitalist State in its Place*. London: Polity Press.
Jessop, B. 2002. *The Future of the Capitalist State*. Cambridge: Polity Press.
Jileva, E. 2002. "Larger than the European Union: The Emerging EU Migration Regime and Enlargement," in S. Lavenex and E.M. Uçarer (eds), *Migration and the Externalities of European Integration*. Lanham: Lexington Books.
Joly, D. 1999. "A new asylum regime in Europe," in F. Nicholson and P. Twomey (ed), *Refugee Rights and Realities: Evolving International Concepts and Regimes*. Cambridge: Cambridge University Press.
Jordan B. and F. Düvell. 2003. *Migration: The Boundaries of Equality and Justice*. Cambridge: Polity Press.
Josephson, M. 1934. *The Robber Barons*. New York: Harvest.
Jospin, L. 2000. "Globalisering—men på våra villkor," *Arena*, 1: 40–2.
Jönsson, P. 1998. "Turkar är väl också européer," *Dagens Nyheter*, 22 January.
Kapteyn, P. 1996. *The stateless market: the European dilemma of integration and civilization*. London: Routledge.
Kettle, M. 1990. "John Paul's grand design for Europe," *The Guardian*, 27 April.
Kinzer, S. 1997. "Top Turkish General Visits Greeks, Bearing Good Will," *The New York Times*, 29 March.
Kofman, E. 1995. "Citizenship for some but not for others: spaces of citizenship in contemporary Europe," *Political Geography* 14(2): 121–37.
Kofman, E. 2002. "Contemporary European migrations, civic stratification and citizenship," *Political Geography* 21(8): 1035–54.
Kopp, K. 2007. "Rights on the Edge—The EU's Common Asylum Policy," Goethe-Institut: Kulturen In Bewegung. Retrieved 18 August 2008 from http://www.goethe.de/ges/pok/prj/mig/mgr/en2081562.htm.
Koslowski, R. 1998. "European migration regimes: emerging, enlarging and deteriorating," *Journal of Ethnic and Migration Studies* 24(4): 735–49.
Kostakopoulou, T. 2001. "Invisible Citizens? Long-term Resident Third-country Nationals in the EU and their Struggle for Recognition," in R. Bellamy and

A. Warleigh (eds), *Citizenship and Governance in the European Union*. London: Continuum.

Kostakopoulou, T. 2002. "Long-term resident third country nationals in the European Union: normative expectations and institutional openings," *Journal of Ethnic and Migration Studies* 28(3): 443–62.

Kostakopoulou, D. 2005. "Ideas, Norms and European Citizenship: Explaining Institutional Change," *Modern Law Review* 68(2): 233–67.

Kubosova, L. 2006a. "EU has limits in respecting Muslim traditions, says Frattini," *EUobserver*, euobserver.com, 9 October.

Kubosova, L. 2006b. "EU launches first immigration border patrols," *EUobserver*, euobserver.com, 14 August.

Kubosova, L. 2007. "African states fear brain drain through EU blue card," *EUobserver*, euobserver.com, 29 October.

Kubosova, L. 2008. "EU gives blessing for Italy's Roma fingerprint scheme," *EUobserver*, euobserver.com, 5 September.

Kveinen, E. 2002. "Citizenship in a Post-Westphalian Community: Beyond External Exclusion?" *Citizenship Studies* 6(1): 21–35.

Kymlicka, W. and W. Norman. 1994. "Return of the Citizen: A Survey of Recent Work on Citizenship Theory," *Ethics* 104(2): 352–81.

Lafontaine, O. 1998. "The Future of German Social Democracy," *New Left Review* 227: 72–87.

Landler, M. 2007. "Germany Cites Koran in Rejecting Divorce," *The New York Times*, 22 March.

Lange, P. 1992. "The Politics of the Social Dimension," in A. M. Sbragia (ed), *Euro-Politics: Institutions and Policymaking in the "New" European Community*. Washington, D.C: The Brookings Institution.

Lavenex, S. 1999. *Safe Third Countries: Extending the EU Asylum and Immigration Policies to Central and Eastern Europe*. Budapest: Central European University Press.

Lavenex, S. 2001. "The Europeanization of Refugee Policies: Normative Challenges and Institutional Legacies," *Journal of Common Market Studies* 39(5): 851–74.

Lavenex, S. 2002. "EU Trade Policy and Immigration Control," in S. Lavenex and E.M. Uçarer (eds), *Migration and the Externalities of European Integration*. Lanham: Lexington Books.

LCEC (Lisbon Council for European Competitiveness). 2004. *A Social Contract for the 21st Century*. Brussels: LCEC.

Lehning, P. 1997. "European citizenship: a mirage?" in P. Lehning and A. Weale (eds), *Citizenship, democracy and justice in the new Europe*. London: Routledge.

Lehning, P. and A. Weale. 1997. "Citizenship, democracy and justice in the new Europe," in P. Lehning and A. Weale (eds), *Citizenship, democracy and justice in the new Europe*. London: Routledge.

Leibfried, S. and P. Pierson. 1995. "Semisovereign Welfare States: Social Policy in a Multitiered Europe," in S. Leibfried and P. Pierson (eds), *European Social Policy: Between Fragmentation and Integration*. Washington D.C: The Brookings Institution.

Levitas, R. 1998. *The Inclusive Society? Social Exclusion and New Labour*. London: Macmillan.

Lisbon European Council. 2000. *Presidency Conclusions*. 23–4 March.

Loescher, G. and J. Milner. 2003. "The missing link: the need for comprehensive engagement in regions of refugee origin," *International Affairs* 79(3): 595–617.
Luedtke, A. 2007. "Uncovering EU immigration legislation: Policy dynamics and outcomes," *European Union Studies Association Conference, Montreal, 17–19 May 2007.* Montreal.
Lundgren, Å. 1998. *Europeisk identitetspolitik: EU:s demokratibistånd till Polen och Turkiet.* Uppsala: Acta Universitatis Upsaliensis.
Lutterbeck, D. 2006. "Policing Migration in the Mediterranean," *Mediterranean Politics* 11(1): 59–82.
Luxembourg European Council. 1997. *Presidency Conclusions.* 12–13 December.
Maas, W. 2005. "The Genesis of European Rights," *Journal of Common Market Studies* 43(5): 1009–25.
Maas, W. 2007. *Creating European Citizens.* Lanham: Rowman and Littlefield.
MacLaughlin, J. 1993. "Defending the frontiers: the political geography of race and racism in the European Community," in C. H. Williams (ed), *The Political Geography of the New World Order.* London: Belhaven Press.
Macshane, D. 1998. "Two Visions of Europe," *Critical Quarterly* 40(4): 119–26.
Mahony, H. 2006a. "EU states bicker over immigration issues," *EUobserver*, euobserver.com, 22 September.
Mahony, H. 2006b. "Barroso letter pleads for EU immigration 'solidarity'," *EUobserver*, euobserver.com, 7 September.
Maier, R. 2002. "Does a Supranational Europe Stimulate and/or Combat Racism?" in The Evens Foundation (ed), *Europe's New Racism? Causes, Manifestations and Solutions.* New York: Berghahn Books.
Majone, G. 1993. "The European Community Between Social Policy and Social Regulation," *Journal of Common Market Studies* 31(2): 153–70.
Mandel, E. 1970. *Europe vs. America: Contradictions of Imperialism.* New York: Monthly Review Press.
Mann, M. 1987. "Ruling Class Strategies and Citizenship," *Sociology* 21(3): 339–54.
Manners, I. 2007. "Critical Approaches," in K.E. Jørgensen, M. Pollack and B. Rosamond (eds), *The SAGE Handbook of European Union Politics.* London: Sage.
Marfleet, P. 1999. "Nationalism and internationalism in the new Europe," *International Socialism* 84: 69–100.
Marshall, T.H. 1950. *Citizenship and Social Class and Other Essays.* Cambridge: Cambridge University Press.
Martiniello, M. 1995. "European citizenship, European identity and migrants: towards the post-national state?" in R. Miles and D. Thränhardt (eds), *Migration and European Integration: The Dynamics of Inclusion and Exclusion.* London: Pinter Publishers.
Martiniello, M. and A. Rea. 1999. "The effects of the construction of Europe on national immigration and refugee policies: the case of Belgium," in A. Geddes and A. Favell (eds), *The Politics of Belonging: Migrants and Minorities in Contemporary Europe.* Aldershot: Ashgate.
Marx, K. 1976. *Capital: Volume I.* London: Penguin.
Mazey, S. 1988. "European Community Action on Behalf of Women: The Limits of Legislation," *Journal of Common Market Studies* 27(1): 63–84.

McDonagh, P. 2008. "Muslim anger at Opposition calls for school ban on hijab," *Independent.ie*, 2 June, Retrieved 12 September 2008 from Independent.ie.

McInerney, S. 2009. "More foreign workers choose to return home," *The Sunday Times*, 15 February.

McNamara, K.R. 1998. *The Currency of Ideas: Monetary Politics in the European Union*. Ithaca: Cornell University Press.

Mead, N. 2005. "Melilla: bloodbath on the African-Europe frontier," *openDemocracy*, http://www.opendemocracy.net/people-migrationeurope/melilla_2905.jsp, 10 October.

Meehan, E.M. 1993. *Citizenship and the European Community*. London: Sage.

Melis, B. 2001. *Negotiating Europe's immigration frontiers*. The Hague: Kluwer Law International.

Mettler, A. 2005. "A Two-Speed Europe, At Last," *Wall Street Journal. Online Edition*, 9 June.

Meulders, D. and R. Plasman. 1997. "European Economic Policies and Social Quality," in W. Beck, L. van der Maesen and A. Walker (eds), *The Social Quality of Europe*. The Hague: Kluwer Law International.

Miles, R. 1993. *Racism after "race relations."* London: Routledge.

Milne, S. 2008. "The persecution of Gypsies is now the shame of Europe," *The Guardian*, 10 July.

Monar, J. 2000. "Justice and Home Affairs," *Journal of Common Market Studies* 38(Annual Review): 125–42.

Monar, J. 2001. "The Dynamics of Justice and Home Affairs: Laboratories, Driving Factors and Costs," *Journal of Common Market Studies* 39(4): 747–64.

Monar, J. 2003. "Justice and Home Affairs," *Journal of Common Market Studies* 41(Annual Review): 119–35.

Monar, J. 2004. "Justice and Home Affairs," *Journal of Common Market Studies* 42(Annual Review): 117–33.

Monar, J. 2005. "Justice and Home Affairs," *Journal of Common Market Studies* 43(Annual Review): 131–46.

Moore, R. 1992. "Foreword," in T. H. Marshall and T. Bottomore (authors), *Citizenship and Social Class*. London: Pluto Press.

Moravcsik, A. 1991. "Negotiating the Single European Act: national interests and conventional statecraft in the European Community," *International Organization* 45(1): 19–56.

Morris, L. 2002. *Managing Migration: Civic stratification and migrants' rights*. London: Routledge.

Morton, A.D. 2006. "The Grimly Comic Riddle of Hegemony in IPE: Where is Class Struggle?" *Politics* 26(1): 62–72.

Moschonas, A. 1996. "The Logic of European Integration," in G. A. Kourvetaris and A. Moschonas (eds), *The Impact of European Integration: Political, Sociological, and Economic Changes*. Westport: Praeger.

Moschonas, G. 2002. *In the Name of Social Democracy: The Great Transformation, 1945 to the Present*. London: Verso.

Mouffe, C. 1988. "The civics lesson," *New Statesman*, 7 October.

Murray Brown, J. 2008. "Irish PM urges Yes vote on EU treaty," *Financial Times*, 8 June, Retrieved 10 September 2008 from FT.com.

Murray, R. 1971. "Internationalization of Capital and the Nation State," *New Left Review* 67: 84–108.
Naudin, T. 1994. "A union whose parts do not yet add up," *The European*, 28 October– 3 November.
Noll, G. 2003. "Visions of the Exceptional: Legal and Theoretical Issues Raised by Transit Processing Centres and Protection Zones," *European Journal of Migration and Law* 5(3): 303–41.
Noll, G. 2006. "The Euro-African migration conference: Africa sells out to Europe," *openDemocracy*, 14 July.
Norman, P. 1999. "Europe's Apathetic Voters Stay Away from the Polls," *Financial Times*, 14 June.
O'Keeffe, D. 1994. "Union Citizenship," in D. O'Keeffe and P.M. Twomey (eds), *Legal Issues of the Maastricht Treaty*. London: Wiley Chancery Law.
Overbeek, H. 1995. "Towards a new international migration regime: globalization, migration and the internationalization of the state," in R. Miles and D. Thränhardt (eds), *Migration and European Integration: The Dynamics of Inclusion and Exclusion*. London: Pinter Publishers.
Overbeek, H. 2003. "Globalization, neo-liberalism and the employment question," in H. Overbeek (ed), *The Political Economy of European Employment: European integration and the transnationalization of the (un)employment question*. London: Routledge.
Painter, J and C. Philo. 1995. "Spaces of citizenship: an introduction," *Political Geography* 14(2): 107–20.
Panitch, L. 1996. "Rethinking the Role of the State," in J.M. Mittelman (ed), *Globalization: Critical Reflections*. Boulder, CO: Lynne Rienner.
Panitch, L. 2002. "Violence as a Tool of Order and Change: The War on Terrorism and the Antiglobalization Movement," *Monthly Review* 54(2): 12–32.
Panitch, L. and C. Leys. 2001. *The End of Parliamentary Socialism: From New Left to New Labour*. London: Verso.
Party of European Socialists. 2007. *Hedge Funds and Private Equity: A Critical Analysis*. Brussels: PES.
Patomäki, H. 2006. "Problems of Global Democracy: A Dialogue," *Theory, Culture and Society* 23(5): 115–133.
Patterson, T. C. 1997. *Inventing Western Civilization*. New York: Monthly Review Press.
Phillips, L. 2008a. "Latin America could halt EU trade talks over return directive," *EUobserver*, euobserver.com, 23 June.
Phillips, L. 2008b. "Latin American leaders condemn "racist" EU law," *EUobserver*, euobserver.com, 2 July.
Pierson, P. and S. Leibfried. 1995. "The Dynamics of Social Policy Integration," in S. Leibfried and P. Pierson (eds), *European Social Policy: Between Fragmentation and Integration*. Washington D.C.: The Brookings Institution.
Platform of European Social NGOs. 2005. *From a strategy to a tragedy: Social NGOs call on political leaders to reject the Barroso approach to Lisbon and reaffirm the European model of society*. http://www.socialplatform.org/module/FileLib/ENSpringSummit2005resolution.pdf.
Polanyi, K. 1957. *The Great Transformation: The Political and Economic Origins of Our Time*. Boston: Beacon Press.

Pop, V. 2009. "EU adopts Blue Card scheme for skilled migrants," *EUobserver*, euobserver.com, 26 May.
Prentoulis, N. 2001. "On the Technology of Collective Identity: Normative Reconstructions of the Concept of EU Citizenship," *European Law Journal* 7(2): 196–218.
Prodi, R. 1999a. "Speech given by Mr. Prodi to the European Parliament – 13 April 1999," http://europa.eu.int/comm/commissioners/prodi/speeches/130499_en.htm.
Prodi, R. 1999b. "Speech by Mr. Romano Prodi, Strasbourg, 4 May 1999," http://europa.eu.int/comm/commissioners/prodi/speeches/040599_en.htm.
Prodi, R. 2000a. "Innovation and responsibility: business and the citizen in a changing world," Speech/00/21411, 11 June, Brussels.
Prodi, R. 2000b. "The new Europe and Japan," Speech/00/27719, 19 July, Tokyo.
Prodi, R. 2000c. "The road to Europe's Future," Speech/00/416, 7 November, Brussels.
Prodi, R. 2000d. "Europe's renaissance," Speech/00/441, 17 November, Frankfurt am Main.
Purcell, M. 2002. "The State, Regulation and Global Restructuring: Reasserting the Political in Political Economy," *Review of International Political Economy* 9(2): 284–318.
Rees, P. 1997. "Worlds apart: The media stereotype of the mad Muslim feeds Islamic insecurity in a dangerous way," *New Statesman*, 1 August.
Rhodes, M. 1991. "The social dimension of the Single European Market: National versus transnational regulation," *European Journal of Political Research* 19(2–3): 245–80.
Rhodes, M. 2000. "Lisbon: Europe's Maastricht for Welfare?" *ECSA Review* 13(30): 2–7.
Romero, F. 1993. "Migration as an issue in European interdependence and integration: the case of Italy," in A. S. Milward, et al. (eds), *The Frontier of National Sovereignty: History and theory 1945–1992*. London: Routledge.
Rosas, A. and E. Antola (eds). 1995. *A Citizens' Europe: In Search of a New Order*. London: Sage.
Rose, N. 1996. "The death of the social? Re-figuring the territory of government," *Economy and Society* 25(3): 327–56.
Ross, G. 1992. "Confronting the New Europe," *New Left Review* 191: 49–68.
Ross, G. 1995. "Assessing the Delors Era and Social Policy," in S. Leibfried and P. Pierson (eds), *European Social Policy: Between Fragmentation and Integration*. Washington D.C.: The Brookings Institution.
Rossilli, M. G. 1999. "The European Union's Policy on the Equality of Women," *Feminist Studies* 25(1): 171–81.
Ruggie, J. G. 1982. "International regimes, transactions, and change: embedded liberalism in the postwar economic order," *International Organization* 36(2): 379–415.
Ryner, M. 2000. "European Welfare State Transformation and Migration," in M. Bommes and A. Geddes (eds), *Immigration and Welfare: Challenging the Borders of the Welfare State*. London: Routledge.
Ryner, M. 2002. *Capitalist Restructuring, Globalization and the Third Way: Lessons from the Swedish Model*. London: Routledge.

Ryner, M. 2005. "International Political Economy beyond the Post-Structuralist Historical Materialist Dichotomy," in M. de Goede (ed), *International Political Economy and Post-Structural Politics*. Basingstoke: Palgrave Macmillan.

Ryner, M. 2008. "Neoliberal European Governance and the Politics of Welfare State Retrenchment: A Critique of the New Malthusians," in B. van Apeldoorn, J. Drahokoupil and L. Horn (eds), *Contradictions and Limits of Neoliberal European Governance: From Lisbon to Lisbon*. Basingstoke: Palgrave.

Sassen, S. 1999. *Guests and Aliens*. New York: The New Press.

Scharpf, F. 1998. "Negative and Positive Integration in the Political Economy of European Welfare States," in M. Rhodes and Y. Mény (eds), *The Future of European Welfare: A New Social Contract?* Houndmills: Macmillan.

Scharpf, F. 1999. *Governing in Europe: Effective and Democratic?* Oxford: Oxford University Press.

Scharpf, F. 2001. "Notes Toward a Theory of Multilevel Governing in Europe," *Scandinavian Political Studies* 24(1): 1–26.

Scharpf, F. 2002. "The European Social Model: Coping with the Challenges of Diversity," *Journal for Common Market Studies* 40(4): 645–70.

Schierup, C-U. 2003. "What Creed in Europe? Social Exclusion, Citizenship, and a Changing EU Policy Agenda," in G. Brochmann (ed), *The Multicultural Challenge*. Amsterdam: Elsevier Science.

Schierup, C-U, P. Hansen and S. Castles. 2006. *Migration, Citizenship, and the European Welfare State: A European Dilemma*. Oxford: Oxford University Press.

Scott, J. W. 2007. *The Politics of the Veil*. Princeton: Princeton University Press.

Scott-Smith, G. 2003. "Cultural Policy and Citizenship in the European Union: An Answer to the Legitimation Problem?" in A. W. Cafruny and M. Ryner (eds), *A Ruined Fortress? Neoliberal Hegemony and Transformation in Europe*. Lanham: Rowman and Littlefield.

Shaw, J. and S. Day. 2002. "The EU Electoral Rights and Political Participation of Migrants in Host Polities," *International Journal of Population Geography* 8: 183–99.

Shore, C. 1993. "Inventing the 'People's Europe': critical approaches to European Community 'cultural policy'," *Man* 28(4): 779–800.

Shore, C. 1996. "Transcending the Nation-State?: The European Commission and the (Re)-Discovery of Europe," *Journal of Historical Sociology* 9(4): 473–96.

Shore, C. 2000. *Building Europe: The Cultural Politics of European Integration*. London: Routledge.

Singer, D. 1998. "Ils Accusent...," *The Nation*, 16 February.

Singer, D. 1999. *Whose Millennium? Theirs or Ours?* New York: Monthly Review Press.

Smith, C.S. 2005. "Spain's African Enclaves Are Migrants' Portals to Europe," *The New York Times*, 5 November.

Smith, S.J. 1995. "Comment: Citizenship: all or nothing?" *Political Geography* 14(2): 190–3.

Soininen, M. 2003. "Exploring EU Ethnic Diversity and Anti-discrimination Policy," in E. Zeybekoglu and B. Johansson (eds), *Migration and Labour in Europe: Views from Turkey and Sweden*. Istanbul and Stockholm: Marmara University and NIWL.

Solty, I. 2008. "The Historic Significance of the New German Left Party," *Socialism and Democracy* 22(1): 1–34.

Soysal, Y.N. 1994. *Limits of Citizenship: Migrants and Postnational Membership in Europe.* Chicago: University of Chicago Press.
Špidla, V. 2005. *The 2005 Jean Jacque Rousseau Lecture for the Lisbon Council: Modernizing the European Social Model.* 20 June, Brussels.
Statewatch. 2003. "EU: Mass deportations by chartered flight." *Statewatch Bulletin*, 13(2).
Statewatch. 2004a. *Statewatch European Monitor,* 4(6).
Statewatch. 2004b. *Killing me softly? "Improving access to durable solutions": doublespeak and the dismantling of refugee protection in the EU.* Statewatch Analysis, Prepared by B. Hayes, July.
Statewatch 2005. "European Commission technical mission to Libya: exporting Fortress Europe," *Statewatch Bulletin*, 15(2).
Steedman, H. 1979. "The Education of Migrant Workers' Children in EEC Countries: from assimilation to cultural pluralism?" *Comparative Education* 15(3): 259–68.
Stockhammer, E. 2005–6. "Shareholder Value Orientation and the Investment-Profit Puzzle," *Journal of Post Keynesian Economics* 28(2): 193–216.
Stoop, C. de. 1997. *Utan papper: människohantering i dagens Europa.* Stockholm: Ordfront.
Streeck, W. 1995. "From Market Making to State Building? Reflections on the Political Economy of European Social Policy," in S. Leibfried and P. Pierson (eds), *European Social Policy: Between Fragmentation and Integration.* Washington, D.C: The Brookings Institution.
Streeck, W. and P. C. Schmitter 1996. "Organized Interests in The European Union," in K. A. Kourvetaris and A. Moschonas (eds), *The Impact of European Integration: Political, Sociological, and Economic Changes.* Westport: Praeger.
Svenning, O. 2000. *Vänstern i Europa: De nya liberalerna?* Stockholm: Atlas.
Swann, D. 1988. *The Economics of the Common Market,* 6th ed. Harmondsworth: Penguin.
Swardson, A. 1998. "Are French Warming Up For Another Explosion," *International Herald Tribune,* January 3–4.
The Economist. 1993. "Enough of Le Pen," 30 January.
The Economist. 1994. "Apathy Within, Enthusiasm Without: Europe," 18 June.
The Economist. 2008. "Ireland's no vote: not about immigration," 20 June. Retrieved 10 September 2008 from Economist.com.
The New York Times. 2009. "As Jobs Die, Europe's Migrants Head Home," 24 April.
Thomas, D. 2009. "Sarkozy's law: The institutionalization of xenophobia in the new Europe," *Radical Philosophy* 153: 7–12.
Thomassen and Schmitt. 2004. "Democracy and Legitimacy in the European Union," *Tidskrift for Samfunnsforskning* 45(2): 377–410.
Tilly, C. 1995. "The Emergence of Citizenship in France and Elsewhere," *International Review of Social History* 3: 223–236.
Times Online. 2005. "Paris isn"t burning," 19 November, Retrieved 10 July 2008 from http://timescorrespondents.typepad.com/charles_bremner/2005/11/whitegloved_wai.html.
Tindemans, L. 1976. "European Union: Report by Mr. Leo Tindemans, Prime Minister of Belgium, to the European Council," *Bulletin of the EC,* Supplement 1/76.

Trubek, D. M. and J. S. Mosher. 2003. "New Governance, Employment Policy, and the European Social Model," in J. Zeitlin and D. M. Trubek (eds), *Governing Work and Welfare in a New Economy: European and American Experiments.* Oxford: Oxford University Press.

Turner, L. 1993. "Prospects for Worker Participation in Management in the Single Market, in L. Ulman, B. Eichengreen and W. T. Dickens (eds), *Labor and an Integrated Europe.* Washington D.C.: Brookings Institution.

Uçarer, E. M. 2003. "Justice and Home Affairs," in M. Cini (ed), *European Union Politics.* Oxford: Oxford University Press.

UK Government. 2003. "New Vision for Refugees." March 7, http://www.proasyl.de/texte/europe/union/2003/UK_NewVision.pdf.

UNHCR. 2003. *Towards more accessible, equitable and managed asylum systems, COM (2003) 315 final, 4 June.* UNHCR Summary Observations on the European Commission Communication.

Urth, H. 2005. "Building a Momentum for the Integration of Third-country Nationals in the European Union," *European Journal of Migration and Law* 7(2): 163–80.

van Apeldoorn, B. 2002. *Transnational Capitalism and the Struggle over European Integration.* London: Routledge.

van Apeldoorn, B. 2003a. "The Struggle over European Order: Transnational Class Agency in the Making of 'Embedded Neo-Liberalism'," in N. Brenner, et al. (eds), *State/Space: A Reader.* Oxford: Blackwell.

van Apeldoorn, B. 2003b. "European unemployment and transnational capitalist class strategy," in H. Overbeek (ed), *The Political Economy of European Employment: European Integration and the Transnationalization of the (Un)Employment Question.* London: Routledge.

van Apeldoorn, B. 2008. "The Contradictions of 'Embedded Neoliberalism' and Europe's Multilevel Legitimacy Crisis: The European Project and its Limits," in B. van Apeldoorn, J. Drahokoupil and L. Horn (eds), *Contradictions and Limits of Neoliberal European Governance: From Lisbon to Lisbon.* Basingstoke: Palgrave.

van Apeldoorn, B. and L. Horn. 2007. "The Marketisation of European Corporate Control: A Critical Political Economy Perspective," *New Political Economy* 12(2): 211–35.

van Apeldoorn, B., Overbeek, H. and M. Ryner. 2003. "Theories of European Integration: A Critique," in A. Cafruny and M. Ryner (eds), *A Ruined Fortress? Neoliberal Hegemony and Transformation in Europe.* Lanham: Rowman and Littlefield.

van der Klauuw, J. 2002. "European Asylum Policy and the Global Protection Regime: Challenges for the UNHCR," in S. Lavenex and E. M. Uçarer (eds), *Migration and the Externalities of European Integration.* Lanham: Lexington Books.

van der Pijl, K. 1998. *Transnational Classes and International Relations.* London: Routledge.

van der Pijl, K. 2006. "A Lockean Europe?" *New Left Review* 37: 9–37.

Verkaik, R. 2007. "Major airline refuses to help with forcible removal of immigrants," *The Independent,* 8 October.

Vucheva, E. 2008. "Brussels calls for Lisbon treaty ratification to continue," *EUobserver,* euobserver.com, 13 June.

Vucheva, E. 2009. "Cool reception to compulsory EU sharing of asylum 'burden'," *EUobserver,* euobserver.com, 5 June.

Wahl, A. 2002. "European Labor: Social Dialogue, Social Pacts, or a Social Europe," *Monthly Review* 54(2): 45–50.
Wallace, W. and J. Smith. 1995. "Democracy or Technocracy? European Integration and the Problem of Popular Consent," *West European Politics* 18(3): 137–57.
Ward, I. 1997. "Law and the Other Europeans," *Journal of Common Market Studies* 35(1): 79–96.
Warleigh. A. 2001. "Purposeful Opportunists? EU Institutions and the Struggle over EU Citizenship," R. Bellamy and A. Warleigh (eds), *Citizenship and Governance in the European Union*. London: Continuum.
Watkins, S. 2005. "Continental Tremors," *New Left Review* 33: 5–21.
Watson, M. 2005a. *Foundations of International Political Economy*. Basingstoke: Palgrave.
Watson, M. 2005b. "Hedge Funds, the Deutsche Börse Affair and Predatory Anglo American Capitalism," *The Political Quarterly* 76(4): 516–28.
Weiler, J. 1997. "To be a European Citizen: Eros and Civilization," *Journal of European Public Policy* 4(4): 495–519.
Weiss, F. and F. Wooldridge. 2002. *Free Movement of Persons Within the European Community*. The Hague: Kluwer Law International.
Wiener, A. 1998. *"European" Citizenship Practice: Building Institutions of a Non-State*. Oxford: Westview Press.
Wiener, A. and V. Della Sala. 1997. "Constitution-making and Citizenship Practice – Bridging the Democracy Gap in the EU," *Journal of Common Market Studies* 35(4): 595–614.
Williams, A. M. 1994. *The European Community: The Contradictions of Integration*, 2nd ed. Oxford: Blackwell.
Willis, R. F. 1971. *Italy Chooses Europe*. New York: Oxford University Press.
Wincott, D. 2003. "The Idea of the European Social Model: Limits and Paradoxes of Europeanization," in K. Featherstone and C.M. Radaelli (eds), *The Politics of Europeanization*. Oxford: Oxford University Press.
Wood, E. M. 1995. *Democracy Against Capitalism: Renewing Historical Materialism*. Cambridge: Cambridge University Press.
Wood, E. M. 2002. *The Origins of Capitalism: A Longer View*. London: Verso.
Woollacott, M. 1996. "Reduced to the religion of cuts," *The Guardian*, 18 May.
Younge, G. 2007. "To believe in a European utopia before Muslims arrived is delusional," *The Guardian*, 10 December.
Yuval-Davis, N. 1997. "Women, Citizenship and Difference," *Feminist Review* 57(1): 4–27.
Zeitlin, J. 2003. "Introduction: Governing Work and Welfare in a New Economy: European and American Experiments," in J. Zeitlin and D.M. Trubek (eds), *Governing Work and Welfare in a New Economy: European and American Experiments*. Oxford: Oxford University Press.

Index

Adonnino, P., 71
Africa, 150, 158, 180, 185, 187–93, 195, 196n5
    African Union (AU), 192
African, Caribbean and Pacific countries (ACP), 151
Agrela, B., 39
d'Alema, M., 98
Amnesty International, 188
Amsterdam Treaty, 29, 39, 95, 97, 101–102, 104, 127–31, 134, 136–7, 139, 145–8, 158, 160–1
anti-discrimination policy, EU, 10, 15–16, 27, 95, 110, 129–30, 136–8, 142, 159–60, 163–5, 174–6, 196
anti-immigration/immigrant, viii, 1, 7–8, 26, 84, 146, 159, 180, 194, 203, 206. *See also* extreme right
Arbour, L., 188
Archibugi, D., 36n2
asylum policy, viii, 3–4, 9–10, 15–16, 29, 35, 40, 61, 79–86, 88–89, 127–30, 139–40, 144–9, 151–60, 161n8, 161n11, 163–4, 166–7, 169, 183–6, 188–9, 191, 193–4, 196, 204–6.
    Common European Asylum System (CEAS), 129, 146–7, 149, 163, 183–4
    Dublin Convention (1997), 81, 147
Attac, 94
Auschwitz, 8, 11

Balibar, É., v, 168
"Balkanization", 8, 11

Balkenende, J.P., 8
Balzacq, T., 163
Barnard, C., 102
Barroso, J.M., 2, 16, 97–98, 115–20, 124–5, 187, 191, 202
Beck, U., 8, 27, 36n2. *See also* post-national cosmopolitanism
"becoming a citizen", 34, 96, 130. *See also* Castles, S. and Davidson, A.
"being a citizen", 34, 96, 130. *See also* Castles, S. and Davidson, A.
Berlusconi, S., 204
Bieling, H-J., 126n1
Blair, T., 95, 100, 153, 202
blue card, 178–80, 183, 196n2, 204
Blunkett, D., 135
Bornschier, V., 67
Bourdieu, P., 94
"brain drain", 179–80
Brandt, W., 51
Brecht, B., 1
Bretton Woods, 47. *See also* embedded liberalism
Broad Economic Policy Guidelines (BEPG), 106–107
Brussels European Council (2004), 162, 165
Brussels European Council (2005), 116
Business Week, 100

cadre, 98, 119, 122
Cafruny, A., 123
Canary Islands, 191–2
Caporaso, J., 35

245

Carrera, S., 163, 171–2, 204
Castles, S., 34, 96, 194
Central and Eastern Europe
  "Polish plumber", 7, 10–11
  enlargement, 93, 108, 116, 148, 182, 197
  transition rules, 10–11, 43, 57n2, 182
Ceuta, 189–90
Chalmers, D., 106, 109
Charter of Fundamental Rights of the European Union, 132, 136
Chirac, J., 11, 77
Christianity, 14, 75–77, 88, 121
circular migration, 176, 179–81, 183, 205
"Citizens' Europe", 4, 52, 55, 58, 60, 70–71, 76, 87
Claes, W., 77
Clarke, C., 171
colonialism, 48–49
commodification/de-commodification, 3, 122, 124, 203
Community Charter of the Fundamental Social Rights for Workers (1989), 66
"constitutional patriotism", 24, 28
Copenhagen European Council (1993), 93
Correa, R., 188
cosmopolitan democracy, *See* post-national cosmopolitanism (PNC)
Cotonou Agreement, 151
Council of Europe, 171
Cowen, B., 1
critical history, *See* critical political economy
critical political economy, 12–13, 21–22, 197–8, 206
critical theory, 23, 25–27
Crouch, C., 65
customs union, 43

Dannreuther, C., 32
Davidson, A., 34, 96, 194
Deacon, B., 70
Deakin, S., 102

Della Salla, V., 73
Delors, J., 4, 25, 59, 62–63, 65–68, 70, 75, 90n4, 96, 104, 126
"democratic deficit", 3. *See also* legitimacy
demography, 9–10, 117, 139, 141, 164, 176, 178
deportation, 10, 54, 149–51, 153, 155, 158, 161n8, 167, 185, 187–9
development, *See* "migration-development nexus"
Dietz, G., 39
Dinan, D., 102
Draft Treaty Establishing the European Union (1984), 58
Drainville, A., 26

Economic and Monetary Union (EMU), 4, 59, 68, 70, 72, 93–94, 102–3, 106, 109–10, 198, 200
economic/financial crisis
  dot com, 116
  1970s, 3, 46, 50–51
  Russian and East Asian, 94
  2008–, ix, 125, 194, 203
embedded liberalism, 14, 47–48, 50, 198–200
embedded neo-liberalism, 14, 16, 70, 93, 95–97, 109–110, 112–13, 115, 122, 198, 200–1, 205
Employment Taskforce, 109–112
Equal Program, 138
Essen European Council (1994), 93
ethno-culturalism, 11, 14, 26, 40, 60, 74–78, 86–88, 94, 121–2, 159, 165, 171, 173, 200–1, 206. *See also* identity and migrant integration policy, EU
EU Constitution (Treaty establishing a Constitution for Europe), viii, 6–8, 98, 125–6, 132, 202. *See also* Lisbon Treaty
EU referendum/referenda, viii, 1–2, 5–11, 17, 17n3, 126, 197, 202
  Danish, 5
  Dutch, viii, 6–11, 98, 125, 202
  French, viii, 6–11, 98, 125, 202
  Irish, viii, 1–2, 6–7, 9, 11, 202

EU Regional Protection Program (EU-RPP), 152, 157–8, 163, 184–6
EUobserver, 191
"Euro-optimism", 5, 60–61, 82
Euro-pessimism, 3, 55–56, 58, 200
Eurodac, 147, 161n5, 161n7
European Central Bank (ECB), 93, 98–100
European Council on Refugees and Exiles (ECRE), 152, 155
European Employment Strategy (EES), 95, 102, 106–107, 138
European External Borders Agency (FRONTEX), 191
European Fund for the integration of third-country nationals, 169
European Monetary System, 58
European Monitoring Centre for Racism and Xenophobia, 137
European Pact on Immigration and Asylum (2008), 204
European Refugee Fund (ERF), 146
European Roundtable of Industrialists (ERT), 62, 69, 96, 103, 113, 119–121, 200
European Social Fund, 45, 118–19, 138
European Social Model (ESM), 4, 8–9, 28, 59–60, 65, 67–70, 87, 96–97, 99–100, 103, 105, 107–111, 116, 120, 122, 164, 201
European Trade Union Congress (ETUC), 96, 103
European Year against Racism, 137
Eurosclerosis, *See* Euro-pessimism
externalization, of migration policy, 130, 148, 151, 154, 163–4, 183–4, 186–7
extreme right, viii, ix, 83–84, 94, 137, 146, 159, 173, 180, 182, 203–4

Faist, T., 27
Ferrero-Waldner, B., 177
flexibility, 9, 68–69, 88–89, 102, 106, 108–111, 114–16, 118–24, 129, 133–4, 136, 140–3, 155, 157, 159–60, 164, 177, 179, 181, 183, 205–6
flexicurity, 118–9

Fontainbleau European Council (1984), 58, 71
four freedoms, 38
Frattini, F., 166, 168, 170, 173, 179, 191, 204
free movement, 3–4, 10, 12, 14–15, 29, 38–45, 47–50, 54–55, 57n5, 59, 61, 72, 78–82, 97, 128, 131–134, 140, 142, 145, 159, 172, 182, 198–9
"French winter of discontent", 94, 99

Gaddafi, M., 186
Geddes, A., 80
gender equality, 51, 56, 57n3, 111, 166–7, 173–4
Geneva Refugee Convention, 81, 147, 205
Giddens, A., 8, 95
global citizenship, 23
globalization, 7, 23–25, 30, 65, 69, 99–100, 103, 117, 119–20, 160, 201
   European Globalization Fund, 119
Glorious Revolution (1688), 32
Gross, T., 172
Growth and Stability Pact, 93, 100, 106
Guild, E., 204

Habermas, J., 7, 23–24, 26. *See also* post-national cosmopolitanism (PNC)
Hague Program, 16, 130, 158, 161–96, 201, 204
Hallstein, W., 47
hedge funds, 124
hegemonic projects, 33, 35–36, 115, 198, 203
Held, D., 36n2
High Level Group chaired by Wim Kok, 117
High Level Group on the future of social policy in an enlarged European Union, 109–110
Hofheinz, P., 120
Holman, O., 198
Hooghe, L., 63
Huntington, S., 77

identity
    European, 4, 14, 22, 24, 26, 28–29, 36, 40, 52, 58, 60, 71–72, 75, 81, 84–85, 87, 94, 159, 161, 173. *See also* migrant integration policy, EU
    national, 39, 94, 169
International Centre for Migration Policy Development (ICMPD), 189
"ideal" EU citizen, 7, 17, 121, 197, 205–6
international crime, *See* organized crime
Italy
    labour migration from, 42–43
    Roma and Sinti, treatment of, 203–4

Jessop, B., 33, 97. *See also* hegemonic projects
Jospin, L., 99–100
Justice and Home Affairs, EU, 82, 127, 129, 158, 168, 186, 191–2

Keynes, J.M., 50, 62, 98, 100–101, 114
Keynesian Welfare National State (KWNS), 34, 113, 199
Khan, I., 188
knowledge-based economy (KBE), 15–16, 96–97, 103, 111, 114, 120. *See also* Lisbon Strategy/Agenda
Kofman, E., 73
Kostakopoulou, T., 49, 131
Kouchner, B., 1

Laeken European Council (2001), 148
Lafontaine, O., 95, 98–101
legitimacy, ix, 2–5, 12–13, 17, 17n1, 21–22, 27–30, 36, 41, 56, 58, 75, 86, 94, 97, 113, 125, 127, 197, 202–3
Leibfried, S., 73
Libya
    EU migration cooperation with, 158, 185–6, 196n3
Lisbon Council for European Competitiveness (LCEC), 98, 119–21

Lisbon European Council (2000), 95, 104–105, 120
Lisbon High-level Conference on Legal Immigration (2007), 173
Lisbon Strategy/Agenda, 8–10, 15–16, 95–98, 102–125, 126n5, 130, 133, 138, 141, 159, 160–4, 173–4, 176, 178–9, 195, 201–2, 204–5
Lisbon Treaty, viii, 1, 8, 132, 202. *See also* EU Constitution (Treaty establishing a Constitution for Europe)
Lodge, M., 106, 109
Loescher, G., 152
"logic of no alternative", 25, 120
Luxembourg European Council (1997), 95

Maastricht Treaty, ix, 4–5, 12, 14, 17n2, 39, 46, 60, 66, 68–70, 75–76, 78, 82–83, 85–86, 88–89, 93, 96–98, 100, 102, 105–6, 127–8, 131, 199
"market correcting", *See* positive integration
"market making", *See* negative integration
McNamara, K., 62
Melilla, 189–90, 196n5
Merkel, A., 202
Mettler, A., 120
migrant integration policy, EU, 34, 40, 46, 82–85, 88, 130–9, 145, 156, 158–61, 165–76, 193–4, 196, 201, 204–5. *See also* identity
"migration-development nexus", 140, 151, 179–81, 186–7, 190
    Ministerial Euro-African Conference on Migration and Development, 190–1
Moschonas, G., 101
multi-level governance (MLG), 21–37
multiculturalism, 24, 84, 88, 134, 173
Muslim
    anti-Muslim, viii, 7, 10–11, 27, 170, 206
    integration, 10–11, 166, 168, 196

nation-state, 22-37
nationalism, 6-8, 11, 24, 26, 65, 168, 171, 201, 206
negative integration, 4, 8, 14, 25, 28, 35, 44, 59-60, 63-67, 87, 93, 96, 133, 198
neo-assimilationism, 122, 159, 168-9, 173, 175-6, 181, 201-3, 206
neoliberal communitarianism, 96-98, 112-15, 117, 119, 121-4, 133, 136, 138, 159, 171, 201-3. *See also* embedded neoliberalism
"New Vision for Refugees", U.K., 152-5
NGOs, 89, 103, 124, 127-8, 131, 138, 175, 180, 195
Nice European Council (2000), 102, 132
Noll, G., 154, 161n10, 161n12, 190

d'Oliviera, H.U.J., 82
Open Method of Coordination (OMC), 29, 96, 104-8, 137, 141
organized crime, 4, 61, 82, 86, 125, 160, 190
Overbeek, H., 21

Paris European Council, 51, 56
Paris Treaty, 42
"People's Europe", *See* "Citizens' Europe"
permanent residence, 79, 130-1, 133, 141, 159, 177, 179, 183, 191, 194
Petit, P., 32
Pierson, P., 73
Plan D for Democracy, Dialogue and Debate, 125
Pochet, P., 109
Pofalla, R., 170
Polanyi, K., 99, 123-4
Pope John Paul II, 77
de la Porte, C., 109
positive integration, 25, 64, 68, 70, 96, 173
post-national cosmopolitanism (PNC), 7, 21-37
problem solving theory, 14, 21, 30, 36, 198

Prodi, R., 76, 97, 101-103, 109-110, 112, 114-19
Protocol on Social Policy (1991), 66, 102

qualified majority voting (qmv), 59, 66, 128

racism, 7, 16, 54, 79, 84, 129, 137-8, 144, 146, 155, 157, 159-60, 174-5, 196
readmission policy, EU, *See* deportation
refugee policy, *See* asylum policy
regularization, 191-2, 204
regulation theory, 32
remittances, 180, 191
resettlement, 155-8
return policy, EU, *See* deportation
Rhodes, M., 105
Rome Treaty, 38, 41-45, 47-49, 59, 64
Ross, G., 68
Ryner, M., 21, 123

Santer, J., 75, 101
Sarkozy, N., 1, 202, 204
Sassen, S., 40
Scharpf, F., 28-30, 64. *See also* multi-level governance (MLG)
Schengen Agreement, 40, 80-81, 129, 148
Schröder, G., 95, 202
Schumpeterian Workfare Regimes, 97, 113, 126n2. *See also* Jessop, B.
seasonal labor migration, 141, 177-8, 183, 192-3
securitization, 15, 83-85, 88, 155, 160, 196, 202
Seville European Council (2002), 140, 148
Shore, C., 76
Single European Act (SEA), 3, 58-59, 62-63, 65-67, 81, 87, 90n3, 93, 127. *See also* Single Market
Single Market, 3, 4, 5, 14, 17n1, 35, 46, 56, 59-68, 70-72, 74-76, 78-80,

82–83, 87–89, 93, 160, 198, 200. *See also* Single European Act (SEA)
Smith, J., 5
Social Action Program (1974), 51, 53, 57n8
social dumping, 47, 99, 182
"social Europe", *See* European Social Model (ESM)
social exclusion, viii, 16, 60, 66, 69, 84, 101–102, 104, 107–108, 110, 124, 130, 133–4
Social Inclusion Strategy, EU, 107
Social Policy Agenda (SPA), 96, 102, 107–108, 115, 164
social purpose, viii, 12, 14, 22, 31–32, 36, 73, 125, 198. *See also* critical political economy
Soininen, M., 137–8
Spaak Report (Brussels Report on the General Common Report), 41–42
Spaak, P-H., 42
Špidla, V., 119
Statewatch, 156, 158
Stockhammer, E., 50
Stockholm Program, 162, 204
Stoiber, E., 170
de Stoop, C., 161n8
Streeck, W., 65, 74

Tabaksblat, M., 120
Tampere European Council (1999), 129, 148
Tampere Program, 16, 127–63, 165–6, 169, 173, 175–6, 181, 183–5, 187, 201, 204
temporary residence, 141, 181, 183
Terezin, 8

terrorism, 4, 9–10, 82, 88, 101, 116, 125, 145, 153, 160, 162–3, 167, 171–2, 186, 188
The Daily Telegraph, 186
The Economist, 6
Third Way, 95, 97, 100–102, 106, 112–15, 119, 122, 124, 136, 138, 171, 202
Tindemans Report, 52–53, 57n7
trafficking
  drug, 4, 81–82, 86
  human, 10, 139, 145, 148, 163
Turkey
  EU membership, 7, 77

Uçarer, E., 80
UNHCR, 151–4, 186

van Apeldoorn, B., 21, 70, 114
van der Pijl, K., 119
van Mierlo, H., 77

Wahl, A., 100
Wallace, W., 5
Wallström, M., 8, 125
West Germany
  labour migration to, 43, 50
Wiener, A., 73
Wincott, D., 105
Wood, E., 31–2
Yuval-Davis, N., 74

Zeitlin, J., 105
"zero" labour immigration, 130, 139, 143–4, 159
Ziltener, P., 67

www.ingramcontent.com/pod-product-compliance
Ingram Content Group UK Ltd.
Pitfield, Milton Keynes, MK11 3LW, UK
UKHW021850210426
5322IPUK00022B/571